REACHING TOWARD A STATE WHERE YOU WEAR THE UNIVERSE LIKE A GLOVE...AND IT WEARS YOU!

The Medium, the Mystic, and the Physicist is an exploration of the paranormal . . . by psychologist Lawrence LeShan, a practicing psychic healer and a pioneer in parapsychological research. It is another way of looking at the world, through a higher reality described by mediums, mystics and physicists in strikingly similar terms.

"If we have learned one thing from science," LeShan says, "it is that the atypical case, the unusual incident, is one that—if looked at closely—teaches us all about the others." The author gives us a picture of reality above and beyond the sense, with implications in the areas of magnetic healing, hauntings, personality survival after biological death, telepathy, and energy transmission . . . in a way that will grip skeptics and believers alike.

the medium, the mystic, and the physicist

by lawrence leshan

BALLANTINE BOOKS • NEW YORK

*Dedicated to Edgar N. Jackson, who was guide
and comrade-in-arms on this adventure.*

*Acknowledgment is made to the following for permission to
quote.*

E. P. Dutton & Co., Inc.: From the book *Mysticism* by Evelyn
Underhill. Published by E. P. Dutton & Co., Inc., and used
with their permission.

Journal of Transpersonal Psychology: "Physicists and Mystics:
Similarities in World View" by Lawrence LeShan. Reprinted
by permission, Transpersonal Institute, from Volume 1, No. 2,
1969, of the *Journal of Transpersonal Psychology*, 2637 Mar-
shall Drive, Palo Alto, California 94303.

Main Currents in Modern Thought: "Human Survival of Biological Death" by Lawrence LeShan. November–December
1969 issue.

Open Court Publishing Company: From *Albert Einstein: Philosopher-Scientist* by P. A. Schilpp.

Perceptual and Motor Skills: Krippner, S., and Ullman, M.,
"Telepathic Perception in the Dream State: Confirmatory
Study Using EEG-ECG Monitoring Techniques," *Perceptual
and Motor Skills*, 1969, 29, 915–918.

Kenneth Rexroth and *Saturday Review:* From *The Works of
Rimbaud* by Kenneth Rexroth. Copyright © 1967 by Kenneth
Rexroth. First appeared in *Saturday Review*. Used with per-
mission.

The Society for Psychical Research: "A Spontaneous Psychometry Experiment with Mrs. Eileen Garrett" by Lawrence
LeShan. *Journal of Society for Psychical Research*, 1968.

Blanche Stace: From *The Teachings of the Mystics* by W. T.
Stace.

An Esalen Book, published by arrangement with The Viking
Press

ISBN 0-345-30312-1

Manufactured in the United States of America

First Ballantine Books Edition: March 1975
Third Printing: March 1982

acknowledgments

This work was made possible by a grant from Dr. Frederick Ayer II, who has the writer's profound gratitude. It would not have been possible without the patience and help of Mrs. Eileen J. Garrett, who let me question her and work with her for many hundreds of hours.

It is also a pleasure to thank those who took the time and energy to read this manuscript in its various stages of development and to give me the benefit of their reactions. These include Anne Applebaum, Graham Bennette, Gotthard Booth, Roberto Cavanna, Douglas Dean, Martha Gassmann, Max Grossman, Rosalind Heywood, Ensor Holiday, Edgar Jackson, Douglas Johnson, Robert Laidlaw, Eda LeShan, John Levy, Henry Margenau, Abraham Maslow, Lewis Mumford, Jacob Needleman, Fraser Nicol, Bob Ornstein, Karlis Osis, A. R. G. Owen, Bram Pais, J. B. Rhine, Nina Ridenour, Henry Rosenthal, Gertrude Schmeidler, Raymond Van Over, Rebecca Waldinger, and Richard Worthington.

Much of the research on psychic healing reported in Chapter 7 was made possible by a grant from Life Energies Research, Inc. Their encouragement and support has my deep gratitude.

contents

pReface

This book is the story of an adventure, of a search for the meaning of impossible events. The paranormal by definition is impossible. What does it mean for man when the impossible happens? What are the implications for us that sometimes—both in everyday life and in the laboratory—individuals reveal knowledge of things that they cannot know of, knowledge of things so separated from them by space or time that their senses could not under any condition have brought them the information they demonstrate having? What do these things tell us about the nature of man and the universe?

A few definitions may be of help here. If an individual knows something that will occur in the future and there is no information available now from which he could figure it out, we call this "precognition." If an individual knows something in the present and he could not have known it from his senses, or figured it out from other available information, we call it "telepathy" if it is known to any other living person and "clairvoyance" if it is not.[1]

It is usually believed by people seriously working in

this field (who are called *psychical researchers* or *para-psychologists*) that all these terms—*precognition, te-lepathy,* and *clairvoyance*—refer to the same general process (frequently called ESP—extrasensory percep-tion) manifesting itself in different ways. However, it has not been possible up to now to come to a clear understanding of exactly what this process is.

A *sensitive* is a person who demonstrates precogni-tion, telepathy, and /or clairvoyance with unusual fre-quency. A *medium* is a sensitive who explains her (most frequently in Western culture these are women) acquisition of paranormally gained information by say-ing that she gets it from "spirits" or "the souls of people who have already died." Some mediums go into a trance in which they identify themselves as being some-one else than they usually identify themselves as. Very frequently in trance a good medium will demonstrate a very high level of paranormally acquired information. Whether or not it comes from "spirits"—as most medi-ums sincerely believe—is anybody's guess.

For excellent general surveys of the field of psychical research, I recommend C. D. Broad's *Lectures on Psy-chical Research* [2] and Gardner Murphy's *The Chal-lenge of Psychical Research.* [3] C. D. Broad was a very serious British philosopher and well-trained in this area. Gardner Murphy is the outstanding psychical re-searcher of our time and his ability as a psychologist is also at this level. He has been president of the Amer-ican Psychological Association, which is the highest honor psychologists can give to one of their own, and has received similar recognition from psychical re-searchers.

I have written that this book is the story of an adven-ture. This is what it has been for me during the past nine years, and I hope you will find it as exciting as it was for me. The adventure of the search for the mean-ing of impossible events, however, is a very old one, which human beings have participated in during all history and which every culture and every individual has needed to undertake. Each society has come to its own conclusions about the meaning of these happenings.

In our present culture there have been three general explanations of these happenings, each accepted by some of us. The first explanation is that these things do not happen; they are nonsense, and reports of them are due to hysteria, softheadedness, or fakery. The second is that they do happen, but let's ignore them for sanity's sake and maybe they will go away. Another way of putting this one is to say they do happen and we can mildly titilate ourselves with tales about them, but we leave them for the story hour and never look at them seriously. The third explanation is that they do exist, and let's use them for a little happy regression and get out a Ouija board and talk to our dead great-aunt Mary and play spooks and chills. None of these explanations is particularly constructive.

Psychical research today is an unmitigated disaster area. It is doubtful if there are more than twenty-five full-time researchers in this field in the whole world. Funds for research are terribly scarce, and as I sit writing this the most important single research laboratory in the entire field (the William C. Menninger Dream Laboratory) is about to close for lack of funds. On the other hand, most of the interest in this field is aborted by being diverted to kookiness of one sort or another ranging from books on "Edgar Cayce on Atlantis" or "Astrology and Sex" to lectures on "ESP and Reincarnation." [4]

As for the present cultural interest in ESP, Western society has been there before. There have been bursts of excitement about this area (generally, as now, including the "occult," spirits, demons, and the like, which are even *more* fun to titillate yourself with) and they have all died down and nothing was left of any value.

For a psychologist there is a clear explanation for these facts. The occurrence of an "impossible" event makes us anxious and frightened, and when people are anxious they behave in irrational ways. The paranormal raises deep hidden fantasies, and our anxiety level goes up with them. "After all," we nonconsciously conclude, "if this is possible, then anything is possible and nothing is impossible. I may find myself living in a universe in which I understand nothing and can predict nothing. A world gone mad." The psychiatrist Kurt Goldstein called this type of anxiety "a catastrophic reaction" and pointed out that it is the most terrifying of all fears.

On another psychological level, a paranormal event raises a different type of anxiety. As children, we all confused thoughts and actions and believed that thoughts and feelings had power of their own, that our angry thoughts could do actual harm to others. All of us felt guilty over our "bad" thoughts and feelings, and it took a long time for us to emotionally comprehend the difference between these and actions. Parapsychology seems to reinforce our childhood fantasies of thoughts having power (they don't, but this seems the implication of the paranormal) and, as we all know that we have "bad" thoughts and feelings, the old anxiety and guilts return. Will we—or have we already— hurt others in this way? This too makes us anxious about the acceptance of the paranormal.

It is interesting to note that even those doing research in the field respond to these anxieties. Experiments showing strong positive results frequently never get finished or never get repeated. Data gets misplaced. Indeed, if the Society for Psychical Research had established in 1882, when it was founded, one more department, our supply of basic data in this field would have been tripled; this would have been a department to collect basic research protocols left by accident on trains running out of Waterloo Station in London! The number of experiments in which the basic records were lost in this way is quite impressive.

One of the great psychic-research specialists, D. J. West, said on his retirement that looking back over his years of research, he was startled to find how much time he spent looking for good results and how little time he spent following up the few good results he found. Indeed, anxieties raised by this field affect psychical researchers also.

These are some of the reasons that this book is written as an adventure. When a map is of far-away and unexplored areas, we have a strong tendency to fill it with marvelous possibilities and tales of the Seven Cities of Cibola and the Fountain of Youth and to mark on it "Here there be Tygers" and "Here be the land of the soul-eaters and the Upas tree." Exploring these areas in the necessary step-by-step manner, as Livingston marched through Africa or Newton searched out the meaning of observations of the planets, reduces the magic and mystery to levels we can deal with under natural law and science and enables us to find out how the most human use and growth can be made out of our new knowledge. Perhaps this accounting of one adventure in the realm of the paranormal can be of help in making this strange and beautiful land a place where human beings can live and grown with less anxiety.

The book, then, starts with a look at two questions: "Why do we believe the paranormal exists?" and "If it does exist, why is it important?" Since the conclusions I reach are made clear in Chapter 1, "That it *does* exist and is *very* important," a side issue—Why is it not generally accepted in our society and by scientists generally?—is discussed at some length in an appendix (A) for those who are interested in this problem. The next chapter (2) describes the beginning of the exploration and how it started. Chapter 3 is the story of what occurred when I went to the basic source—the serious sensitives who had a high frequency of paranormal events in their lives and tried to understand how this happened. It became clear during this several-year search that at the moment the paranormal information was acquired (when "telepathy" or "clairvoyance" or "precognition" was happening) they were reacting to the world *as if* it were constructed and "worked" on different grounds than those grounds on which we normally believe it to be constructed. At those moments they used a different metaphysical structure of the world than our ordinary, everyday metaphysical structure.

After analyzing this different picture of the world, I realized that two other groups of searchers into the meaning of things had reached identical conclusions: that there are two ways of being-in-the-world, our usual one and another, and what this other way is. These two other groups are the great Eastern and Western mystics and the Einsteinian physicists. Chapters 4 and 5 are an exploration of this agreement and the way in which each of these three groups stated the same conclusions in different terms.

Out of these findings a theory of the paranormal emerged. This is based on the idea that each metaphysical system permits certain activities and events (which are "normal" when you are using the system) and does not permit other activities and events (which are therefore "paranormal" when you are using it). In the everyday metaphysical system (the "Sensory Reality") ESP is "paranormal." In the other system (the "Clairvoyant Reality") ESP is "normal." ESP-type events occur when an individual is relating to the world as if its metaphysical structure were that of the Clairvoyant Reality. This theory seems to account for most of the data we have in parapsychology.

To be useful, however, a theory must do more than account for old data. It must also predict new material, broaden our understanding, and help us learn to accomplish things we could not do before we had the theory. This is the real way to evaluate it. Two tests were devised for the theory: a "practical" one—Could we learn to do something new from it?—and a theoretical one—Could it be applied to a theoretical problem so far unsolved by previous theories?

The practical test chosen was to see if the theory of the two "realities" could point out a way to learn and teach the ability to perform a specific "paranormal" skill. The skill I chose was "psychic healing," a paranormal process in which the "healer" performs certain activities within his own head and the "healee"—often at a considerable distance and often not consciously aware that the healer is doing this—responds (sometimes) with positive biological changes. Chapter 7 describes this test of the theory and its positive conclusion. The first test of the theory was successfully passed.

The theoretical test chosen was to apply the theory to the problem of what happens to the "personality" at biological death. Since the necessary reasoning was quite close and complex and since many of the best examples I found to illustrate it were repetitions used elsewhere in the book, I have included this as an appendix rather than a chapter of this book. The conclusion reached by the exploration was—much to my surprise —that conscious, personal survival was unquestionable if one applied to the problem the methods and standards of field theory in modern physics.[5] However, as no experimental test of the conclusion appears to me to be indicated by the findings, each person who is interested enough in the subject to read Appendix C will have, at this time, to judge for himself whether or not this theoretical test of the theory appears to be successful.

After these two tests of the theory, I believed that the first stage of the research was finished and wrote this book, summing it up with Chapter 8. Showing it to various knowledgeable friends produced some unexpected reactions and led me to the experience and analysis of a third metaphysical system (altered state of consciousness) associated with certain kinds of psychic healing. This exploration is described in Chapter 9, which— since it has been the last part of the adventure so far— is the final chapter of this book.[6]

I know the general outline of how I plan to proceed from here: to further explore the meaning of impossible events and of the wide range of human potentialities they indicate. I do not know where the exploration will lead, what lies around the next corner.

G. N. M. Tyrrell, one of our greatest psychical researchers, summed up far better than I can what became my own views on the nature of this field of endeavor:

> Let us now, before the restricted view of the laboratory worker gains too firm a hold, try to realise how how wide our subject is. We should try once more to see it through the eyes of Frederic Myers as a subject which lies at the meeting place of religion, philosophy and science, whose business it is to grasp all that can be grasped of the nature of human personality.[7]

If you will come with me on this adventure, then perhaps, in the words that Oliver Wendell Holmes wrote to the philosopher Morris Raphael Cohen, "We will twist the tail of the cosmos 'till it squeaks." [8]

part one | three roads to one reality

"I would not" says Socrates, "be confident in everything I say about the argument: but one thing I would fight for to the end, both in word or deed if I were able—that if we believed we should try to find out what is not known, we should be better and braver and less idle than if we believed that what we do not know it is impossible to find out and that we need not even try."

—THE MENO

1 | what is important about the paranormal?

Psychical research, whether one calls it "parapsychology," "psi," "the study of the paranormal," or "ESP research," is far more than it appears to be at first glance. In the most profound sense it is the study of the basic nature of man. To demonstrate its meaning for us today, let us begin by examining our present cultural conception of what man "is." We might begin with a quotation, the implications of which we shall return to later:

> What is man that his welfare be considered? An ape who chatters of kinship with the archangels while he very filthily digs for groundnuts. And yet I perceive that this same man is a maimed God. He is condemned under penalty to measure eternity with an hourglass and infinity with a yardstick and what is more, he very nearly does it.
>
> —James Branch Cabell

We ask, "What is man?" and in our antimetaphysical age regard the question as having little importance. It is, however, the most crucial question of all. How we

3

treat other men and how we treat ourselves depends on our answer. If we believe that man is basically good, we treat him as if he were, and—as Goethe pointed out long ago—thereby tend to make him likely to be a little better. If we believe that man is evil, and treat him as such, it not only makes him worse, but, since we know ourselves to share a common humanity, tends to stifle our own inner being with a consequent loss of joy and spontaneity.

A change in our concept of man leads to changes in our behavior. For example, the new understanding given us by Freud in recent decades changed one part of our concept. The knowledge that man has an unconscious which strongly influences him has led to considerable changes in education, medicine, art, child-rearing practices, law, and a host of other fields.

When we look at our present cultural picture of man, we see that it is one we can describe as "rational" and "sensible." Man is made up of flesh, bone, and nerve. He is the material of earth in an unusually complex form, and that is all he is. Within this picture, each of us is seen as separate from all others in the same way that one bicycle is separate from another. We are perceived as cut off from the world and from other men by the limits of our skin. (This in itself strongly influences how we treat one another. If I see you as separate and different from me, I am likely to treat you differently that I treat myself. If I perceive you and me as part of one another, I am likely to treat you the same way I treat myself.) Only in moments of love, compassion, religious awe, ecstasy, laughter, or dedication are we able to bridge the gap and become a part of one another. Each man is separate, although made up of the same type of atoms, molecules, and physical structure. "If you prick me, do I not bleed?" asks Shylock. Of similar structure we may be, but we see each man as locked in his skin, knowing the world only through the narrow windows of his senses and touching others only through these.

The scientific facts we know seem to point to the

validity of this viewpoint that man is understandable in terms of the same basic physical concepts we use to understand cars and computers. There are, we all agree, more details to understand, but we know the outlines. The major conceptual tools we need are of the same type and order as those described above.

Do *all* the facts we know support this view, or *almost all?* If we look carefully and honestly, we find it is *almost all.* There are some that do not. *There are facts that do not fit in.*

Parapsychology is the scientific study of what Charles Fort used to call "the damned facts": the facts that do not fit in. These facts cannot be reconciled with the concepts we ordinarily use to explain man and his world. But if we have learned one thing from science, it is that the atypical case, the unusual incident, is the one that—if looked at seriously—teaches us about all the others.

It is the one substance in Madame Curie's workshop that glows in the dark that teaches us about the basic structure of all the others. It is the one Petri dish in Fleming's laboratory in which the germs die unexpectedly that leads us to the discovery of the antibiotics. It is the one set of flasks in Pasteur's experiments in which life does *not* appear that teaches us the source of life in the others. It is the atypical paralysis in which neurology can *not* find the lesion that leads Freud to the discovery of the unconscious. It is the one problem in physics (the addition of velocities problem) that cannot be solved in the usual way that leads to an Einsteinian revolution and gives us a deeper understanding of the problems we had been able to solve in the old way.

Almost all the facts agree with our picture of man, but there *are* exceptions. There are facts that do not fit in with our neat ideas of our separateness, or with our just being ordinary matter like rocks, airplanes, and computers. There are facts we cannot reconcile with our preconceived ideas.

About three years ago, a physician in a town more

than a thousand miles from New York, where I was living, went to a five-day medical meeting several states away from his home. He checked into the hotel at nine in the morning, checked out at five the same afternoon, and vanished. I had never met or spoken to the man or to any member of his family. Several weeks later there was still no trace of him, and he was on the police missing-persons list from coast to coast. Through a rather complex chain of connections, the man's wife heard that I was doing research with Eileen Garrett, one of the most gifted and dedicated clairvoyants of all time. The wife wrote to me, asking if I could help her locate her husband, and enclosing a two-inch square from a shirt he had worn the day before he left for the meeting. The morning I got the letter I phoned Mrs. Garrett asking for an appointment without telling her why I wanted one. She told me to come in at two that afternoon. When I arrived at her office we went into the séance room without saying one word about the problem. After she was in trance, I told her two sentences: "A man has disappeared; his wife is very worried. Can you help?" She fingered the scrap of cloth and presently said, "He is in La Jolla. He went there due to a psychic wound he suffered when he was fourteen years old and his father disappeared."

That evening I telephoned the wife and asked her, "Did anything happen to your husband between the ages of thirteen and fifteen?" She replied, "When he was fourteen his father deserted the family and was not heard of again for twenty-five years." Three weeks later when the physician was located, it turned out he had been in La Jolla on the date of the séance.

Here is a fact that does not fit into our picture of man and his relations with other men. Nor does it fit into any science based on the idea of separateness of individuals in the usual sense of the term.

"But," we say as we try to save our nice, accustomed, materialistic picture of man and his world, "perhaps it is something like radio waves. He gave them off, and she received them, perhaps tuned in somehow by the piece of his shirt. It would simply be a case of her receiving his broadcasts. A radio station and a radio set are separate, and neither has to know where the other is for one to receive signals from the other. What is the problem?"

It just won't work that way. To show why this explanation is not at all adequate, let us take one of the older cases in the literature of psychical research. (I will present a more modern, laboratory-type example of this shortly, but an older example may be helpful in getting more of the "flavor" of one aspect of this field).

Mrs. Verall (one of the most talented and carefully studied sensitives of all time) recorded in her daily journal on December 11, 1911, the following paranormal perception:

> The cold was intense and a single candle gave poor light. He was lying on the sofa or on a bed and was reading Marmontel by the light of a single candle. . . . The book was lent to him, it did not belong to him. [On Dec. 17 she continued the note.] The name Marmontel is correct. . . . A French book, I think his memoirs. The Passy may help him to remember. Passy or Fleury. The book was bound in two volumes, the binding was old and the book was lent to him. The name Marmontel is not on the cover.

On March 1, 1912, Mrs. Verrall was told by a friend, Mr. Marsh, that he read the memoirs of Marmontel on a bitterly cold night in Paris on the twentieth and twenty-first of February, 1912, by the light of a candle. Once he was in bed, another time he reclined on two chairs. He had borrowed the book (it had three volumes), and on February 21, he had read the chapter in which the finding of a picture painted at Passy is described by Marmontel, the discovery being associated with a Mr. Fleury.[1]

You can work all you wish with radio waves and all the other concepts of our everyday world and everyday science, but you *cannot* get the radio waves to go ahead in time and be received *before* they are sent. To explain "damned facts" like this one, you need a new concept, a new definition of man and his relationship to the cosmos.

I should remark that for every example of "psi" or "the paranormal" I will refer to here, many dozens of others, just as good or better, have been published by serious people.

There are four major sources of our "damned facts." We might term these Laboratory Experiments, Spontaneous Cases, Mediumistic Cases, and Psychotherapy Cases. Let us look at a fairly typical example from each.

1. Laboratory Experiments

Dr. Gertrude Schmeidler, a psychologist, has repeated the following experiment many times and in many modifications. A group of subjects (such as a class of college students) is asked, "Do you believe (or not) in the possibility of ESP existing?" After they have written their answer, she gives each of them a form with spaces to record a great many guesses. They are then told that on the following day a pack of special cards will be thoroughly shuffled and the order they fall into will be written on a similar form. They are to "guess" the order the cards will fall into tomorrow, and to record their guesses now. After everyone has recorded his guesses, the forms are collected and safely put away. The next day the cards are thoroughly shuffled and their final order compared to the guesses. The group of students who stated that they believed in the possibility of ESP existing can be scientifically demonstrated to have guessed more accurately than the other group.[2]

This type of study is not only a scientific demonstration of the existence of psi, but is also valuable in helping us to develop our beginning understanding of the relationship between ESP and personality. Experiments of this type—precognition experiments—are among the easiest parapsychological experiments to do. There are hundreds of serious, laboratory demonstrations of precognition in the literature.

2. Spontaneous Cases

A ten-year-old girl was walking in a country lane near her home but out of sight of it. She was studying geometry. "In a moment, I saw a bedroom known as the White Room in my house, and upon the floor lay my mother, to all appearances dead. The vision must have remained some minutes, during which time my real surroundings appeared to pale and die out; but as the vision faded, actual surroundings came back, at first dimly and then clearly."

Unable to doubt that what she had seen was real, the child did not go home, but went immediately to the home of the family physician. When he came back with her to her home, the vision was found to be true "even to intimate details." The mother had had a heart attack and would have died without quick medical intervention.[3]

3. Mediumistic Cases

The two cases described previously, the "vanished man" and "Marmontel" cases, are fairly typical of this type.

4. Psychotherapy Cases

Several years before the following incident I had worked with a patient named Marla. She was an artist and an expert on modern art. Obviously a psychotherapist never mentions one patient's name to another.

At the time this incident occurred, I was working with a fairly new patient. She was an amateur painter and one day brought in a painting of hers to show me. We talked about it for a while and I told her I did not know much about this type of art and asked if I might show it to a friend of mine who did, and get an opinion on it. The patient replied, "Of course," and then, for a moment, looked curiously blank. She then asked me,

"Tell me, did anyone named Marla ever sit in this chair?" When I—quite startled—asked her why she had asked, she could only reply that she just felt that she had to ask. She herself knew no one by that name, she said.

It is important to note again that we have been talking about a few typical examples out of the many hundreds of carefully studied cases and precise laboratory experiments that have been published in the professional literature of this field.[4]

Outside of the fact that ESP (telepathy, clairvoyance, precognition) exists, what does all this mean? Primarily, it indicates that there is far more to man than we have known. We have data that are strong and clear, but they could not exist if man were only what we have believed him to be. If he were only flesh and bone, if he worked on the same type of principle as a machine, and if he were as separate from other men as we have thought, it would be impossible for him to do the things we know he sometimes does. A new concept of man, a new way of looking at others and ourselves, a knowledge that there is more to man than our old concepts allow is scientifically demonstrated by these facts. And *that* is the real importance of ESP.

The changes in viewpoint about the nature of man implied by these "damned facts" is a tremendous one. And we must not underestimate how terribly we need a new concept of man. The philosophical legacy of the seventeenth century, which Western civilization has been living on, is used up. The materialistic metaphysics that gave us the Industrial Revolution is now destroying us. Our institutions are foundering one after the other; our way of life is becoming unworkable. Our ways of relating to each other are driving our species toward extinction and making our only planet an unlivable garbage dump.

In 1969, United Nations Secretary-General U Thant stated:

I do not wish to seem overdramatic, but I can only conclude from the information that is available to me as Secretary General [of the United Nations] that the members of the United Nations have perhaps 10 years left in which to subordinate their ancient quarrels and launch a global partnership to end the arms race, to improve the human environment, to defuse the population explosion and to supply the required momentum to world development efforts. If such a global partnership is not forged within the next decade, then I very much fear that the problems I have mentioned will have reached such staggering proportions that they will be beyond our capacity to control.[5]

Most ecologists and most students of the effects of population pressure upon behavior give us between ten and thirty years to make changes before it is too late to save mankind. This places the crucial period between A.D. 1979 and 1999, a terribly short time to change our long-standing ways of acting and reacting to the degree necessary to save ourselves.

One thing is clear: we cannot hope to change our ways of relating to ourselves and others without a major change in how we perceive ourselves and others. It is imperative that we now develop a new and more complete concept of what man is or we will perish.

Psychical research has given us the clues and clear signposts to a new concept, a more accurate picture based on a deeper understanding. This new picture is hard to see as yet. It flies in the face of all our preconceptions and of what we think of as our experience. It flies in the face of these as much as:

The earth goes around the sun. "Ridiculous, who has not seen the sun rise, circle the heavens and set?"

The earth is round, not flat. "Idiotic. Those on the bottom would fall off."

Emotions can contribute to the cause of an ulcer. "Nonsense; everyone knows mind is one thing, body another."

These preconceptions have now been broken and the new concepts accepted. But the old ideas were very strong and were accepted as "obvious common sense" at the time the new ideas came in.

Because they go against all of our preconceptions, it is very hard for most of us to evaluate objectively the "impossible facts" of ESP—those that cannot happen, but do. As Dr. Gardner Murphy has observed, "If there were one-tenth of the evidence in any other field of science that there is in parapsychology, it would be accepted beyond question."

Why then is it so difficult for psi to be accepted? It is partly because of the theoretical bind it seems to lead us into. The "impossible facts" seem to put us into a logically impossible and insane position. This position might be stated as follows:

1. If what we generally know about how the world works is basically true, then certain things—such as seeing ahead in time—are impossible.
2. What we know about this subject is, generally speaking, true. We function far too effectively in our everyday life to make it possible for us to be operating on a set of false assumptions.
3. But these things do happen.

Stated this way, which is the way it has generally been formulated, it *is* an illogical position and a reasonable mind can only assume that (in spite of the overwhelming evidence) statement number 3 is not true, that these things do not happen. Most individuals (and most scientists) shy away from the whole contradictory mess by simply not looking at the data, and thus are able to ignore the problem completely.

There is, however, another answer, one that fits in well with all the evidence and seems clearly indicated if the problem is approached scientifically. This answer is that what we know is true, but there is more to man and his relationship to the cosmos than we have accepted. This "more" is also of a different kind and order than the parts we know about. This answer flies in the face of only one preconception—that we really know all that is important to know about man. And that is a preconception that no rational mind would consciously accept on any subject. It is this specific preconception that has seemed to make so hopeless our attempts to keep the human race from following the path of the dinosaurs. The evidence is clear that it is not a valid conception, and that courage to follow the clues already found can lead to new, fresh answers.

Coleridge wrote somewhere: "What if you slept? And what if, in your sleep, you dreamed? And what if in your dream you went to heaven and there plucked a strange and beautiful flower? And what if, when you awoke, you had the flower in your hand? Ah! What then?"

The human race *has* dreamed. We have dreamed of men like angels and have awakened with the long gold-tipped feathers of angels' wings in our hands. The "impossible facts" of ESP are these feathers. They tell us of a part of man, long hidden in the mists of legend, art, dream, myth, and mysticism, which our explorers of reality in the last ninety years have demonstrated to be scientifically valid. At the least, we have learned that man is far more than he seems to be, more than the materialist philosopher has ever conceived of: He can and does touch others and the universe in a way we do not yet understand, but a way obeying quite different laws than do his senses; his separation from others and his loneliness in the world are, at least partly, illusion.

Psychical research offers a new and deeper understanding of the ancient, crucial question "What is Man?" This understanding awaits us beyond the next horizon. Let us try to reach it in time.

2 | the Beginning of the exploration

In 1964, I had finished a fifteen-year research project on a problem in psychosomatic medicine. It seemed to me then, for the reasons described in the first chapter, that if there was any validity in the whole field of ESP, it was of tremendous importance and really worth studying. I did not really believe that there could be any such validity; I had been trained as an experimental psychologist and it seemed obvious that such evidence as there was must be due to bad experimental design, false memories, hysteria, and chicanery. After all, these things could not happen. I was fairly sure that I would wind up trying to figure out how it was that serious men like William James, Gardner Murphy, and a half dozen Nobel Prize winners had been deluded into believing such nonsense. Nevertheless, on the faint chance the evidence was valid, I considered it worth examining.

To my intense surprise, as I began to read the scientific journals and serious books in the field, it became obvious that the material *was* valid. The standards of research were extremely high and the evidence scientifically valid. The only alternative explanation to the

hundreds of carefully studied "spontaneous" incidents
reported, and the hundreds of scientifically controlled
laboratory experiments, was that the greatest conspiracy in history had been going on for more than
eighty years. This conspiracy would have to involve a
tremendous number of men and women, including
many of otherwise unquestionable probity. It seemed
that, impossible as the evidence for ESP was to accept,
this explanation was even more impossible. It smacked
of the attitude "I have made up my mind. Don't bother
me with the facts." This is not a good attitude for
someone who thinks of himself as a scientist! Science
had frequently fallen into the trap of deciding in advance that certain things are impossible. The great
chemist Lavoisier *knew* that meteorites were an impossible fable because it was obvious that there were no
stones in the sky. This kind of thing has happened so
often in science that knowledge of the danger of assuming that our present beliefs and frame of reference are
absolutely and eternally true is a very real part of the
scientific attitude today. The present viewpoint is rather
something like this: "All scientific knowledge is completely true and valid until the first day of next month.
At that time the new journals come out and everything
is up for grabs!" To the degree that we accept this or a
similar statement, we have a scientific attitude.

The evidence in the scientific publications was of two
general types: anecdotal (events that just occurred, in
or out of the laboratory) and experimental (events that
were carefully planned to occur under precise conditions and continued observation). I had been trained
to be extremely skeptical of any anecdotal material in
science. Nevertheless, some of this material struck me
as having an extremely high order of probability of
being valid. An anecdotal account of a laboratory event
is presented here just as it appeared in the *Journal of
the Society for Psychical Research* in 1968.[1] Although
it is a case I was a part of myself, it is typical of hundreds of reports in the professional journals of this

field, and is the kind of occurrence that anyone who seriously investigates this area will observe:

During the course of a pilot study of fingertip vision at the Parapsychology Foundation, I—as a specialist in research design—was asked to come in and help to tighten up the experimental procedure. This was the third time I had even met Mrs. Garrett, who was the subject in the pilot study. The first two meetings had been exclusively discussions of parapsychology with no personal information talked of. However, she had seen a professional *curriculum vitae* of mine, and a colleague (Dr. Ivan London) had told her that I was married and had a daughter.

After discussing the pilot study procedure with Mrs. Garrett and Dr. Roberto Cavanna, we made an appointment for the next morning to do some test runs.

That evening, thinking the matter over, I decided to try a modification in the next morning's procedure. The targets had been 4-inch cardboard squares of different colors. Knowing something of Mrs. Garrett's orientation to life and nature from her books, I decided to try some targets with more "life" in them. I obtained three identical transparent plastic boxes and looked around for something to put in them. My daughter walked by at this moment and I took a small lock of her hair and put it in the first box. From our backyard garden I cut a rosebud and put it in the second. Some neighbors had just moved in next door that week and, as they and their dog were then on their back porch, I asked them for a tuft of hair from their dog's tail.

The next morning (May 14, 1964) I brought the three boxes into the experimental room. Present were Mrs. Garret, Mrs. Bethe Pontorno as shorthand notetaker, and myself. I told Mrs. Garrett that I had decided to change the targets and showed her the three boxes one at a time. Each one—after my comments—she simply held and looked at for 10–20 seconds. My comments were as follows:

"This is a lock-of hair from my daughter Wendy."

"This is a tuft from the tail of our neighbor's dog. He is a purebread Welsh terrier named 'Charlie'."

"This is a rosebud."

After this without further conversation, I took the three boxes behind the visual screen set-up (the "Cavanna Box"—a special screen system designed to study fingertip vision*) and put them out of sight. Mrs. Garret put her right arm through the sleeve of the screen system. I picked each box in turn (in an order determined by random number tables) and slid it beneath her fingers. Her comments were as follows:

Mrs. Garrett's Comments	Discussion
Box #1	
"Oh, that's your daughter. I think I'll call her 'Hilary.' She'd like that."	When my daughter was 4 years old (8 years previous to this date), she

* The "Cavanna Box" was designed for studying "dermal vision" by Dr. Roberto Cavanna. It is a five-sided box about 2″ by 1½″ by 1½″. It is lit electrically from inside and is open on the side facing the experimenter. The side facing the subject has a hole in it, circular, about 5″ in diameter; attached to the hole is a sleeve, about 20″ long of heavy, double black cloth. The subject thrusts an arm through the sleeve and thus can hold his hand above objects (in this case the boxes containing the lock of hair of Wendy, the hair from the dog's tail, and the rosebud) which he cannot possibly see visually.

Mrs. Garrett's Comments	Discussion
	had a "crush" on a girl of 6 named "Hilary." For a year she begged us to change her name to Hilary. Nothing like this had ever happened before or since. It was a private family joke for several years thereafter that had never been—to the recollection of my wife or myself—mentioned outside the immediate family. It had certainly *not* been mentioned in at least 4 years by any of us.
"She should ride horses. There is something between her and horses. They understand each other."	This is true. My daughter rides like a cavalry officer and can gentle the most upset horse. However, many girls of her age enjoy horseback riding and are very interested in it. An estimate of my daughter's approximate age could have been easily made intuitively from my age or from the lock of hair.
"She has a special relationship with her father. She loves her mother, but is particularly close to her father at this time."	True, but this is valid for a very large number of girls of her approximate age.

Mrs. Garrett's Comments	*Discussion*
"She is nice. She's better and more interested in art and literature than the sciences."	This is true. (I certainly believe she is a "nice" person.) The "interest" statement is true, but rather general. It could apply to many people.
"She has been very interested in American History these past few weeks, hasn't she?"	Three weeks before my daughter had been given an English assignment in school to do a book review of Howard Fast's book on the American revolution, *April Morning.* For the first time in her life she became interested enough in a subject to go to the school library and ask for more books about it. During these last three weeks she had read several other books on the American revolution and the period, Fast's *Conceived in Liberty, Johnny Tremain* by Esther Forbes, and others. She was fascinated by the subject during that time. To the strong belief of my wife and myself, this was not mentioned outside the house although her teachers and schoolfriends may have known of it.

Mrs. Garrett's Comments	*Discussion*
"The Peace Corps? She wants to join the Peace Corps this summer. That doesn't seem right."	We had recently decided to send Wendy to a work camp the following summer. She had hearily disliked the idea. The night before, Wendy, my wife and I were discussing the matter. My wife said, "It's a sort of junior Peace Corps." Wendy immediately grasped this concept, became quite excited at the idea and began to look forward to going to the work camp. The discussion had not been mentioned to anyone else by my wife, my daughter or myself.

At this point, Mrs. Garrett stopped talking. I waited a moment, took the first box back and slid the second one—the tuft of hair from the dog—beneath her fingers.

Mrs. Garrett's Comments	*Discussion*
Box #2 "Oh, he's a nice dog. I'd like to take him hunting. He gets a lot of burrs in his coat."	He does often get burrs in his coat, but so do most dogs in the suburbs and country, I imagine.
"I think he once had a very bad pain in his paw. It really hurt him badly didn't it?"	I answered this by saying, "I don't know. The neighbors just moved in." That evening I asked the

Mrs. Garrett's Comments   *Discussion*

neighbors if the dog had any trouble with a paw. They answered that the previous year he had cut a forepaw on a piece of glass in the garden of their home. It had become infected and they had expected it to be fatal. He spent six weeks at the veterinary hospital.

"Tell me, didn't he once have a Sealyham companion."

I replied again that I did not know. (Further I did not add, but it was true, that knowing nothing about dogs, I would not have known a Sealyham if one came up and bit me.) That evening when I asked our neighbor about this he replied, "I thought you didn't know anything about dogs. He's a purebred Welsh terrier with Kennel Club papers to prove it, but there is something about his bone structure so that every time we show him to a real dog fancier, he says, 'Oh, come now, there's a little Sealyham in him somewhere.'"

Mrs. Garrett again stopped speaking and I took back the second box and slid the third (the rosebud) under her fingers.

Mrs. Garrett's Comments   **Discussion**

Box #3

"It's the rosebud. It comes from a very small garden. The garden needs a lot of work before it's ready for the summer."

These statements are true but could have been intuitively guessed by anyone who had formed a fairly accurate picture of my personality. Knowing that I lived in a suburb it would be a reasonable guess that I took it from my own garden. Knowing me, it would also be a reasonable guess that—if I had a garden—it would be a small one and that it would be very likely to be neglected and need a lot of work to be ready for the summer.

"The soil is too acid for it to grow well."

I had been told this several times by people who knew something about gardening. However it is entirely possible that someone raised in the country—as Mrs. Garrett was—could have known this from looking at the rosebud. Further, this soil condition is very common—almost universal—in the area in which I lived.

In this "spontaneous" psychometry experiment, all the statements made were accurate. Some were extremely precise—as the "American History" statement. Some

—as the statements about the dog's paw and the "Sealyham companion"—were unknown to anyone present and presumably to anyone Mrs. Garrett had ever met. Interestingly enough the statement about the "Sealyham companion" and the statements of the dog fanciers that ". . . there's a little Sealyham in him somewhere" (referring to his bone structure) appears to illustrate the typical clairvoyant problem of finding it difficult to differentiate realistic and symbolic levels of perception and description.

The facts that the decision to bring new materials to the experiment was made after seeing Mrs. Garrett, and in her absence; that the materials were chosen pretty much at random and that no one was told of this until they were handed to her; increases the impressiveness of this "spontaneous experiment." It should be emphasized perhaps that the procedure we were working on at the time was dermal vision and not psychometry and that her statements were "off-the-cuff" and spontaneous.

A tremendous number of good experimental studies also have been published. An example of one of these is also presented at the back of this book as Appendix E. It is by Stanley Krippner and Montague Ullman and is from a psychological journal called *Perceptual and Motor Skills*.[2] Those not trained in statistical methods may prefer to skip this as it can make pretty laborious reading. However, it is presented for the benefit of those who would like an example of "hard-core" research in parapsychology.

The very large number of cases of the sort I have described so far, demonstrating that people sometimes have information that—by all the common-sense knowledge and by the laws of how-the-world-works that we know—they could not possibly have, made it plain to me that ESP existed. And that if it existed, it was important and could not be left to be considered a sort of "bubble of mystery floating around in an otherwise normal universe" (as the philosopher Jacob Needleman has described one of the usual attitudes toward it). I felt that I had to try to study and understand further whatever was going on. "Impossible" things were clearly happening, and in science this is not permissible. The answer to this sort of situation in science has been to broaden our understanding of the possible so as to include the new data. To attempt to do this seemed to me to be the task I should now engage in.

3 | the way of the clairvoyant: the first road

If the paranormal abilities of man are indeed important, how could I go further? What could I do with the knowledge that they exist? If this knowledge was to be extended, two things were needed first: a useful and fruitful theory to deal with the facts we have and a method of training paranormal abilities so that they can be used in the service of individuals and society. The quest for these two things is what the rest of this book is about.

First there must be a theory. "Without a theory facts are a mob, not an army," wrote the physicist W. F. Barrett in 1940. Unless there is a coherent way of looking at a collection of facts that clearly have *something* to do with each other, we can do nothing with these facts except be upset, confused, or amused by them. Without a theory, facts tend to be forgotten or distorted by our memories. We find it hard to keep track of them unless they are in a framework that makes some kind of sense to us. Certainly, without a theory, we have no guide to tell us where to look for new facts, or how to use our inherent paranormal abilities. Clearly the development of some sort of theory was the first step necessary for an advance in knowledge.

This is just what we have been unable to develop. Since the beginning of the Society for Psychical Research in 1882 (and long before), serious men of very high caliber have been trying hard to answer the question "How does the sensitive do it?" "How does she get information she simply cannot have?" It has seemed impossible to arrive at a meaningful explanation. The whole situation flies so much in the face of common sense that we mentally stagger in circles trying to understand it.

There is, however, a scientific article of faith that seemed helpful to me. It is the knowledge that if serious people work for a long time on a question and do not get an answer, they are asking the wrong question. So often in scientific history what has seemed to be an absolute impasse, a totally hopeless situation in our quest for understanding has opened up and been bypassed when someone has asked a new question about the problem.

What question should I ask? Psychical research had failed with "How does the sensitive get the information?" and "How is it transmitted?" I decided to try this new one: "What is the relationship between the sensitive and the rest of reality at the moment when paranormal information is being acquired?" Instead of asking "how" it is done, I was now asking "What is going on *when* it is done; what is the structure of the total situation when the paranormal event happens?" This is a quite different question, and one I thought might, perhaps, lead me further.

How should I try to arrive at an answer to the new question? The simplest ways are best, if they work, and should be tried first. I decided to *ask,* to ask those most likely to know—the great sensitives, people like Eileen Garrett, Rosalind Heywood, Mrs. Willett, Phoebe Payne, Douglas Johnson. (One might define the "great sensitives" as people who over a long period of time have had a very high number of paranormal acquisitions of knowledge, who have done this under a wide variety of conditions, including carefully controlled laboratory investigations, and about whom there has never been the slightest question of fakery or chicanery. There have been a half dozen or so of these great ones carefully investigated in our century, and it is to them and to their writings that I decided to go.)

When I approached them with this question, something fascinating immediately happened. "Oh yes," they said, "when we are getting the paranormal information the world looks quite different than at other times." "Different?" I asked, as this clearly seemed very important. "Different how? What does the word 'different' mean here?"

As I searched the writings of these serious sensitives and questioned them (I must have questioned Eileen Garrett for at least five hundred hours and read and reread every line of the four to five thousand pages of her writing I could locate), I saw that again and again they said that they somehow shift to another way of perceiving the world, of being at home in it, just before they "achieve" the paranormal information. As far as they are concerned, the relationship between them and the rest of reality *is* different at these moments. Here are two examples of how Mrs. Garrett described the fact that there *is* a shift (exactly what the shift consists of I will come to shortly):

The supersensory experiences of clairvoyance, trance, telepathy and so on depend upon a fundamental shift of one's awareness. The field of stimulation is itself changed.[1]

I can now consciously shift my breathing when I choose and by doing so I can constantly change my activity from one phase to another.[2]

Again and again I discovered that the sensitives use phrases like these: the "fundamental shift of one's awareness," the "field of stimulation is itself changed," "the change of activity from one phase to another." Clearly, these were important in the search for understanding my question, What is the relationship between the sensitives and the rest of reality when paranormal information is being acquired? The relationship seems to change. How? To what? Is it really different?

I began to get a clue to *how* different the world looks at these moments of "shift awareness" in an incident that happened when I was working closely with Mrs. Garrett. She was in Florida, and I was going to fly there from New York the next day to do an experiment with her. On the spur of the moment I decided we might as well do another experiment on the same trip, and began assembling materials for a study in psychometry—a procedure in which the sensitive holds an object previously unknown to her and attempts to describe details of its history that cannot possibly be figured out from the object itself. (Thus from a tuft of hair from a dog's tail it might be possible to figure out the dog's breed and description, but not—as Mrs. Garrett did on the occasion I described earlier—figure out that the previous year it had had a badly infected paw.)

The materials I assembled for the experiment were all small and very different. They included an old Greek coin, a tiny fossil fish, a woman's comb, a bit of stone from inside Mt. Vesuvius, a used scrap of bandage from a hospital emergency room, and so forth. Each was wrapped in tissue, sealed in a small box, put into an envelope, and given a code number. These envelopes were then given to someone who did not know what was in them and who—working by himself—put each envelope into a large manila envelope with a new code number. Only he had both code numbers, so the end result was that there was no one, not even I, who knew which object was in which large manila envelope. This is typical research procedure in this field. It prevents, for example, the experimenter from unconsciously giving clues to the clairvoyant as to what is in the envelope.

As I was finishing wrapping and boxing the objects

in my office (where Mrs. Garrett had never been), I
found that I was one box short. The last object I
planned to use was an ancient Babylonian clay tablet
written in the old cuneiform method. It was somewhere
between 3000 and 3500 years old and I have never had
it translated. It could be anything from a laundry list
to a peace treaty! Certainly a dramatic and interesting
object.

Not having a box, I went to a neighboring office and
asked the secretary there (a woman I knew only
slightly) if she had one. She asked what size and came
into my room to see the ones I had been using. There
she noticed the clay tablet, picked it up and asked what
it was. We chatted about it for three minutes and she
departed to look for a box. While she was gone, I found
one of my own, identical with the others I had used,
and put the tablet in that. This seemed a very minor
incident in the history of this tablet, and one that
quickly slipped out of my consciousness.

Two weeks later and 1500 miles away, Mrs. Garrett sat before a tape recorder. I sat in another corner
of the room, facing away from her. A third person,
Jean Andoire (who had no knowledge of the objects
either), ran the recorder and took notes. Mrs. Garrett
picked up one of the large manila envelopes, which I
later learned contained the tablet, read the double-
coded number on the outside and started to talk about
"a woman associated with this." She then proceeded to
describe the secretary from the office next to mine
(whom she had never met nor heard of) in such detail
that it would have been possible just from the description to pick the secretary out of a line-up of ten thousand women. She described the two scars she bore on
her body (which later checking showed to be precisely
where Mrs. Garrett had indicated), her distinctive hair
style, her job history, and the special relationship she
had with her daughter. However, Mrs. Garrett did not
say one word that could possibly be interpreted as
having anything to do with an ancient Babylonian clay
tablet, or with the area of the little shops next to the

British Museum where I had bought it, or even with my desk in whose top drawer it had rested for the past year.

Clearly then, the "field of stimulation" Mrs. Garrett was responding to when gaining this paranormal information was a different one from that which we ordinarily respond to. All the aspects of the tablet that would be regarded as important in our view of the world, or our way of being at home in the world, went unmentioned. What was described—unquestionably true and unquestionably paranormally known as it was——were things that in our everyday view of the world were very minor and unimportant. What was important in my "field of stimulation" was unimportant in hers, and vice versa.

I began to see from this and similar incidents in the literature that the paranormal field of stimulation—the-way-the-world-looks to a clairvoyant—is indeed different from the normal one; and that the sensitive *is* looking at the world in these special moments as if it were constructed along different lines from the way we ordinarily believe it to be constructed. And a thousand different experiments in parapsychology bear this out.

It has long been known in physical research that we need a new concept to understand our data. Louisa Rhine, one of the leading specialists in the field, discussed this need for a new concept:

Parapsychological research has discovered a modality of perception unlimited by space and time which as a phenomenon is still quite unexplainable. It looks as if a different concept than the present one of the structure of the objective universe is necessary before it can be fitted in. The facts of mental ability already discovered in parapsychology no more fit the current idea of a space-time world than such a fact that ships disappear bottom-first over the horizon fit the model of a flat earth. The contradiction in the latter case called for a new and revolutionary idea; this one in parapsychology does too.[3]

Perhaps the statements and evidence offered by sensitives, that they conceive the universe to be constructed on different lines during moments when they are paranormally acquiring information than in "ordinary" moments, was the beginning of the new concept I needed, the clue for which so much searching had been done. How could I begin to understand this different way of comprehending reality? I started by continuing to look at the writings and statements of the serious sensitives. What did they say about it?

As I searched their writings and questioned those I could for an answer to this problem, it gradually emerged that all my sources appeared to agree on four basic differences between the ordinary and the paranormal ways of understanding how the world is constructed. These four differences, which I shall shortly describe in detail, raised these questions:

1. What is the most important aspect of a "thing"?
2. What is "time"?
3. How should one look at "good and evil"? What do these words mean?
4. What is the best way of gaining information?

The sensitives agreed that in the moments when they were acquiring paranormal information they felt differently about these four aspects of reality than they did at other times. Their relationship to reality changed in the special "paranormal" moments and these four differences were aspects of that change. I was beginning to see a glimmer of light illuminating my question "What is the relationship between the sensitive and the rest of reality at the moment when paranormal information is being acquired?" Now I had to explore in more detail each of these four differences.

The first one, "What is the most important aspect of a 'thing'?" was by far the hardest one for me to comprehend. It was also the most central and most crucial one: eventually it became clear that the other three rested on it. I shall describe it here and return to it

from time to time in this book, each time attempting to
further define my understanding of it.

I might start by asking what is most important about
John K. Jones. Clearly, the most important thing about
him is that he is this individual, unique person, John K.
Jones. The second most important thing is that he is a
man, the third is that he is a mammal, the fourth that
he is an animal, the fifth that he is a living organism,
the sixth that he is a collection of matter here and now,
the seventh that he is a field of energy interacting with
other energy fields of all kinds, and so on, until we
come to what is ordinarily considered the *least* important thing about him; that he is part of the total
cosmos, that he is one with all and everything, with the
total universe.

This is our ordinary way of looking at things. Certainly we vary it to some degree; for certain purposes
the most important thing about our mythical John K.
Jones may be that he is a man, or an American citizen.
However, if we consider a scale of aspects ranging
from his most individual and unique aspects (the extreme being that he is *him* and no other) to his most
general and related aspects (the most extreme being
that he is a part of the total universe), we usually tend
to consider that the most important aspects are the ones
clustering around the unique and individual end of the
spectrum.

In the special moments of paranormal perception, I
discovered from the writings of the clairvoyants, this
consideration is reversed. The most important aspects
of a thing are seen as clustering around the general or
relationship end of the scale. It is the *unity* of all things
that is seen as most important, their *relationships* rather
than their individual and unique characteristics that are
seen as crucial. The ordinary way of perceiving starts
with each "thing" (entity or event) seen first as separate and unique and that is what is most important
about it. Only secondarily do we go to its relationships
with other entities or events. In the paranormal moment
of perception (which I called the "Clairvoyant Reality,"

the reality perceived when ESP is taking place) we start just in the opposite manner. All "things" (entities and events) are related, and that is what is most important. Only secondarily do we go to its separate or individual charatceristics. It is as if we are turning reality upside down. In the ordinary way of looking at things (which I called the "Sensory Reality," the reality in which we gain information through our senses), we start with the individual thing and then proceed to its relationship with other things. In the Clairvoyant Reality we start with the relationships and then go on to the individual.

One great British sensitive, Mrs. Willett, wrote of the Clairvoyant Reality, "It's so heavenly to be out of myself—when I'm everything, you know, and everything else is me." [4] In one of her scripts (Mrs. Willett's mediumship was mostly done with automatic writing), she defined mediumship as the capacity for *excurisis* (a "going out"). In a later script she struggled to define it further, and in this struggle gives some of the flavor of the differences in operating in these two modes of being, these two ways of relating the self to the rest of reality.

> The falling of the barriers say that there is the dual process . . . the hemming in the partitioning off the localizing the selfing. All that is one process. Now reverse it and say the escape the unifying the delocalization of the soul that is nearer get the thought clear testifying to the existence of a whole. . . .[5]

As one reads this over, one begins to sense how fundamentally these two ways of perception differ. They give different answers to the question "Which is more important, an entity's individuality or its relationships?" No one would say that one of these is important and the other is not. Both clearly are. There is, however, a difference as to where you start from, which end of the spectrum you consider primary, and which end you consider secondary. In our ordinary moments of perception (when we are in the Sensory Reality), we say it is the individuality end of the scale. In moments of paranormal perception (when we are in the Clairvoyant Reality), we say it is the relationship end that is most important.

I shall return to this point later and hope to clarify it further. Now, however, let us go to the second way in which the sensitives say that the Sensory Reality and the Clairvoyant Reality differ: the nature of time.

In the Sensory Reality we know that time "flows" inexorably in one direction. Time proceeds at an absolutely steady pace from the future, through the moment of the present, into the past. It cannot be changed or reversed; it simply proceeds. It is "time's arrow," a concept of time that goes only in one direction. In this flow of time, events "happen," they "occur." Events are located in the past, in the present, or in the future. They "have happened," or "are happening," or "will happen." If they happen in the past, we can (theoretically at least) observe them or their effects. If they are in the future, we can (theoretically at least) intervene in their course: have an effect on them.

In the Clairvoyant Reality, say the sensitives, time takes on quite a different structure. All events *are*, they do not happen. The past, the present, and the future are all equally in existence, even though we can ordinarily only observe those events located in the present. It is as if one were describing what happens when a movie is being shown. All the events of the movie are in existence: they are on the celluloid film already, but we can only see a very narrow slice of the film already, but we can only see a very narrow slice of the film at any one time. As the frames of the film pass behind the lens of the projector and flash on the screen, it looks to us as if the events were happening, but in reality the entire film and all the events on it (those that have already "happened" on the screen and those yet to "happen") already exist. All these events can (theoretically at least) be observed. None can be acted on any more than we can act on the events in the film, even if we were an actor in it. This is similar if we are an actor in a play. The events *exist* in the script. We can participate, feel, observe. Any attempt to change the events as they occur (if for example we were playing Romeo and "wished" he would not take the poison) would disrupt and end the play. Any attempt in the Clairvoyant Reality to "change" events disrupts this reality and returns us to the Sensory Reality.

In the Clairvoyant Reality, time is seen in this way: all events of the past, present, and future exist; it is only the narrow window we usually look through that makes them seem to "happen," that makes only the present visible. "Everything that was, is, and if you are a sensitive you stumble on it," said Mrs. Garrett. She has also described clairvoyance as

> an intensely acute sensing of some aspects of life in operation, and since at clairvoyant levels time is undivided and whole, one often perceives the object or event in its past, present and/or future phases in abruptly swift successions.[6]

And elsewhere Mrs. Garrett wrote:

> On clairvoyant levels there exists simultaneity of time, and the clairvoyant message may concern future events and future relationships which today seem impossible, or meaningless to the person to whom they are revealed.[7]

This concept of time leads to the third aspect of the Clairvoyant Reality which, the sensitives say, differs from our ordinary way of perceiving the world, from the Sensory Reality. This third aspect concerns the nature of good and evil. If everything that *is, was* and *will continue to be* (like the nature of the celluloid film that is the "reality" of the movie we see), then every events *is,* and is above and beyond the concept of good and evil. In Mrs. Garrett's words "What I see in clairvoyance is neither *good* nor is it *right*. It *is*. It is inevitable."

This is a difficult point to which I shall return in more detail later. Yet here it is important to note that the clairvoyant would never say that pain, disease, suffering, the stunting of human growth and potential are not evil and are not to be avoided. In the Sensory Reality these *are* evil. However, in the Clairvoyant Reality one simply observes and does not judge. Everything and every event is seen as a part of everything else and a part of everything that (from our ordinary view) was and will be. Thus to judge any specific event as good or evil is to judge the entire cosmos, the complete space-time fabric of being. If no thing can be separated from all other things, then neither can the judgment of any one thing be separate. It is partly in this sense that the clairvoyant says that from this view, "good" and "evil" are concepts that are irrelevant to her perceptions. Certainly, however, when the clairvoyant is in the Sensory Reality (as she is the great majority of the time), she knows good and evil and takes action for the former and against the latter.

There were four aspects by means of which the sensitives differentiated the Sensory Reality and the Clairvoyant Reality. These were: the most important aspect of a thing; the nature of "time"; the nature of "evil"; and the best way of gaining information.

In the Sensory Reality, the best way of gaining information about a thing is to use our sense organs: to examine, listen to, touch, and taste it. We would use our intelligence to interpret this information, and sharpen our intelligence with philosophical and scientific methods. Basically, in this view of the world, our senses are the best way of gaining information.

In the Clairvoyant Reality, however, the best way is not the way of the senses. Since everything—including the observers (you and I)—is primarily and fundamentally related to and a part of everything else—then the best way of gaining information about something is to accept this "oneness," to accept that you and it are the same thing, and then you "know" about it in the same way you ordinarily know about yourself through self-observation. One of the greatest contemporary experts in psychical research is Emilio Servadio, an Italian psychoanalyst. Of this area he wrote, "In telepathy, a dualism appears to be temporarily cancelled, and for some moments a 'unity in plurality' reestablished." [8]

Let me put this another way. In the way-the-world-works, as seen in the Clairvoyant Reality, you and I are really one. We are part of the total "One" that makes up the entire cosmos. If I know that this is true and am reacting to you as if this were true, then—being one—there is nothing to bar information exchange between us. So to speak, nothing can come between a thing and itself. Thus we have "telepathy" between us from the viewpoint of the Sensory Reality, and from the viewpoint of the Clairvoyant Reality we simply have information circulating inside one "thing." This is the way that the clairvoyant's concept of reality "explains" telepathy and clairvoyance, just as it explains precognition with the concept that all events *are* and that one can perceive this by "knowing" it and widening the narrow lens through which we ordinarily perceive reality (or to continue the analogy with the movie, to simply lift the film off the projector reel and look at it to observe that "events are" before they flash on the screen, which we call the "present").

This then is the "reality" that the clairvoyant experiences during the moments of paranormal acquisition of information. This is the way it seems to her the world is put together during these moments. When I had analyzed it to this degree, two things seemed clear. First, that I still had much distance to go in order to understand it deeply enough to arrive at a useful and fruitful theory about the paranormal. These were bare bones and it would be necessary to bring life to them by adding flesh and muscle. Second, that this *Weltbild*, this picture of the world, was familiar; I had seen it described before. As it developed, another group of people, starting from a different point, with different techniques and goals, had arrived at the same world picture, had described identically the Clairvoyant Reality, and helped me immeasurably in understanding it more deeply.

4 | the clairvoyant
and the mystic:
the second road

The second group of people I found who has described
the Clairvoyant Reality in the same way as the clairvoyants came from a wide variety of times and places. In
Europe, there were the Roman Plotinus, and later
Meister Eckhardt, Richard Rolle, Isaac Luria, St.
Richard of Victor, St. John of the Cross, St. Teresa of
Avila, the Baal Shem Tov, George Fox, Evelyn Underhill, and many others. From the East, there were the
Lord Buddha, Sankara, Kabir, Dogen, Rumi, Vivekananda, Ramakrishna, and a host more. All had a great
deal in common. They spoke of something other than
our usual way of conceptualizing reality, another way
of describing how-the-world-works and, whatever their
specific differences, all agreed on this idea of its structure. Evelyn Underhill (the most literate and one of
the greatest of modern Western mystics) wrote:

> The most highly developed branches of the human
> family have in common one peculiar characteristic.
> They tend to produce—sporadically it is true, and
> often in the teeth of adverse external circumstances—
> a curious and definite type of personality; a type

which refuses to be satisfied with that which other men call experience, and is inclined, in the words of its enemies, to "deny the world in order that it may find reality." We meet these persons in the east and west; in the ancient, medieval, and modern worlds . . . whatever the place or period in which they have arisen, their aims, doctrines and methods have been substantially the same. Their experience, therefore, forms a body of evidence, curiously self-consistent and often mutually explanatory, which must be taken into account before we can add up the sum of the energies and potentialities of the human spirit, or reasonably speculate on its relations to the unknown world which lies outside the boundaries of sense.[1]

The British philosopher C. D. Broad also described this group:

To me, the occurrence of mystical experience at all times and places, and the similarities between the statements of so many mystics all the world over, seem to be a really significant fact. *Prima facie* it suggests that there is an aspect of reality with which these persons come in contact in their mystical experience, and which they afterwards strive and largely fail to describe in the language of every day life. I should say that this *prima facie* appearance of objectivity ought to be accepted at its face value unless and until some reasonably satisfactory explanation of the agreement can be given.[2]

"All mystics," wrote the visionary Louis Claude de Saint-Martin, "speak the same language and come from the same country."

Bertrand Russell did not think very much of the mystical approach to reality, although he confessed himself to be puzzled by the very high quality of the people who believed in it. He did, however, turn that superb analytical brain of his to the problem of exactly what it was that the mystics believed in. He reported that in the moments when they believed that they were really comprehending "reality," really perceiving and being at home in it, they all agreed on four of its characteristics. These, said Russell, are:

1. That there is a better way of gaining information than through the senses.
2. That there is a fundamental unity to all things.
3. That time is an illusion.
4. That all evil is mere appearance.[3]

I found Russell's analysis of the mystic after I had completed my own analysis of the Clairvoyant Reality as described by the clairvoyants. The identical nature of the two was overwhelming. It was clear that the two groups of individuals were talking about the same thing. Each had come to the conclusion that two ways of looking at reality exist: our ordinary way and another way, and they agreed completely on the nature of this other.

Describing this second way, and training techniques for perceiving it, Evelyn Underhill spoke of changing the "field of perception" in words almost identical with those of Eileen Garrett given on page 29:

> The act of contemplation is for the mystic a psychic gateway: a method of going from one level of consciousness to another. In technical language it is the condition under which he shifts his "field of perception" and obtains his characteristic outlook on the universe.[4]

In another place, Underhill makes it even clearer that the mystic relates to and *unites with* a different conceptualization of reality than the one we ordinarily use:

> The distinction between mystic and nonmystic is not merely that between the rationalist and the dreamer, between intellect and intuition. The question which

divides them is really this: What, out of the mass of
material offered to it, shall consciousness seize upon—
with what aspect of the universe shall it "unite". . . ?[5]

Let us take these four aspects in the same order as
in my discussion of the sensitives' conception. The
most central of the four aspects is that there is "a
fundamental unity to all things." Basically this is a
statement that the general and relational aspects of a
"thing" are the really important aspects, and its individual and unique characteristics are less so. Literally,
all things are connected. All is One.

From this viewpoint, everything is a part of the All
that makes up reality, the total cosmos. To see, to
understand anything means first to see and understand
that it is a part of everything else, that nothing is
separate, nothing stands alone. The most important
thing about a man is that "no man is an island." He is
"a part of the main." It was to this point that the
mystic-poet Francis Thompson addressed himself when
he wrote:

> All things by immortal power
> Near or far
> Hiddenly
> To each other linked are
> That thou cans't not stir a flower
> Without troubling of a star.

W. T. Stace, one of the great scholars of the subject,
wrote of this aspect of mysticism:

> The whole multiplicity of things which comprise the
> universe are identical with one another and therefore
> constitute only one thing, a pure unity. The Unity,
> the One . . . is the central experience and the central
> concept of all mysticism, of whichever type.[6]

On this fundamental unity and oneness of all things,
including the person who observes in the Clairvoyant
Reality, Mrs. Garrett wrote:

You are both question and answer. You are the total consciousness for which you seek, but bound by life's many experiences. One thing must be clear to you: there is no interruption; the experiences and you are the same.[7]

Compare this statement with, for example, a stanza of Emerson's poem "Brahma," which is regarded by many as a profound statement of the Eastern mystical point of view.

> They reckon ill who leave me out,
>> When me they fly, I am the wings.
> I am the doubter and the doubt.
>> I am the hymn the Brahmin sings.

Indeed, Evelyn Underhill defines mysticism as "the art of union with Reality."[8] And this may be further compared with this extract from a trance session:

> Question:
> ". . . the man upon the road to Mecca
> realizes that the city . . ."
> Mrs. Garrett's reply:
> "He is both the city and the route."[9]

The mystic sees as his major life task understanding this in such a complete way that he *knows* it is true, that in his perception of the world it *is* true. It is this state of being—in the parlance of today, this "altered state of consciousness"—for which he strives. He strives toward knowing this so completely that he perceives himself at one with the total cosmos, and knows it to be so valid that he can never be lost from it. It is toward this state that his exercises, his training, his meditations are directed. He seeks to know his oneness with the One so that with Giordano Bruno he can say, "Out of this world we cannot fall." It is from this total being at home in the universe that he participates in the serenity, the peace, the *hitlavut,* the joy, that is so typical of the mystical adept.

There are many roads of training for this comprehension, and I will discuss them in some detail later. However, whether one sits in a lotus position, prays on one's knees in a church, moves in the whirling dance of the dervish, or pores over the words of the Cabala, what is being sought is a way to be at home in the world under a different metaphysic, to be one with the cosmos in such a way that the general and relational aspects of oneself (and everything else) are paramount and the separate, cut-off, unique, and individual aspects are secondary and illustory. This is what the Christian mystic means when he says, "Come to know the hidden unity in the Eternal Being"; what the Eastern Vedantist means when he says one can and should say to everything, "Tat tvam asi"— "That art thou"; and what the Talmud means when it says, "No place is empty of Him."

This is the meaning of the statement of Rabbi Dov Baer, one of the leading mystics of the Hasidic school, that his task as a teacher was "to change the something back into the nothing." This statement is clearer if we break up the words "something" and "nothing" to "some thing" and "no thing." His task, as a teacher, was to show that a "thing," with its implications of being separate and distinct from all other "things," did not exist. It is no "thing" but a part of the all. Similarly, the Mandyyuka-Rarita Upanishad states:

All objects are in origin unlimited like space
And multiplicity has no place in them in any sense.[10]

A clear statement of this is the story of the Zen student who asked what was his enemy barring his path to enlightenment. Yasutani-Roshi, the Zen Master, replied, "your enemy is your discursive thinking which leads you to differentiate yourself on one side of an imaginary line from what is not you on the other side of this non-existent line." [11] And we might compare this to a statement of the Roman mystic Plotinus: "No doubt we should not speak of seeing but, instead of seen or seer, speak boldly of a simple unity. For in the seeing we neither distinguish nor are there two." [12]

Of the four aspects of reality as perceived by the mystic (which, in Russell's analysis, differs from our usual, everyday perception), the first is the importance of the general and relational aspects of a thing rather than its unique and individual aspects. The second is that time is an illusion.

When I examined what the mystic means by the statement that time is an illusion, I found that he is saying that it is our usual concept of past, present, and future as separate, differentiated states that is an illusion. If all is one—and this is the basic statement of the mystical world-picture—then there is unity in time as well as space. In this view, the separation in space between two entities is an illusion and the separation in time between two events is an illusion. Since in this metaphysical system we are most concerned with the relational aspect of "things," all events and entities "flow" into one another. Sharp dividing lines are an illusion, and this includes the sharp dividing lines we customarily make between the past, the present, and the future. Time, says the mystic, is "a seamless garment" on which man customarily makes arbitrary seams and separation lines.

The Absolute, the One, the Real, Brahman, from the mystic's viewpoint, *is*. It was, is, and will be, and is not divided into "has happened," "is happening," "will happen," into past, present, and future. The Real contains no such characteristics and divisions any more than the movie film resting in the can, or the play's script on its pages, has them. We view the real through the narrow lens of the film projector (or through reading one line of the script at a time), and it therefore appears to us as if events were happening in motion and as if the universe were divided into what *has, is,* and *will be* happening. That this is the *only* way to perceive is an illusion arising from the structure of our nervous system and the false way we are trained as children to perceive.

The mystic thus says that there are two ways of looking at time: the everyday way and the way of mystical perception. (The way of the mystical perception of reality is what we have previously called the Clairvoyant Reality.) Meister Eckhardt, the great medieval mystic, wrote:

> Perception here means seeing in the light that is in time, for anything I think of I think of in the light that is in time and temporal. But angels perceive in the light that is beyond time and eternal. They know in the eternal now. . . . Yet take away this now of time and thou art everywhere and hast the whole of time.[13]

The statement of Jesus, "Before Abraham was, I am," expresses this insight of two different ways of perceiving time even more clearly.

I found that our present-day, common-sense view of time as one-way, linear, and irrevocable, is a view peculiar to our culture, and neither completely accepted by modern physics (see Chapter 5) nor by the ancient world. It is a viewpoint brought into the Western world by Christianity, which insisted on a unique event that could be dated: That Christ had come into the world and died for our sins at a definite time. The unique, datable event, never having happened before and never to be repeated, forces us to a concept of time as linear and unidirectional. The older religions did not have unique events that occurred at a time that could be dated. Apollo might have been born at Delos, or Athena might have emerged from the brow of Zeus, but no one could date the event. It happened in a different conceptual scheme of time. In some of the older religions, the great events were essentially cyclical and repeating, sometimes on a seasonal basis. Others considered the Gods in a perpetual state of being. In either case, they were not in our common-sense time; they could not be dated. The Jews had prepared the way for the new concept of time with Jehovah handing down the tablets at Mt. Sinai, and a Messiah who was to appear only once, but it was Christianity that spread the concept throughout the world.

The Australian aborigines(and many other primitive societies) also conceive of two kinds of time. The first is our irresistible, passing time. The second is "the Great Time." The latter is the time of the myths, the Gods and Heroes, and of the dream. It is the time of all-at-once instead of the time of one-thing-after-another. What occurs in the Great Time has sequence, but it cannot be dated as to *when* it happened. The time concept of the sensitive and of the mystic seems structurally akin to the primitives' concept of the Great Time.

The third of Russell's characteristics of the mystical world-view (in the order we considered them in our analysis of the Clairvoyant Reality) is that "all evil is mere appearance." This is indeed a strange and disturbing statement. It appears to lead toward a way of life that would ignore the pain and suffering in the world, and would choose not to participate in the great struggle for human freedom and dignity. Indeed it is true that some Eastern mystical traditions have historically made this decision, and seen their major life tasks to be to withdraw from the world of everyday reality and to pay no attention to human suffering. These traditions, however (which were never widespread in the West), have been largely abandoned by Eastern mystics in the past fifty to a hundred years as a misinterpretation. It comes as a surprise to many that there are invalid mystical paths in the same way as there are invalid materialistic paths. In the modern phrase, "bum trips" occur in both kinds of searching.

The prevalent viewpoint of the mystics concerning the meaning of this aspect is quite different. They say that when one is being in the world of the One, the Unity, one does not judge, one only observes and *is*. Since—from this viewpoint—everything flows into everything else, one observes and is a part of the total harmony of the All, the Cosmos, and in this great harmony, nothing is superfluous or disharmonious. If a single event or entity did not exist, the total harmony would be destroyed. It is only by including everything that the total being is possible. The Italian playwright Ugo Betti put it: "If there were one drop of water less in the universe, the whole world would thirst." The total, from this viewpoint, is a dynamic, complete harmony that if one comprehends, one does not desire to change. Rosalind Heywood, who is both a serious sensitive and a serious mystic, once tried to explain this to me. I found it very difficult to understand. Finally, in some desperation, she said, "Look Larry, if you hear music being played perfectly, you do not say, 'Play it out of tune.' "

Gary Snyder in his *Earth House Hold* has written to this point:

> Avatamsaka (Kegon) Buddhist philosophy sees the world as a vast interrelated network in which all objects and creatures are necessary and illuminated. From one standpoint, governments, wars, or all that we consider "evil" are uncompromisingly contained in this totalistic realm. The hawk, the swoop and the hare are one. From the "human" standpoint we cannot live in these terms unless all human beings see with the same enlightened eye. The Bodhisavata lives by the sufferer's standard, and he must be effective in aiding those who suffer.

> The mercy of the West has been social revolution; the mercy of the East has been individual insight into the basic self/void. We need both. They are both contained in the traditional three aspects of the Dharma path: Wisdom (prajna), meditation (dhyana), and morality (sila).[14]

The serious mystic is involved in and united with both ways of beings in the world. Both are valid for him, both are part of man's being. According to Plotinus, man is an amphibian who must live in both worlds to attain his full growth. He can live in one of them, in water or on land (the world of the One or the world of the many), but living in just one stunts the development toward his full potential. Ramakrishna used an almost identical concept when he spoke of man in his youth being like a tadpole that must live in water. Later in his development, he said, "when the tail of ignorance drops off," he becomes a frog that needs to live both on land and in water. "To give our Lord a perfect hospitality," wrote St. Teresa of Avila, "Mary and Martha must combine."

The anonymous author of "The Cloud of Unknowing" (one of the great medieval mystical manuscripts), writes again and again of the need for "listy" behavior if one is seriously concerned with spiritual growth. "Listy" here means the opposite of "listless"; it means being active, eager, involved.

In the Hasidic tradition it is repeated over and over that if the Zaddick, the wise man, serves only God and not the people, he will descend from whatever "rung of the ladder of perfection" he has ascended to. "If the Zaddick serves God," typically wrote Rabbi Nahman of Bratislav, "but does not take the trouble to teach the multitude, he will descend from his rung." [15]

The great mystics have understood this, and functioned strongly in both worlds. W. R. Inge, a scholar of the subject, has pointed out that "all the great [Western] mystics have been energetic and influential, and their business capacity is specially noted in a curiously large number of cases." [16] The lives of St. John of the Cross, St. Teresa of Avila, Kabir, Vivekananda, and many others show this understanding, concern, and active involvement with the world of multiplicity. In her usual incisive way, St. Teresa once stated the situation clearly. At dinner, a dish of roast partridges had been served, and she was eating with great gusto and enjoyment. Someone reproached her that it was unseemly for a bride of Christ to have such zest for and participation in the mundane aspects of the world. St. Teresa replied,

"When it's prayer time, pray; when it's partridge time, partridge!"

Further, there is an ethical aspect implicit in the Clairvoyant Reality. If I *know* that in a real and profound sense you and I are one and are both integral parts of the total One, I treat you in the same way I treat myself. In addition, I treat myself with love and respect because I am part of the total harmony of the universe (or "a part of God" or "contain the indwelling light" or "an expression of Brahma"). If I regard you and me as separate, and do not accept that we are part of one another, I tend to treat you differently than I treat myself. Further, because of my cut-off-from-the-universe state, I may treat either or both of us badly. The Clairvoyant Reality contains within it the answer to the question of Cain: we *are* each our brothers' keepers and we are each our brothers.

The fourth aspect of Russell's analysis of the mystics' description of how-the-world-works is that "there is a better way of gaining information than through the senses." The senses are "blind guides leading to the morass of illusion." To comprehend the truth about reality, one must see beyond the apparent multiplicity of the world, beyond the illusory separateness of events and entities to the Oneness that makes them all a part of the great harmony of the One.

Rohit Mehta (a serious mystic who wrote the introduction to A. W. Osborn's book *The Expansion of Awareness*), said in this regard:

There are indeed fundamentally two categories of knowledge—Knowledge by Ideation and Knowledge by Being. All scientific knowledge, whether physical or super-physical, belongs to the first category. Such knowledge is based on the duality of the observer and observed. In spiritual perception, however, there is Knowledge by Being—it arises in that state where the duality of the observer and the observed has vanished. This is the very core of direct or what is otherwise called the Mystical experience.[17]

Again, I must emphasize that the great majority of mystics know and say that both ways of looking at and being in reality are valid. For a feel understanding one must see both. In the center of Shinto temples stands a mirror symbolizing the fact that to see reality one must see both oneself and the illusory nature of the self, see the reality of the separate entity and see that—from another viewpoint—it is not reality, but illusion.

Kabir, the beautiful Indian mystic of the fifteenth century, describes this in terms of the reality of both the One (the water) and the Many (the waves):

The river and its waves are one surf: where is the difference between the river and its waves?

When the wave rises, it is the water; and when it falls, it is the same water again. Tell me, Sir, where is the distinction?

Because it has been named a wave, shall it no longer be considered as water?

Within the Supreme Brahma, the worlds are told like beads: Look upon that rosary with the eyes of wisdom.[18]

The mystic says that to preceive reality we must go beyond the data of the senses. Our senses show us the world of multiplicity, which has reality and in which we must live. (Ramakrishna states that if one perceives only in the world of the One, the body cannot stay alive for more than twenty-one days). Truth, however, consists of more than the world of multiplicity, and for this we must go beyond the senses to view the other metaphysical possibility: the world in which everything flows into and is connected to and is a part of everything else. It is for this going beyond the senses that the disciplines, the long, hard training, the meditations of the mystical training schools and traditions have been devised. And the lives of the great mystics—of the Lord Buddha, of Jesus of Nazareth, of Meister Eckhardt, Jalal-ud-din Rumi, Jacob Boehme and the Baal Shem Tov—all bear testimony to the fact that they were basing their actions and lives on data that did not come to them through the narrow windows of their sensory channels.

It should be noted here that Gardner Murphy has also examined the relationship of the mystical and paranormal viewpoints and has reached a conclusion different than the one reached in this book. He concludes that they are *not* the same. He notes that until he carefully considered the matter, he had agreed with the psychical researcher Frederick Myers that "these two classes of experience are closely related expressions of the same deep powers of the human mind." [19] It may be that the different conclusions reached by Murphy and me are dictated by different approaches to the problem. Murphy is primarily concerned with the *why* and *when* of the experience, and sees it as a *response to a need*. I am more concerned with the *what*, and view it as a method of interaction with reality. Our differences may well stem from this.

(The conceptualization in this book, however, owes much to Gardner Murphy's field-theoretical, biosocial approach. He has made what psychoanalyst Jan Ehrenwald has called "the decisive step toward . . . the open, non-Cartesian or non-Euclidean model of personality." [20])

In one area, there tends to be real disagreement between the mystic and the medium. This disagreement centers on their attitude toward the paranormal. For the mystic, concentration on, or interest in such things as telepathy, precognition, clairvoyance, and psychokinesis tends to move the individual away from the path of psychological change he is interested in. The mystics, particularly the Eastern mystics, report that paranormal abilities naturally arise as the person moves into the perception and being of the world of the One. However, the mystic tends to believe that interest in them prevents further growth. This viewpoint of the mystic was expressed by Aldous Huxley:

> The Sufis regard miracles as "veils" intervening between the soul and God. The masters of Hindu spirituality urge their disciples to pay no attention to the *Siddhis,* or psychic powers, which may come to them unsought, as a by-product of one-pointed contemplation. The cultivation of these powers, they warn, distracts the soul from Reality and sets up insurmountable obstacles in the way of enlightenment and deliverance. A similar attitude is taken by the best Buddhist teachers, and in one of the Pali scriptures there is an anecdote recording Buddha's own characteristically dry comment on a prodigious feat of levitation performed by one of his disciples. "This," he said, "will not conduce to the conversion of the unconverted, nor to the advantage of the converted." Then he went back to talking about deliverance.[21]

Thus, I had, at this point in my research, found that there were two groups that agreed that man is capable of perceiving the world as put together in two different ways and what these two ways are. It may be useful to examine a few statements of these two ways of being at home in reality. Two of these statements are by a medium, one is by a historian, one by a physicist, two by mystics, and one by a psychiatrist.

In a subjective view, Eileen Garrett summed up her feelings about her experience:

> But there are certain concentrations of consciousness in which awareness is withdrawn as far as possible from the impact of all sensory perceptions. . . . Such withdrawals of consciousness from the outer world are common to all of us in some measure, in the practice of prayer, meditation, and abstract thought.
>
> What happens to us at these times is that, as we withdraw from the environing world, we relegate the

activities of the five senses to the field of the subconscious, and seek to focus *awareness* (to the best of our ability) in the field of the superconscious—the timeless, spaceless field of the as-yet-unknown. . . .

In such types of consciousness-activity all our illusions of present time, our situation in space, and differentiations in consciousness (individuality) are transcended.[22]

And in an exuberant tone, Mrs. Garrett said elsewhere:

And so today I build in space my own roadways from there to there and back, where I enjoy the advantage of living in two worlds at once—the mundane world and the world "out-there" where the sun never sets and adventure lurks in every breath, where destiny and free-will meet, and like past and future are irrevocably wedded.[23]

Arnold Toynbee, the historian, has differentiated the sensory and clairvoyant realities in an interesting manner:

[There is a] distinction between two facets of truth which cannot be focused into a unity by imperfectly united faculties of the Human Mind. In the Human Psyche there are two organs: a conscious, volitional surface and a subconscious, non-volitional abyss. Each of these two organs has it own way of looking at, and peering through, the dark glass that screens Reality from Man's inward eye and, in screening it, dimly reveals it; and therefore each mode of imperfect apprehension calls its findings "the Truth." But the qualities of the two different facets of a latent unitary truth are as different as the nature of the two organs of the human psyche that receives these "broken lights." [24]

The physicist J. Robert Oppenheimer made the same point when he wrote:

These two ways of thinking, the way of time and history and the way of eternity and timelessness, are both parts of man's efforts to comprehend the world in which he lives. Neither is comprehended in the other nor reducible to it. They are, as we have learned to say in physics, complementary views, each supplementing the other, neither telling the whole story.[25]

Evelyn Underhill put it this way:

Now it is a paradox of human life, often observed by the most concrete and unimaginative philosophers, that man seems to be poised between two contradictory orders of reality. Two phases of existence— or, perhaps, two ways of apprehending existence— lie within the possible span of his consciousness. That great pair of opposites which metaphysicians call Being and Becoming, Eternity and Time, Unity and Multiplicity, and others mean, when they speak of the Spiritual and the Natural Worlds, represents the two extreme forms under which the universe can be realized by him.[26]

And we might compare these quotations with a statement of the mystic Meister Eckhardt:

The soul has something within it, a spark of supersensual knowledge that is never quenched. But there is also another knowledge in our souls, which is directed outward towards objects; namely knowledge of our senses and the understanding; this hides that other knowledge from us. The intuitive higher knowledge is timeless and spaceless, without any here and now.[27]

Kurt Goldstein, one of our most thoughtful and wisest psychiatrists, wrote:

I have come to the conclusion that man always lives in two spheres of experience: the sphere in which

subject and object are experienced as separate and
only secondarily related, and another one in which
he experiences oneness with the world. . . . Because
we observe these experiences in normal human beings,
we must say that they, and the world in which they
appear, belong to man's nature.[28]

If one compares these—particularly perhaps the
statements of J. Robert Oppenheimer and Evelyn Underhill—one perceives clearly they are all saying the
same thing.

If there are two ways of comprehending reality,
which one is "better"? If one has two different choices
as to how to do something, we ask which one we should
choose.

The answer to this question is clearly that each is better for different things. It depends upon what you are
trying to do. Both are equally valid even though they
are quite different. Which one is chosen at a particular
time does not depend on which is more true, but on
what you are trying to accomplish at that particular
moment. Each has assets and liabilities. I am reminded
here of the old Spanish proverb " 'Take what you
want,' said God. 'Take it and pay for it.' "

If one wishes to bring food to his body, dodge the
speeding truck, invent air conditioning, or inject Novo-
cain into a painful jaw, one had better be operating
primarily in the world of multiplicity, in the Sensory
Reality. This is the reality in which one can select goals,
and plan and carry out action. It is a reality we *must*
learn to operate in in order to stay alive physically. As
D. J. West has said, "From sheer biological necessity,
life is organized around the limited but sharply focused
morsel of environment presented by our senses." [29]
G. N. M. Tyrrell, another very serious psychical re-
searcher, stated: "normal perception tends to oust the
supernormal and keep the field to itself." [30]

If, however, instead of the necessary, practical goals
of the biological and physical world which we can
work toward so well in the Sensory Reality, we wish to

work toward another type of goal, we need the Clairvoyant Reality. If we wish to choose as our goals a
sense of serenity, peace, joy in living, being fully at
home in the cosmos, a deeper understanding of truth,
our fullest ability to love, we need the world of the
One.

Beyond this, however, is the crucial fact that to
attain our full humanness we need both. Plotinus's
analogy had a deep validity; we are Amphibia. With
only one reality, we are crippled and stunted, achieving
only part of our being. Laurens van der Post discussed
this when he wrote:

> There, for instance, we have the key to the signifi-
> cance of the one-eyed giants who stride so strangely
> through Greek and Roman mythology. I suspect that
> their gruesome presence there does not mean that a
> race of one-eyed colossi once walked the earth with
> seven-leagued strides and brushed the thunder clouds
> out of their hair. Only on the most elementary levels
> can they be taken to represent a man grown into a
> monstrous physique with only one eye in the middle
> of his forehead. But in the aboriginal language of the
> spirit, in the underlying thought processes of man it
> is a different and meaningful story, and the giant is
> in the image of a man who has grossly exceeded him-
> self in a part of himself. Only one eye is planted in
> the cretin head to indicate that he has not the two-
> way vision that the complete spirit needs but only
> this one-way look into a world of outward-bound
> senses. So also the two eyes of contemporary man
> when they focus *as one* on the outer physical world
> give him only one-way sight and admit only one-way
> traffic.[31]

Deep within us all is the knowledge that we need the
development of that other side of us, the part of us we
have so neglected and undernourished, to be complete.
We know that we have lost something of our heritage
and potentiality and are thereby less. One student of

mysticism was asked why he meditated. He replied, "It's like coming home." The sense of the loss of part of our selves lets us understand the mystic Louis Claude de Saint-Martin when he wrote, "We are all in a widowed state, and our task is to remarry." [32]

The deepest goal is to integrate the two in our lives, so that each viewpoint is heightened and sharpened by the knowledge of the other. This is the lesson of the magnificent Rodin statues which shade off into the raw unfinished rock of our planet. The tremendous individuality and uniqueness given by the finished parts of the statue, the vibrancy and thrust of being they provide, is accented by the part that shades into the raw stone and thus into oneness with the stuff of the world. The background of the One heightens our perception of the specialness and uniqueness of the individual, as the special quality of the individual note of music may be accentuated by its being a part of the symphony.

5 | the clairvoyant, the mystic and the physicist: the third road

As I examined, and tried to understand more fully the picture of reality presented by the medium and the mystic, it seemed to me that I had also seen their description somewhere else. It was not only these two groups who had agreed on the potential twofold nature of man's perception of "what is," but another group as well. This third group was the Einsteinian physicists, those who explored and worked with relativity theory.

This was a real surprise. I suppose I had felt that it was all right for mediums, mystics, and such to believe in another way of perceiving reality, but not tough-minded, hard-headed people like physicists! They are realists! It was a shock to find that my own prejudice about the nature of reality was still so strong. In spite of the fact that I now knew that scientific standards in parapsychology were far more exacting than in many other branches of science, in spite of the knowledge I had gained of the rigorousness of the mystical path (the mystics are, in the words of Josiah Royce, "the most thorough going empiricists in the history of philosophy" [1]), something in me still believed that only the way we ordinarily look at reality is the "real" way. Certainly physicists, I felt, would not be like mediums and mystics; they would not say that there was another, equally valid way of viewing the world. Not only did it come as a surprise to find the physicists in agreement with the mystics and mediums, but it was a surprise to find that I was surprised!

And yet as I examined the nature of reality as it is presented in the Einsteinian view of the world, it became apparent that it was identical with what I had called the Clairvoyant Reality. The Einsteinian world-picture is often called the "Minkowski, four-dimensional, block universe," and it did not seem possible to find any real differences (someone once defined a "real difference" as "a difference that makes a difference") between the descriptions given by Minkowski, by Eileen Garrett, and by Vivekananda.

It is true that the three groups started from different places, used different training and exploratory techniques, had different goals in view, and accomplished different ends, but they arrived at, and used, the same view of reality. Again, Rosalind Heywood helped me to understand this. At one point in our discussion she said, "James Bond and I may both use the telephone, but we say different things over it!"

Before I go into the details of the similarities between the Clairvoyant Reality and the picture of reality given by modern physics, however, I should ask whether the physicist actually believes that there are two ways of conceptualizing the world. The medium and the mystic would speak of "a shift of awareness," the physicist of "a different way of understanding" or "a different conceptualization," but—whatever their words—do they agree on the fact that there is another valid way?

Alfred North Whitehead described this:

When we survey the subsequent course of scientific thought throughout the seventeenth century up to the present day, two curious facts emerge. In the first place, the development of natural science has gradually discarded every single feature of the original commonsense notion. Nothing whatever remains of it, considered as expressing the primary features in terms of which the universe is to be interpreted. The obvious commonsense notion has been entirely destroyed, so far as concerns its function as the basis for all interpretation. One by one, every item has been dethroned.

There is a second characteristic of subsequent thought which is equally prominent. This commonsense notion still reigns supreme in the workaday life of mankind . . . in general (between the scientific and commonsense views of the nature of the universe) there is no conciliation.[2]

And J. Robert Oppenheimer's statement, cited earlier, bears repetition here:

These two ways of thinking, the way of time and history and the way of eternity and timelessness, are both parts of man's effort to comprehend the world in which he lives. Neither is comprehended in the other nor reducible to it. They are, as we have learned to say in physics, complementary views, each supplementing the other, neither telling the whole story.[3]

Quotations to this effect could easily be multiplied. In addition, there is a small experiment anyone can do which will make it clear that the modern physicist frequently operates in a world-view, a frame of reference that is very far from our usual, everyday way.

One asks a physicist the question "If light travels in waves through a vacuum, what is waving?" The answer one gets will be something like "What makes you think that because there are waves, something must be waving?"

Fifteen minutes later, as you stumble back from the

merry-go-round of confusion and noncommunication into which you have fallen, you will be very clear about the fact that the physicist frequently operates in a system of how-the-world-works that is very different from the one we ordinarily use and ordinarily believe is the only valid, common-sense one.

The physicist speaks of two ways of conceptualizing reality: the common-sense, everyday way (the Sensory Reality) and another way. Is this other way the same as the way I have termed the Clairvoyant Reality, the one the medium and the mystic agree on?

There are four central aspects of the Clairvoyant Reality:

1. There is a central unity to all things. The most important aspect of a "thing" is its relationships, its part in the whole. Its individuality and separateness are secondary and/or illusory.
2. Pastness, presentness, and futurity are illusions we project onto the "seamless garment" of time. There is another valid view of time in which these separations do not exist.
3. From this other view of the world, evil is mere appearance: when we are in this other understanding (a term which originally meant to "stand under," "to be a part of"), we do not judge with the criteria of good and evil.
4. There is a better way of gaining information than through the senses.

What does the physicist say about these four points? I shall describe this quite briefly. The Einsteinian worldview has been expressed readably by such experts as Henry Margenau, Sir James Jeans, Lincoln Barnett, Alfred North Whitehead, Werner Heisenberg, and J. Robert Oppenheimer. It would be both repetitious and arrogant on my part to repeat in detail what they have said so well, but some examples of what they have written may illustrate why I came to the conclusion that medium, mystic, and physicist had arrived at the same picture of reality.

The critical and central point of the Clairvoyant Reality is that of the central unity of all things, that each object and event (including the observer—medium, mystic, or physicist though he be) must be regarded first and "really" as a part of the All, and only secondarily (if at all) as separate, bounded, and cut off. All three other aspects (the three other "basic limiting principles," to use the term given by C. D. Broad) flow out of this one. What does the physicist say about this?

Max Planck wrote:

> In modern mechanics . . . it is impossible to obtain an adequate version of the laws for which we are looking, unless the physical system is regarded *as a whole*. According to modern mechanics [field theory], each individual particle of the system, in a certain sense, at any one time, exists simultaneously in every part of the space occupied by the system. This simultaneous existence applies not merely to the field of force with which it is surrounded, but also its mass and its charge.

> Thus, we see that nothing less is at stake here than the concept of the particle—the most elementary concept of classical mechanics. We are compelled to give up the earlier essential meaning of this idea; only in a number of special border-line cases can we retain it.[4]

Einstein described the history of this viewpoint succinctly:

> Before Clerk Maxwell, people conceived of physical reality—insofar as it is supposed to represent events in nature—as material points, whose changes consist exclusively of motions. . . . after Maxwell they conceived physical reality as represented by continuous

fields, not mechanically explicable. . . . This change in the conception of reality is the most profound and fruitful one that has come to physics since Newton.[5]

Werner Heisenberg, a modern theoretical physicist, wrote that the methods of modern physics classify the world

. . . not into different groups of objects but into different groups of connections. . . . The world thus appears as a complicated tissue of events, into which connections of different kinds alternate or overlap or combine and thereby determine the texture of the whole.[6]

Alfred North Whitehead put it in terms that would delight a serious mystic:

The new view is entirely different. The fundamental concepts are activity and process. . . . Nature is a theatre for the interrelations of activities. All things change, the activities and their interrelations. . . . In the place of the Aristotelian notion of the procession of forms, it [the new physics] has substituted the notion of the forms of process.[7]

Albert Einstein put it simply and clearly:

It therefore appears unavoidable that physical reality must be described in terms of continuous functions in space. The material point, therefore, can hardly be conceived any more as the basic concept of the theory.[8]

Summing up his discussion of this viewpoint, Whitehead writes, "in the modern concept . . . there is no possibility of a detached, self-contained existence." [9]

The philosoper of science Hans Reichenbach wrote:

When I, on a certain occasion, asked Professor Einstein how he found his theory of relativity, he answered that he found it because he was so strongly convinced of the harmony of the universe.[10]

Both physicist and mystic say that they themselves are a part of this Unity and cannot realistically be separated from it. The mystic says this openly. His "Tat Tvam Asi" ("That art Thou") is a basic element of all serious mysticism of any form. The physicist says that he himself influences and effects his observations to such a degree that he cannot separate them and himself, and that the concepts he arrives at in his attempt to understand the world are a function of an interaction between himself and reality. Few physicists would disagree with the mystic Evelyn Underhill when she refers to "the game of give and take which goes on between the human consciousness and the external world." [11]

The physicist Niels Bohr put it beautifully:

The development of atomic physics, which forces us to an attitude toward the problem of explanation recalling ancient wisdom, that when searching for harmony in life one must never forget that in the drama of existence we are ourselves both actors and spectators.[12]

One might compare the following two quotations. The first is by the thirteenth-century Zen Master Dogen. The second is by the physicist Sir Arthur Eddington.

Man disposes himself and construes this disposition as the world.[13]

The mind has by its selective power fitted the processes of Nature into a frame of law of a pattern largely of its own choosing; and in the discovery of this system of law the mind may be regarded as regaining from Nature that which the mind has put into Nature.[14]

There is an ancient saying, attributed to Padma Sambhava, the eighth-century founder of Tantric Yoga:

All appearances are verily one's own concepts, self-contained in the mind, like reflections in a mirror.[15]

Werner Heisenberg, in a somewhat similar vein, wrote:

For our experiments are not nature itself, but a nature changed and transformed by our activity in the course of research.[16]

The second aspect I have described in the Clairvoyant Reality is that pastness, presentness, and futurity are illusions when one is in the clairvoyant way of perceiving and being in the world. Here again, the physicist agrees. Herman Weyl has written of this:

The objective world simply *is*, it does not *happen*. Only to the gaze of my consciousness, crawling along the life-line of my body, does a section of the world come to life as a fleeting image in space which continually changes in time.[17]

Lincoln Barnett, in his excellent review of relativity theory, *The Universe and Dr. Einstein,* wrote:

In man's belief tenancy on earth he egocentrically orders events in his mind according to his own feelings of past, present and future. But except on the reels of one's own consciousness, the universe, the objective world of reality, does not "happen"—it simply exists. It can be encompassed in its entire majesty only by a cosmic intellect.[18]

The same point was made by J. G. Whitrow when he wrote that in the picture of the world as given by relativity theory, "external events permanently exist and we merely come across them."

The physicist Louis de Broglie puts the same thing differently:

> In space-time, everything which for each of us constitutes the past, the present and the future is given in block, and the entire collection of events, sucessive for each of us which forms the existence of a material particle is represented by a line, the world line of the the particle. . . . Each observer, as his time passes, discovers, so to speak, new slices of space-time which appear to him as successive aspects of the material world, though in reality the ensemble of events constituting space-time exist prior to his knowledge of them.[19]

De Broglie is writing about the Minkowski, four-dimensional universe, but I do not believe any serious mystic would disagree with a single word of the paragraph. One might, for example, compare it with the following statement of Sri Vivekananda:

> The absolute [is] everything that exists. . . . This Absolute has become the universe [as we perceive it] by coming through time, space and causation. . . . Time, space and causation are like the glass through which the Absolute is seen, and when It is seen . . . it appears as the universe. Now we at once gather from this, that in the Absolute, there is neither time, space or causation. . . . What we call causation begins after, if we may be permitted to say so, the degeneration of the Absolute into the phenomenal and not before.[20]

Although it is obvious that physicists tend to write somewhat more clearly and succinctly than mystics, they do seem to be describing the same point of view.

The third of the four basic principles is that from the viewpoint of the Clairvoyant Reality, events cannot be judged as good or evil. Henry Margenau, probably the leading present-day theoretician of relativity theory, wrote:

> In my view . . . natural science contains no NORMA-
> TIVE principles dealing with ultimate goals; physical
> reality is the quintessence of cognitive experience and
> not of values. . . . To know physical reality is to know
> where to look when something is wanted or needed
> to be seen; it is to be able to cure when a cure is
> desired, to kill when killing is intended. But natural
> science will never tell whether it is good or bad to
> look, to cure or to kill. It simply lacks the premise
> of an "ought." [21]

No one who knows of his work and life could ac-
cuse Henry Margenau of a lack of concern for his
fellow man or of not being deeply and passionately
involved in helping to better the human condition.
What he is saying, however, is that a viewpoint (valid
for some purposes, not for others) exists that does not
have the categories of good and evil.

The fourth of the basic limiting principles of the
Clairvoyant Reality is that there is a better way of
gaining information than through the senses. This is
essentially a statement that the channels of sense give
a picture only of the Sensory Reality. In order to know
the Clairvoyant Reality we must find another way of
knowing. Einstein wrote on this point:

> Since, however, sense perception only gives informa-
> tion of this external world or of "physical reality"
> indirectly, we can only grasp the latter by speculative
> means. [22]

The physicist Ilse Rosenthal-Schneider was dealing
with this when she wrote:

> Planck, too, like Einstein, pointed to the remarkable,
> and at first sight paradoxical, fact that the physical
> world picture is becoming more and more perfect, in
> spite of its continuously growing distance from the
> world of the senses. [23]

If indeed, as seems clear, there is a very great similarity between the world-view of the mystic, the medium, and the physicist, and this view is different from our everyday view of how-the-world-works, then it should lead also to similarities in their ways of solving problems, and their ways should sometimes be different from our everyday ways. The following quotations illustrate they do tend to come to the same kind of solution to problems, a kind of solution very foreign to our usual ways of solving difficulties.

In the Pali Canon, a document of mystical Buddhism,

Vaccha asked the Buddha:

"Do you hold that the soul of the saint exists after death?"

"I do not hold that the soul of the saint exists after death."

"Do you hold that the soul of the saint does not exist after death?"

"I do not hold that the soul of the saint does not exist after death."

"Where is the saint reborn?"

"To say he is reborn would not fit the case."

"Then he is not reborn."

"To say he is not reborn would not fit the case." [24]

J. Robert Oppenheimer wrote:

If we ask, for instance, whether the position of the electron remains the same, we must say "no"; if we ask whether the electron's position changes with time, we must say "no"; if we ask whether the electron is at rest, we must say "no"; if we ask whether it is in motion, we must say "no." [25]

And Eileen Garrett gives us this formulation:

I asked these spirit figures if I was seeing them or if I was seeing what was in my own brain. They answered, "both." [26]

It may be of interest here to have two more quotations, by the physicist Sir Arthur Eddington and by the mystic Dionysus the Areopagite, which also speak to this point:

It is a primitive form of thought that things either exist or do not exist: and the concept of a category of things possessing existence results from forcing our knowledge into a corresponding frame of thought. Everyone does this instinctively. [27]

Nor does it belong to the category of existence or to the category of non-existence. [28]

One can try in vain to fit these five statements into the Sensory Reality in which we ordinarily carry on our lives, but in it they are meaningless and disturbing. In the Clairvoyant Reality they make perfect sense.

In another way, the mystic and the modern physicist show a similarity. Neither can describe his data adequately in the ordinary language of common sense. The findings of both are ineffable: they cannot be directly stated in clear language. Both groups give the same reason for this: they are dealing in concepts for which everyday language is inadequate. As W. T. Stace wrote,

The position of every great mystic in every land and clime [is] that the supposed ineffability is due to some kind of a basic and inherent logical difficulty, and not due to mere emotional intensity.[29]

From our viewpoint, this is perfectly reasonable and the only thing to be expected. The language we use was designed to describe discrete entities and events and their relationships. If no discrete entities or events exist in a frame of reference, the language breaks down. The Clairvoyant Reality does not have discrete or separate entities in it; attempts at describing experiences and perceptions in it are bound to fail. The physicist has his mathematics which he can use to describe and manipulate concepts in the Clairvoyant Reality. Perhaps the most successful modes of expression for *experiences* in this reality are music and non-representational art. When we listen to Haydn's *The Creation* or the *Brandenburg Concertos* or respond to a Klee, a Miró, or certain Picassos, we are likely to get a strong sense of much that the mystic is talking about.

The sixteenth-century Hebrew mystic Isaac Luria was once asked why he did not write out his ideas and teachings. He replied: "It is impossible because all things are interrelated." [30]

At one time, in order to test out more fully the idea that the physicists and mystic agreed on the nature of reality, I performed a small experiment.[31] I took sixty-two statements of how-the-world-works. Half of them were written by physicists, half by mystics. Then I mixed them up, took out the author's name, and gave them to various people to see if they could tell what persuasion the author of each statement followed. I gave this list to people trained in physics, to people trained in mystic disciplines, and to others. None of these groups has done well on it. Physicists tend to guess with about 50 to 60 percent accuracy. Individuals knowledgeable in mysticism guess with about 60 to 70 percent accuracy. It is literally impossible to distinguish the statements accurately, so consistent are the conclusions of both groups.

Before turning the page, for example, try to determine which of the following quotations (taken from the experiment) were written by mystics and which by physicists.

1. "The stuff of the world is mind-stuff."
2. "The reason why our sentient, percipient, and thinking ego is met nowhere in our world picture can easily be indicated in seven words: because it is ITSELF that world picture. It is identical with the whole and therefore cannot be contained in it."
3. "It is the mind which gives to things their quality, their foundation, their being."
4. "It is necessary, therefore, that advancing knowledge should base herself on a clear, pure and disciplined intellect. It is necessary, too, that she should correct her errors, sometimes by a return to the restraint of sensible fact, the concrete realities of the physical world. The touch of Earth is always reinvigorating to the Sons of Earth. . . . It may even be said that the superphysical can only be really mastered in its fullness . . . when we keep our feet firmly on the physical."
5. "Thus the material world . . . constitutes the whole world of appearance, but not the whole world of reality; we may think of it as forming a cross section of the world of reality."
6. "As far as the laws of mathematics refer to reality, they are not certain, and as far as they are certain, they do not refer to reality."
7. "Pure logical thinking cannot yield us any knowledge of the empirical world; all knowledge of reality starts from experience and ends in it. Propositions arrived at by pure logical means are completely empty."

The important thing about a game like this is not how many one guesses correctly (turns of phrases and ways of verbalizing, for example, will often point to the persuasion of the author), but that it was *difficult* to guess correctly. The similarity in viewpoints is so great, the conclusions about the nature of reality so identical, that in a specific situation it is very hard to know whether the author is a medium, a mystic, or a physicist.

No. of Quotation	Source
1.	Physicist—Sir Arthur Eddington
2.	Physicist—Edwin Schrodinger
3.	Mystical Document—The Dhammapada
4.	Mystic—Sri Aurobindo
5.	Physicist—Sir James Jeans
6.	Physicist—Albert Einstein
7.	Physicist—Albert Einstein

The physicist and the mystic follow different paths: they have different technical goals in view; they use different tools and methods; their attitudes are not the same. However, in the world-picture they are led to by these different roads they perceive the same basic structure, the same reality.

And, when we view the two over a long perspective, we should not be surprised by this. Rudolph Otto [32] has suggested that from the mystical intuition of a oneness behind the various phenomena of the world arose the beginning of the search for the underlying substance that made up the cosmos, and that it was this search that started the development of science. The approach of the mystic is to understand this oneness and see it behind the veil of illusion and multiplicity. The approach of the scientist is to understand the fundamental nature of whatever is behind the great diversity we view with our senses. Lincoln Barnett in his *The Universe and Dr. Einstein* has described the scientific quest as

the long course of science towards the unification of man's concepts of the physical world. Through the centuries the varied currents of discovery, theory, research, and reason have steadily converged, mingled, and flowed onward into ever widening and deepening channels. The first long advance was the reduction of the world's multifarious substances into some 90 natural elements. Then these elements were reduced to a few fundamental particles. Concurrently the various "forces" in the world came to be recognized one by one as varying manifestations of electro-magnetic force, and all the different kinds of radiation in the universe—light, heat, X-ray, radio waves, gamma rays—as nothing more than electro-magnetic waves of varying wave length and frequency. Ultimately the features of the universe distilled down to a few basic quantities—space, time, matter, energy, and gravitation. But in Special Relativity, Einstein demonstrated the equivalence of matter and energy and in General Relativity he showed the indivisibility of the space-time continuum. His Unified Field Theory sought to culminate and climax this coalescing process. For from its august perspective the entire universe appears as one elemental field in which each star, each atom, each wandering comet and slow-wheeling galaxy and flying electron is seen to be but a ripple or tumescence in the underlying space-time unity. And so a profound simplicity would supplant the surface complexity of nature. The distinctions between gravitational force and electro-magnetic force, matter and energy, electric charge and field, space and time, all fade in the light of their revealed relationships and resolve into configurations of the four-dimensional continuum which Einstein revealed the universe to be. Thus all man's perceptions of the world and all his abstract intuitions of reality would merge finally into one, and the deep underlying unity of the universe would be laid bare.[33]

As one reads this last sentence and realizes how well a Plotinus, a Sankara, or a Meister Eckhardt would have accepted it, or how similar it is to the way a serious sensitive describes the clairvoyant view of the world, the similarity of the world-pictures of the physicist, the mystic, and the sensitive becomes clear.[34]

I am reminded here of the Eastern concept that as one explores deeper and deeper into oneself, he comes finally to the true essence of the self—Atman. As one searches more and more deeply into outside reality, tearing apart veil after veil of illusion, one finally discovers the true nature of reality—Brahman. And Atman and Brahman are the same.

6 | some implications of the two realities

It is certainly clear to all of us that clairvoyance and precognition are impossible. They simply cannot exist in the world as we commonly know it and respond to it. To make the problem worse, this picture we have of reality, the "everyday" picture is clearly valid. We are too successful in predicting the effects of actions and events when we use this conceptual scheme to believe that it is based on false premises. Not only does it work too well to be false, but we know in our hearts that it is valid; clairvoyance and precognition cannot occur. The problem is that they do occur. The evidence, and it is there—hard, scientific, and factual —for anyone who looks at it, is not refutable. We must do something about the paradox.

It is perfectly useless from a scientific viewpoint to try to "explain" this paradox by saying "spirits do it." Spirits (or "discarnate entities," "people who have passed beyond this plane of existence," or what have you) may or may not exist; that is not the question. Suppose that they do exist: the problem remains. We say that the cosmos is put together ("works") in a certain way, and therefore certain things cannot happen. Then we say there is a class of beings who can make these impossible things happen. We have not solved the problem; we have hidden and obscured it. We must still ask—if we accept "spirits" as a factor—"How do the spirits do it? How do they violate the laws of the cosmos and produce impossibilities like clairvoyance and precognition?" We can complicate the question all we wish by adding hypothetical factors like spirits, but the problem and the paradox remain.

However, there *is* a way past the problem. We are not hopelessly boxed in by this paradox. The apparent absolute impossibility of the problem is not due to its nature, but due to the fact that we believe that there is only one valid way of looking at reality; that only one *Weltbild,* one picture-of-the-world, can be "right," "real," "valid."

The fact that one way of looking at reality is valid, however, does not mean that a different way may not be equally valid. (There is an old poem about seven blind men and an elephant that has some relevance here.) It *is* valid to conceive of light as traveling in waves. It is *equally valid* to conceive of light as traveling in an entirely different, mutually exclusive, way, in particles. If you use only one concept, you can explain only one part of the data. You explain it well, but you need the other conception to explain, equally well, the other part of the data. Using both, we can understand a little more about the behavior of light. J. Robert Oppenheimer described the situation in physics:

You know that when a student of physics makes his first acquaintance with the theory of atomic structure and of quanta, he must come to the rather deep and subtle notion which has turned out to be the clue to unraveling that whole domain of physical experience. This is the notion of complementarity, which recognizes that various ways of talking about experience may each have validity, and may each be necessary for the adequate description of the physical world, and yet may stand in mutually exclusive relationship to each other, so that to a situation to which one applies, there may be no consistent possibility of applying the other.[1]

The basic problem in understanding the Clairvoyant Reality is not in the description of the cosmos given in this view; that is not too difficult to understand. It is the belief that this view of the cosmos cannot be valid, as it is contradictory to the obviously true, everyday view of the world. If we look at it differently—that both may be equally true—we break through the difficulties. No longer are we constrained to try either to explain ESP in terms of the everyday world, or else discard it as untrue. We can explain it in terms of a concept of the cosmos in which it makes sense. We can explain everyday phenomena in terms of another concept of the cosmos. No paradox remains.

Of this Eileen Garrett wrote:

Awareness becomes concerned with stimuli that occur in a nonsensory field. I have an inner feeling of participating, in a very unified way, with what I observe—by which I mean that I have no sense of any subjective-objective dualism, no sense of I and any other, but a close association with, an immersion in, the phenomena. The "phenomena" are therefore not phenomenal while they are in process; it is only after the event that the conscious mind, seeking to understand the experience in its own analytical way, divides up the unity which, after all, is the nature of the supersensory event.[2]

How *do* we "explain" paranormal abilities in these terms? We do it by starting with the fact that in different metaphysical systems, different things are possible. In the Clairvoyant Reality there are no separate entities or events. Things "flow" into each other instead of being separate: they are overlapping subfields of larger unities. Space cannot be a bar, under these conditions, to the flow of being an "information" between them. Telepathy and clairvoyance "occur" when perceiver and perceived, spectator and spectacle, are *one* in the most profound and "real" sense of the word. The medium is "active" in changing her metaphysical system, but does not *do* anything in the Clairvoyant Reality; she *is;* and in a way we do not understand, the strong emotion in a particular direction she had when she entered this state causes an overlapping between "her" and the "object" or "entity" toward which the emotion was felt. This overlapping between what are now two subfields of a larger entity permits information to flow between them and to be remembered and reported when the medium returns to the Sensory Reality. (It can also be reported during the period when she remains in the Clairvoyant Reality, by a special disassociated part of her personality which may present itself as a spirit control, or simply by her hearing and vocal mechanism.)

The "explanation" given for precognition in this theory is that in this metaphysical system pastness, presentness, and futurity do not exist, although sequences of events remain. (That is to say that there are object-object relationships, or sequences, but not subject-object relationships.) The only time is "the eternal now." Events *are,* they do not *happen,* although we may or may not "stumble across them." A statement relating to this has been made by the mathematician Kurt Gödel:

"[Since the Special Relativity Theory] the assertion that events A and B are simultaneous (and, for a large class of pairs of events, also the assertion that A happened before B) loses its objective meaning, insofar as another observer, with the same claim to correctness, can assert the claim that A and B are not simultaneous (or that B happened before A).[3]

The physicists Lev Landau and B. Rumer have put the same thing more simply:

"[Modern physics has shown that] the words [that two events occurred] "at one and the same time" turned out to be as meaningless as the words "at one and the same place." [4]

Our view is that it is not only the observer position (which is what these physicists are referring to) that determines perceived time relations between events, but also the metaphysical system that the observer uses to structure the universe.

Is it possible that two views of reality can *both* be valid? One of the greatest advances of modern physics is the clear statement, known as the Law of Complementarity, that this can be so. We are not concerned today in science with the question "What is reality?" which Max Planck has described as a goal that is "theoretically unobtainable." [5] (Indeed the great philosopher-logician Morris Raphael Cohen has put it: "The category of reality belongs not to science, but to religion." [6]) We are concerned rather with understanding more deeply the nature of reality, by means of more fruitful theories, theories that lead us forward toward the goal we never expect to fully reach. As in art or in personal growth and becoming, scientific understanding also is a process without an end point: there are always new reaches to strive for—new goals, new depths and heights. The universe is, as are we, open-ended; there is no top to the mountain of possibility of beauty, growth, or understanding. Only our own limitations or courage can determine how far we can go.

There is no limit; there are no end points that say

"Thus far and no further." Our deepest goal is to seek deeper and deeper into ourselves and into outer reality, and into the infinitely rich blending of the two made one. There is no "final knowledge" nor any "enlightenment" which will bring us to a static goal of completion. There is only the exciting, endless process of becoming. Meister Eckhardt has written:

> There is no stopping place in this life—no, nor was there ever one for any man, no matter how far along his way he'd gone. This above all, then, be ready at all times for the gifts of God, and always for new ones.

Although we tend to regard the Sensory Reality as the only valid way to regard reality, other cultures have not always agreed. Benjamin Lee Whorf has shown that:

> The Hopi language contains no reference to "time" either implicit or explicit. At the same time [it] is capable of accounting for and describing correctly, in a pragmatic or operational sense, all observable phenomena of the universe. . . . Just as it is possible to have any number of geometries other than the Euclidian which give an equally perfect account of space configurations, so it is possible to have descriptions of the Universe, all perfectly valid, that do not contain our familiar contrasts of space and time. The relativity viewpoint of modern physics is one such view, conceived in mathematical terms, and the Hopi Weltanschauung is another and quite different one, nonmathematical and linquistic.[7]

Indeed the Hopi conception of the universe, with its *manifest* and *manifesting* replacing our concepts of space and time, is in many ways quite close to the mystic's world-picture. This can be quite a shock to the Western-trained person who further realizes that this metaphysic is held by an extraordinarily strong, coherent, and resilient culture which was able to maintain its integrity in the face of the tremendous impact of European civilization.

Not only have other, often strong and coherent cultures frequently disagreed with our "common-sense" picture of how-the-world-works, but modern science also sees it as a limited view which can only be applied to certain types of problems. The mathematician Henri Poincaré wrote:

Modern man has used cause-and-effect as ancient man used the gods; to give order to the Universe. This is not because it was the truest system, but because it was the most convenient.

And Sir James Jeans, a physicist of the first rank, made much the same point:

In particular, mechanism, with its implications, has dropped out of the scheme of science. The mechanical universe in which objects push one another about like players in a football scrimmage has proved to be as illusory as the earlier animistic universe in which gods and goddesses pushed objects about to gratify their own caprices and whims.[8]

It is clearly accepted in science today that the Law of Complementarity, if used carefully, is valid. Similarly, the mystics and (less clearly) the mediums have told us of the two ways of "being," of the two ways of conceptualizing and reacting to "reality." These three groups have further agreed on the nature and structure of these two views of reality although they are not in agreement on the use they each wish to make of this knowledge. I have termed these two views the Sensory Reality and the Clairvoyant Reality. Table I presents some aspects of the differences between the two.

Table 1 | *Comparison of the Sensory Reality and the Clairvoyant Reality in Reference to Certain Basic Limiting Principles*

Sensory Reality	*Clairvoyant Reality*
1. Objects and events separated in space and/or time are primarily individual and separate, although they may be viewed as being related in larger unities.	Individual identity is essentially illusory. Primarily, objects and events are part of a pattern which itself is part of a larger pattern, and so on until all is included in the grand plan and pattern of the universe. Individual events and objects exist, but their individuality is distinctly secondary to their being part of the unity of the pattern.
2. Information comes through the senses and these are the only valid sources of information.	Information is *known* through the knower and object, being part of the same unitary pattern. The senses give only illusory information.
3. Time is divided into past, present, and future and moves in one direction, irreversibly from future, through now, into the past. It is the time of one-thing-followed-by-another.	Time is without divisions, and past, present, and future are illustory. Sequences of action exist, but these happen in an eternal now. It is the time of all-at-once.
4. An event or action can be good, neutral, or evil, although its con-	Evil is an illusion, as is good. What is, *is* and is neither good nor evil, but a

Sensory Reality	*Clairvoyant Reality*
sequences often cannot be seen until long after the event.	part of the eternal, totally harmonious plan of the cosmos which, by its very being, is above good and evil.
5. Free will exists and decisions that will alter the future can be made. Action can be taken on the basis of will.	Free will does not exist since what will be *is*, and the beginning and end of all enfold each other. Decisions cannot be made, as these involve action-in-the-future, and the future is an illusion. One cannot take action but can only participate in the pattern of things.
6. Perception can be focused by the will in any desired direction, unless it is externally blocked, and thus specific knowledge can be acquired.	Perception cannot be focused, as this involves will, taking action, and action-toward-the-future, all of which are impossible. Knowledge comes from being in the pattern of things, not from desire to know specific information. Perception cannot be externally blocked since knowledge comes from being part of the All, and nothing can come between knower and known, as they are the same.
7. Space can prevent energy and information exchange between two	Space cannot prevent energy or information exchange between two individual

Sensory Reality	Clairvoyant Reality
individual objects unless there is a medium, a *thing-between* to transmit the energy or information from one to the other.	objects, since their separateness and individuality are secondary to their unity and relatedness.
8. Time can prevent energy and information exchange between two individual objects. Exchanges can only take place in the present, not from present to past or from present to future.	Time cannot prevent energy or information exchange between two individual objects, since the divisions into past, present, and future are illusions, and all things occur in the "eternal now."

The differences in the first aspect bring into clear focus the heart of the difference between the two realities, which consists of the way one views a person, object, or event. If one sees its uniqueness, its isolation, its I-stand-alone quality; if one sees its this-is-a-so-and-so, its what-are-important-are-its-boundaries-and-cut-off-points quality, its this-is-where-it-ends-and-something-else-begins quality, one views it from the Sensory Reality.

If, however, one sees as its most important characteristics its harmonious-relationships-to-other-parts-of-the-total quality, its part-of-a-pattern-that-is-part-of-a-larger-pattern quality, its field-theory quality, one views it from the Clairvoyant Reality.

Meister Eckhardt contrasted these two Realities when he wrote:

"When is a man in mere understanding?" I answer, "When he sees one thing separate from another." And when is a man above mere understanding? That I can tell you: "When a man sees All in all, then a man stands beyond mere understanding." [9]

It appears that other differences between the Sensory Reality and the Clairvoyant Reality follow logically from this difference.

As can be clearly seen from this table, a person cannot live fully consciously aware of the Clairvoyant Reality for any length of time. One would not survive biologically in this way for very long. To live completely consciously unaware of it, however, makes man less than he can be, and robs him of much of his potential.

Historically, certain techniques seem to have been evolved to help individuals living in the Sensory Reality to attain some of the information obtainable in the Clairvoyant Reality without losing the security and values of their everyday Weltanschauung. These include astrology, numerology, the I-Ching, and tarot cards.

These techniques appear to function in a definite manner, although this is frequently hidden and overlaid by extra and distorting attributes. Through the use of a structured setting in which the individual is oriented to a strong expectation and mental set for results, plus an enforced passivity of action and will (one has to *wait* to see how the cards fall, and it is out of his control), the person is placed in a conscious psychological situation closely allied to that of the sensitive. The unstructured data (the I-Ching paragraphs, for instance, have no exact or precise meaning) let a possibility arise for the conscious perception of unconscious material. Tension and anxiety are reduced; it appears to the individual as if his information is coming from objective data rather than from unconscious or paranormal sources. Under these conditions, some Clairvoyant Reality perceptions are occasionally likely to take place and to be interpreted as if they were Sensory Reality perceptions.

This is what may well account for the "something valid" that many investigators feel is in the I-Ching and other techniques, but that has so far not been possible to pin down.

It may be important to note that although I have described these two realities as if they were completely separate and discrete, it is much more likely that we are dealing with a spectrum of realities that shade into each other, and that the descriptions given are merely convenient focal points on this range. Tidy compartments are easier to talk about than shades of gray. Compartments may be permissible for discussion purposes, but reality is rarely so neatly divided into sections.

In the Sensory Reality, as we live in it in our everyday lives, there *are* relationships and patterns that made it possible for us to function effectively. This should not hide the fact, however, that these are secondary to our perception of unique objects and events. In this sense, Western common-sense reality (the Sensory Reality as we know it) is not the *pure* state at the extreme end of the scale, but rather a state near the end of the spectrum.

Similarly, for the mystic, the Clairvoyant Reality as he generally uses it does not appear to be the extreme possible *pure* state, but a perceptual mode near the opposite end of the spectrum. Subpatterns of events, and to some degree individual events themselves are perceived, although these are distinctly secondary to the perception of larger patterns and harmonies. Lao-Tze divided the Tao into the Tao of Heaven (T'ien Tao), the Tao of Earth (T'i Tao), and the Tao of Man (Jen Tao). All three are perceived in correspondence and harmony, but are nevertheless perceived as subpatterns.

In the *pure* state of Clairvoyant Reality, for which some mystics strive and which some say they have achieved, all specific content and all events and subpatterns vanish. This, however, seems as hard for most of us to conceive of as a *pure* Sensory Reality state with *only* unique events and *no* relationships.

It also seems important to say here that I am greatly oversimplifying the mystical point of view. This viewpoint arises out of a profound study of the relationship of man and the cosmos, and of man's being and potentiality for being. What I am doing in this book is analyzing one aspect of this study, its Weltbild, its concept of how-the-universe-works; but there is far more to serious mysticism than this.

For example, the special attitude brought by the mystic to the Clairvoyant Reality is *love* in its deepest and most profound sense. It is selflessness, a purity of heart and mind, and a deep humility. When the Sufi poet Jalal-uddin-Rumi writes "The astrolabe of the mysteries of God is love," [10] he is expressing the mystic's way of entering into a union so complete with the harmonious totality of the cosmos that he apprehends it directly and fully. When I state here that the Clairvoyant Reality is the cornerstone of the mystic's world-picture the metaphysical system he uses and is a part of—I am writing of only one small part of what the mystic offers to mankind. This cornerstone is what this book is concerned with, and I believe it is crucial to an understanding of the paranormal, but it must not be interpreted as being all there is to mysticism. Books such as Aldous Huxley's *The Perennial Philosophy* [11] can help illustrate more of the richness of the mystic's understanding than I can show in this work.

The fact that there are disagreements among mystics should not obscure the overwhelming general agreement among them any more than disagreements among physicists obscure the great areas of agreement. Mystics universally agree on the structure of the cosmos, and, in general, tend to agree on how a man should act and what goals he should set in life. Beyond this, there is a good deal of variation. In the ancient Eastern tale, the Three Vinegar Tasters each sampled the brew of life in Chang-An-Sa, the Land of the Morning Calm. Buddha found it bitter; Confucius found it sour; Lao-Tze found it sweet. Each counseled a somewhat different path than the others. Nevertheless, overwhelmingly, they were in agreement.

Thus there are two ways of perceiving and reacting to reality; both potential in man, both necessary for his fullest existence, his fullest potential. (In Abraham Maslow's words, "When we are all well and healthy and adequately fulfilling the concept 'human being,' then experiences of transcendence should in principle be commonplace." [12]) One way of perceiving reality, the Sensory Reality, is thoroughly taught early in life; the other is rejected. It is not totally rejected, but often expressed in art, music, and religion, and mankind has always regarded as its greatest men those who have tried to show a workable formula for integrating the two. "Render unto God . . ." is a more profound statement than is often realized. This is the position of Buddha, Lao-Tze, Socrates, and Jesus of Nazareth. (Rabbi Simeon Ben Yohai, the hero of the Zohar, the thirteenth-century "Book of Splendour," is described in it as "a great tree who stands in both worlds" [13]). The supreme teachers of mankind all tried to show a path encompassing the data from both realities, a way of living as if both were valid, and these are the men for whom a special place of honor has been reserved in history. And indeed does not everything we most highly regard—beauty, love, heroism, laughter, awe, religion—tell us that there is a buried part of us desperately demanding recognition and expression? In the world of the Sensory Reality these things make no sense. We cannot, for example, understand them by a mechanistic, physiological, psychoanalytical, Pavlovian or Skinnerian analysis of the data. They do not fit a human being seen only from the viewpoint of the Sensory Reality. Given a total human being, including both aspects, both realities, both ways of being, they do fit.[14]

It is interesting that in only two areas have we generally accepted that both ways of looking at the cosmos may be equally valid: theology and art.

In theology, in most religions, God is seen as having two aspects. He is the Hidden God who is out of time and space, ineffable—a being of the Clairvoyant Reality. He is also the Revealed God who works in time and history, who acts in space, who wills actions and carries them out—a being of the Sensory Reality.

In art we accept the Sensory Reality expression of a Rembrandt and a Titian, with their deep understanding of the unities of the everyday view of man and the universe. We also accept as valid the other types of unities and interactions of the nonrepresentational painter: those of a Picasso, or a Miró, in their attempts to communicate another view of reality. These artists, like the serious sensitives, attempt to see reality with both eyes—the Sensory Reality and the Clairvoyant Reality.

A recent essay on Rimbaud illustrates what I have been saying here concerning the disruption of the usually accepted unities and the formation of new ones in the field of modern poetry:

What did Rimbaud accomplish in poetry? He developed, refined, and pushed to its final forms the basic technique of all verse that has been written since the idiom of international modernism—the radical dissociation, analysis, and recombination of all the material elements of poetry. This means all, not just the syntactical structure. True, the logical patterns of Western European thought and lanugage begins to break down. The basic form—subject, verb, object, and their modifiers—dissolves. The prosody dissolves too, into doggerel, free verse, and a new kind of incantatory prose quite unlike Baudelaire's. The whole tendency of the prosody is toward hypnotic incantation and invocation of delusion—acoustic magic. For more important, however, the ultimate materials, psychological, descriptive, dramatic—things the poetry is "about"—are shattered beyond recognition and recombined into forms that establish the conviction of a new and different order or reality. The subject and the poetic situation are liquidated. It is impossible to say who the actors in the poem are, or where they are, or what is happening to them. . . .

By the time we get to the painting of Juan Gris, or poems of Pierre Reverdy, Rimbaud's philosophy of composition has been brought under cool control: It has, so to speak, entered the period of Plato, Aristotle, or even Aquinas. But behind Plato lies the demonic Socrates, whom nobody could understand, but only systemize. . . .

To achieve the dissolution and dissociation of all the elements of poetry, it was necessary for Rimbaud to undertake a forced dissociation of the personality—under the strict control of a powerful will and reason. This is the "reasoned derangement of the senses" which has become a byword of all modern art. In Rimbaud it is commonly accompanied and always in his best poems, with the phenomena of dissolution of the personality that are found in natural mysticism and in trance states which result from toxins—whether drugs, or the products of fasting, or manipulation of the breath and nervous system. Cyclones, explosions, blue lights, shattering crystals, colored snow, whirling sparks, shipwrecks, whirlpools, the looming of an alternative reality behind the fiction of the real, the sense of estrangemant of the self; "the true life is absent"; "I am another." . . .[15]

A major aspect of the concept of the "peak experience," as defined and developed by Abraham Maslow,[16] is the change in the formal perceptual system which the individual is using. In the peak experience, the self and the environment (to its most distant conceived parts) are perceived as functioning as a unit. There is no "here-is-where-I-am-and-here-is-where-the-rest-of-the-universe-begins" quality about the perceptions, but rather an "I-am-a-part-of-a-dynamic-everything" quality. Individual unities remain, but their uniqueness is perceived as distinctly secondary to their relational qualities. In a formal perceptual and organizing sense, the person in a peak experience has shifted from the Sensory Reality to a system at least much closer to the Clairvoyant Reality. He has distinctly moved along the spectrum that unites and relates these two states of being.

Perhaps the existence of two alternative sets of conceptualizations of the universe—one where uniqueness of events and objects is the crucial consideration, the other where the relationship of objects and events is the basic consideration—is part of the meaning of the dark sentence of Protagoras: "Man is the measure of all things, of things that are that they are and of things that are not that they are not."

Agreement among sensitives, mystics, and physicists in itself does not imply truth. As W. T. Stace has pointed out, alcoholics all over the world agree that they see pink rats, but this does not mean that there *are* pink rats.[17] However, to carry Stace's example further, if the alcoholics' rats start biting nonalcoholics occasionally, we had better start studying the way the alcoholics perceive and relate to reality. Their rats are real. The sensitives' rats *do* bite nonsensitives with the veridical information they give. The mystics' rats bite nonmystics with the peace, joy, and general efficiency in working toward his goals that the mystic clearly attains. The physicists' rats bite nonphysicists with the immense control over the "external world" it has given them. Under these conditions of proof, it certainly behooves us to study the way these groups of individuals perceive and relate to the world, and to accept that their way is, at least, tremendously fruitful.

part two | testing the theory:
psychic healing

But what are concepts save formulations and creations of thought, which, instead of giving us the true forms of objects, show us rather the forms of thought itself? Consequently all schemata which science evolves in order to classify, organize and summarize the phenomena of the real world turn out to be nothing but arbitrary schemes— airy fabrics of the mind, which express not the nature of things, but the nature of mind.

—ERNST CASSIRER [1]

7 | the next step in the adventure: psychic healing

I have described my analysis of the Clairvoyant Reality as it proceeded from the first question, "What is the relationship between the medium and the rest of reality at the moment paranormal information is acquired?" to the discovery that medium, mystic, and Einsteinian physicist agreed on the structure of the cosmos and the "explanation" of the paranormal implied in this finding. If this long road we have followed has validity, it should be possible to demonstrate this, to acquire new ways of doing things because of our new knowledge. The word "validity" is a tricky and difficult one; it is hard to know exactly what it means. The word "fruitful" is a better one. Is the path we have been following a fruitful one; does it lead us closer to where we wish to go? W. R. Inge, a great student of mysticism, has written:

> One test is infallible. Whatever view of reality deepens our sense of the tremendous issues of life in the world wherein we move, is for us nearer the truth than any view which diminishes that sense.[1]

To this one can only say enthusiastically, "yes!" Today, however, we need more than this. We are faced with extinction as a species because we cannot stop killing each other. One after another of our institutions is failing and we cannot seem to stop polluting our planet. Does the view of man and his potential that I have elaborated have anything to offer for *these* problems? New knowledge today must be evaluated in terms of these disasters. If it is serious it must be applicable to them.

I have been writing here about a part of man that is generally unrealized and unexpressed, about a way of being at home in the universe, of being with himself and others that is repressed early in life for nearly all of us. It may well be that in this repression lies a basic clue to the problem of our own behavior that so puzzles and bedevils us. The price for denying a basic part of one's being is well known to Western psychological science today—its cost is in diminished joy and zest, in a tendency toward pathological symptoms, hate and destruction, self-hate and self-contempt.

Is *this* repression one of the reasons we are such a sick species, that we are so destructive to ourselves and each other? It is interesting to note that nearly all the great sensitives had a very unusual amount of *joie de vivre* and *élan vital,* and that typically the person who follows the mystical path and disciplines finds joy, serenity, and a nondestructive life of peace and fulfillment of purpose.

Behind all the paranormal and the mystical lies the knowledge of the essential unity of man, with his fellows and the rest of the cosmos. This basic unity is reflected again—behind the screen of the mathematics—in Einsteinian physics. A *knowledge* of this, a comprehension of this oneness-with-the-All, that "no place is empty of Him," could only aid our culture in moving forward into a world where we can live with ourselves and each other. Indeed, it is only by grasping a concept new to it, the acceptance of a new idea, that a culture *can* change. Technological inventions only change a society to the degree that they bring a new idea in their wake.

The knowledge of the existence of an unconscious as a part of man's mind is a very old one. Plato wrote of it. In addition, everyone has had an experience that clearly demonstrates its presence. I cannot remember your name in the morning; I can in the afternoon. Where was the memory in the meantime? In spite of the writings of philosophers and of common experiences like this, the concept of the unconscious did not make the slightest impact on society until Freud did two things. First he analyzed it in terms that fit the spirit of the times. Second, he made the concept into a culturally useful tool—psychotherapy. We have now accepted it, and the impact of the concept can be seen in the law, medicine, art, education, fiction, the philosophy and techniques of child-raising, and a hundred other areas. Because of it, we act in a slightly more humane and civilized way toward ourselves and each other.

The implications of man's potential for being at home with himself and the cosmos in the Clairvoyant Reality are many times greater than those of the Freudian unconscious. If we wish the culture to explore and accept these implications, we must first describe the Clairvoyant Reality in terms acceptable to our present-day viewpoint, our *Zeitgeist,* or spirit-of-the-day, and then turn it into a useful cultural tool. There does not seem to be another route.

I have tried here to describe the Clairvoyant Reality in the terms of today, in a scientific frame of reference. I have done this more technically in an earlier publication,[2] but in this book also I have tried to keep the scientific attitude. I approached the problem of turning this concept into a useful cultural tool after my analysis of the physicist's frame of reference, and it is this problem which I will describe now.

Theoretically, once the theory of the paranormal was clear, it would have been possible to test it by devising training methods built on it for any of the "mental" paranormal abilities. The choice seemed to lie between telepathy, clairvoyance, precognition, and psychic healing. In exploring these choices, it seemed to me that for communication purposes, the telephone would be more useful than telepathy, at least in the foreseeable future. As for clairvoyance and precognition, the data arising from the senses and from intellectual analysis would, I believed, generally be more reliable and dependable than data arising from these abilities. The greatest likelihood for a useful cultural tool seemed to lie in psychic healing and for this reason I chose it to test the theory of the paranormal.

The first question was, Does such a phenomenon really exist? With what we know today about hysterical symptoms and hysterical suppression of symptoms, did the phenomena described as "psychic healing" exist apart from these? Prior to my work in parapsychology, I had spent fifteen years working full time on a project in psychosmatic medicine, and so was aware at least of the scope of the problems involved.

A survey of the literature in this field made it plain that the phenomenon of psychic healing *did* exist. There was enough solid experimental work and enough careful evaluation of reported claims to make this clear. After I discarded the 95 percent of the claims that could have been due to hysterical change, suggestion, bad experimental design, poor memory, and plain chicanery, a solid residue remained. In these, the "healer" usually went through certain behaviors inside of his head, and the "healee" showed positive biological changes which were not to be expected at that time in terms of the usual course of his condition.

The "explanation," or theories of explanations, were another matter entirely. Generally speaking, these seemed to be divided into three classes.

The largest group of healers described their work as "prayer" and believed their success was due to the intervention of God. A second group believed the healing was done by "spirits" after they had set up a special linkage between the spirits and the patient. The third group believed that they were transmitters or originators of some special form of "energy" that had healing effects.

With the group that involved God in the healing process I could find no quarrel. I could not, nor did I wish to, disagree with this explanation. Nevertheless, science must go further than this. We are concerned with the "how" of things: "How" does God work? The poet-philosopher Petrarch devised the rationale of science within a religious framework when he described the world as the "theater of God," the "Teatrum Dei," and said man could admire God by understanding His handiwork. Within this framework, I could work in harmony with those who used God as an explanatory force.

A serious difficulty with the use of the concept of God is that, with it, one can do little either to further one's understanding of a process or to increase his efficiency at it. To improve one's healing ability he can learn to pray better, but that is about all. For a scientific approach and a scientific society, more was needed.

The second group used "spirits" as an explanation. I have no particular opinion, one way or another, on the existence of discarnate entities who intervene in human affairs. Even after hundreds of hours spent conversing with mediums in trance during which the medium claimed to be someone who was dead, I still see no scientific way to determine if these spirits are (1) what they claim to be; (2) a multiple personality split-off; or (3) something else. At present we do not seem to have a way to test any of these hypotheses. (In Appendix D, I present a theoretical discussion of one approach to this problem.)

In addition, "spirits" are notably difficult to work with scientifically. If you do not get results today, it is because the "spirits" were not in the mood! In any case, with the "spirit" explanation, I had to concentrate on "how" the spirits do it, how they can heal. I could not prove or disprove the spiritistic answer, but I could go on from there and study the "how" of the healing process, whether spirits existed or not.

The third group explained the healing on the basis of an "energy" which they either originated or transmitted. Certainly this sounded more promising scientifically than the other explanations. However, since no one has been able to define this energy further than by giving it a name presently acceptable to science, nor to find any of its characteristics, it did not seem very useful.

Furthermore, there is a very real problem about the use of a concept such as "energy" if it is accepted into one's thinking too early in the process of exploration. Such a concept has implications; it shapes our thinking in ways we are often unaware of. Energy does "work," for example. Is "work" done in the psychic healing process? Tempting as it is to answer "yes," one had better be careful about it. The Christian Science healers (and they often accomplish very serious results) would certainly not agree with this. In addition, energy "flows" or "travels" between "two things." Are there "two things" in the psychic healing process? If so, it would mean that we find our explanatory system in the Sensory Reality and not in the Clairvoyant Reality.

I could point out other implications of the use of a concept like "energy" that worried me, but these should do to show why I was so cautious about accepting it as an explantory system early in the game. Rather than seeking the understanding of healing in the explanations of the healers, it seemed plain that another approach was needed.

· I assembled a list of individuals who could be described as "serious psychic healers." These included all the individuals whom I felt reasonably certain *did* accomplish results in this area, who worked consistently in it, and about whom there was either autobiographical or good biographical material. It consisted primarily of Olga and Ambrose Worrall, Harry Edwards, Rebecca Beard, Agnes Sanford, Edgar Jackson, the Christian Science group, Paramahansa Yoga-nanda, Stewart Grayson, and Katherine Kuhlmann. A variety of other healers, ranging from Padre Pio to Mrs. Salmon and Sai Baba, were also studied in this way through the material which was available on them.

This group all described behaviors that they felt were related to the healing effect. When I listed these behaviors, I found that they fell into two classes. The first class were "idiosyncratic behaviors," that is, behaviors engaged in by one or a few of the healers. The second class consisted of "commonality behaviors," behaviors engaged in by all of the healers. The assumption was made that it was this second class of activities that was relevant to the healing effect.

At this point in time I had a set of behaviors, a series of activities, that all the serious healers engaged in when they were trying to heal someone. This series had been teased out of the larger mass of activities they described as related to the healing. I could reasonably assume that I had come as close as I could at the moment to the "pure method," to the activities really related to the healing process, and I could discard the other, idiosyncratic behaviors as culturally or personally conditioned and nonessential. Exactly what were these activities? How could I describe them?

I found that, from the viewpoint of the experience of the healer (what he believed and observed himself to be doing), they fell into two classes. From an experiential viewpoint, there seemed to be two separate types of healing here. In a brilliant flash of genius I named these "Type 1" and "Type 2"!

The healers themselves had not made this differentiation as far as I could tell. Some used both, slipping back and forth without apparently noticing that the two phenomena were qualitatively different. Some used only one of them. To my best knowledge, this was the first time they had been separately delineated in detail.

Type 1 seemed to me to be the most important type. Many healers such as Edgar Jackson and the Christian Science group used it exclusively.

In Type 1 healing, the healer goes into an altered state of consciousness in which he views himself and the healee as one entity. There is no attempt to "do anything" to the healee (in Harry Edwards's words, "All sense of 'performance' should be abandoned"), but simply to meet him, to be one with him, to unite with him.[3] Ambrose Worrall put this simply and clearly: "I followed a technique I have of 'tuning in,' to become, in a metaphysical sense, one with the patient." [4] Edgar Jackson defined intercessory prayers (prayers for a patient's recovery) as "a subject-object bridge." [5] And Edwards wrote that in psychic healing the healer ". . . then draws 'close' to the patient so that his being is merged, as it were, into that of the patient, so that 'both' are 'one.' " [6]

These are clear statements. Jackson put the entire matter in a larger frame of reference:

> Prayer as a specialized state of consciousness moves beyond the usual considerations of real or unreal, conscious or unconscious, organic or inorganic, subjective or objective to a place where he is dealing wth the totality of being at one and the same time in a way that produces sensitivity to the whole.[7]

What we have here began to become clear. The healer views the healee in the Clairvoyant Reality at a level close to that in which All is One. However, he is focused by love, by caring, by *caritas,* on the healee: this is an essential factor. In Agnes Sanford's words, "Only love can generate the healing fire." [8] Ambrose and Olga Worrall have said, "We must care. We must care for others deeply and urgently, wholly and immediately; our minds, our spirits must reach out to them." [9] Stewart Grayson, a serious healer from the First Church of Religious Science, said, "If this understanding is just mental it is empty and sterile" and "the feeling is the fuel behind the healing." [10] Sanford wrote: "When we pray in accordance with the law of love, we pray in accordance with the will of God." [11]

It is essential that there be a deeply intense caring and a viewing of the healee and oneself as one, as being united in a universe—the Clairvoyant Reality—in which this unity is possible. This seemed to be the heart of the Type I healing. It seemed only to take a moment, a moment of such intense knowledge of the Clairvoyant Reality structure of the cosmos that it filled consciousness entirely, so that there was—for that moment—nothing else in the field of knowing to prevent the healing results from occurring. "Become conscious for a single moment that Life and intelligence are . . . neither in nor of matter [and] the body will cease to utter its complaints." [12] So wrote Mary Baker Eddy, and there seemed general agreement on the brief span of time of complete consciousness necessary for the biological effects to occur.

The healers used a wide variety of "techniques" to attain this altered state of consciousness. Some prayed, some attempted to look at the healee from God's viewpoint or to see him as he looked from the spirit world, and some were able to describe what they did without much of an explanatory system. All agreed, however, that there must be intense caring and a viewing of the healee within a framework in which healer and healee could become one entity in a larger context without either of the two losing their individuality. Indeed, both would have their uniqueness enhanced by becoming one as do two people who fall in love.

Gradually a theory began to emerge. At one moment, the healer was operating in the metaphysical system of the Clairvoyant Reality to the degree that he "knew" it was true. This was a moment of such complete knowing that nothing else existed in consciousness. In some way this was transmitted to the patient. I could use the word "telepathy" or else could point out that—for a moment—the healer's assumptions about how-the-world-works were true and valid. As has been proved over and over again by mediums, mystics, and physicists using the Clairvoyant Reality to accomplish their own ends, this is a perfectly valid set of beliefs about reality. Since at this moment of intense knowing on the part of the healer it was valid and the healee was an integral and central part of the system, the healee knew it, too.

Knowing this at some deep level of personality, the healee was then in a different existential position. He was back at home in the universe; he was no longer "cut off"; he was now living the full life of the "amphibian" in both land and water. In a way, he was for a moment in what I might call "an ideal organismic position." He was completely enfolded and included in the cosmos with his "being," his "uniqueness," his "individuality" enhanced. Under these conditions there were sometimes positive biological changes.

There is a beautiful Haiku that Nikos Kazantzakis puts into the mouth of St. Francis that seems relevant here:

I said to the Almond tree
"Sister, speak to me of God"
and the Almond tree blossomed.[13]

The healers—and this is particularly true of those with a Christian approach—make this statement quite clearly. They view "wholeness" and "holiness" as having the same meaning, as they did in the original meaning of the words. In describing their healing technique, Ambrose and Olga Worrall wrote: "In true prayer our thinking is an awareness that we are part of the Divine Universe." [14]

I felt that I understood what these healers were saying about their work. But why did it often produce results? How could positive biological changes occur under these conditions? I asked myself this question, and in answering it I looked first at the limitations of psychic healing.

George Bernard Shaw once said that the Shrine at Lourdes was the most blasphemous place on the face of the earth. He explained that while it contained evidence of cures in the form of mountains of crutches, wheelchairs, and braces, it did not have as evidence a single glass eye, wooden leg or toupee. This implied a limitation of the power of God and *this* was the blasphemy.

Like most Shavian wit, there is a grain of biting truth here. Furthermore, in all the serious cases of psychic healing I was able to uncover, there was not a single case of the regrowth of an amputated limb or the re-suturing of a severed optic nerve.

In addition, there is a very serious report by Alexis Carrel, who observed under a lens what happened to an open, visible cancer during a "miraculous healing" in the course of which it regressed and cleared up. Carrel (a very highly trained and reliable observer) reported that the cancer followed the usual, well-known course a cancer follows when it regresses. These include specific courses of development in the formation of scar tissue fibers, changes in blood distribution, etc. This cancer, said Carrel, followed this progression, but many, many times faster than he had ever seen or heard of it happening before.[15]

I began to see the light on a possible way of explaining the biological changes. None of us do anything as well as we potentially can. We can all learn to read faster, jump higher, discriminate colors more precisly, reason more accurately, and so on through practically any abilities you can name. One of these abilities is the ability to heal ourselves, our ability at self-repair and self-recuperation. This too usually operates far below potential.

What appeared to happen in Type 1 healing was that because he was momentarily in an "ideal organismic situation," the healee's self-repair and self-recuperative systems began to operate at a level closer than usual to their potential. Type 1 psychic healing was not a "doing something" to the healee, but a meeting and uniting with him on a profound level, a uniting that permitted something new to happen. The reason then, behind Shaw's comment on the lack of wooden legs at Lourdes is that the regrowth of a severed limb is beyond the ability of the body's self-repair systems. The rapid remission of a cancer is not.

Henry Miller had once written something that was in a curious way very similar to the way I had begun to see this:

> The great physicians have always spoken of Nature as being the great Healer. This is only partially true. Nature alone can do nothing. Nature can cure only when man recognizes his place in the world, which is not in Nature, as will the animal, but in the human kingdom, the link between the natural and divine.[16]

When man is "at home" in both realities, when he is fulfilling himself as an "amphibian," living in both—in Miller's terms of the "natural and the divine"—the healing of many wounds can occur. The healer does not "do" or "give" something to the healee; instead he helps him come home to the All, to the One, to the way of "unity" with the Universe, and in this "meeting" the healee becomes more complete and this in itself is healing. I was reminded here of Arthur Koestler's words: "There is no sharp dividing line between self-repair and self-realization." [17]

This fit very well with one of the analogies used in Christian Science to "explain" this type of healing. Christian Scientists point out that a rubber ball retains its usual shape of roundness (here the analogy for "health") so long as there is no pressure to deform it (here the analogy for "illness"). As soon as the pressure is released, it springs back to roundness. The pressure, they say, is being cut off from God, is the lack of the knowledge that one is a part of God, or, in our terms, the All. When this "pressure" is "released" through the healer setting up a metaphysical system where the healee is included in the All, brought "home" to it, the healee's body responds by a tendency to repair itself and work toward health.

A basic theory had emerged for Type 1 healing.

Now would come the crucial test of the theory: a test that involved learning to meet and unite with another person (and training others to do this) according to the theory, and see if it provided positive physical changes. But I have gotten ahead of myself. Type 2 healing remains to be described, since the analysis of both methods was done at the same time.

Experientially, Type 2 is quite different from Type 1. The healer perceives a pattern of activity between his palms when his hands are "turned on" and facing each other. Some healers perceive this as a "flow of energy," some as a sphere of activity. The hands are so placed— one on each side of the healee's pathological area—so that this "flow of energy" is perceived to "pass through" the troubled area. This is usually conceived of by the healer as "healing energy" which "cures" or "treats" the sick area. In a large percentage of cases (I would estimate about 50 percent in my own experience) healees who do not know the literature and do not know the expected response perceive a good deal of "heat" in the area. Frequently there are surprised comments like "It feels like diathermy!" "It's like an electric blanket!" "Where is all that heat coming from?" A smaller percentage of naïve subjects (about 10 percent in my experience) report a sensation of a great deal of "activity" in the area. A very few report a sensation of "cold." These sensations are almost invariably felt only in an area in which there is a real physical problem. One can "turn on" one's hands to any degree and it is still almost unheard of to get a perceptual response from the healee when the hands are held on each side of a healthy area.

In Type 2 the healer *tries* to heal; he wants to and attempts to do so through the "healing flow." In both Type 1 and Type 2 he must (at least at the moment) care completely, but a fundamental difference is that in Type 1 he unites with the healee; in Type 2 he tries to cure him. Harry Edwards, writing of Type 2, explained his attitude:

When the author is engaged in this work, only one thing exists and that is his hands through which the healing power flows. The healer's whole being is concentrated on his fingers—nothing else seems to exist. The desired result is the only thing that is his concern.[18]

Some healers see themselves as the *originators* of this healing power; others see themselves as the *transmitters* of it. Frank Loehr has called them the "God Withiners" and the "God Beyonders," [19] respectively. In either case, the procedure and the experience is essentially the same.

This much I learned from reading the works of the serious healers, but I could not understand what was going on. Even now I do not have the faintest idea what Type 2 is all about or how it "works." And it frequently does "work," that is, produces positive biological changes in the healee. I know how to "do it," to "turn on" my hands and teach others how to "turn on" theirs. It seems perfectly reasonable to me that we may be dealing with some kind of "energy." It also seems reasonable to me that Type 2 may be a sort of "cop out" on Type 1 in which healer and healee say, in effect: "We are both too frightened of all this closeness and uniting that is a part of psychic healing. Let's pretend with each other that all that is happening is a flow of energy is coming out of the hands and treating the problem. That way we will both be more comfortable." It also seems reasonable to me that the most fruitful explanation of Type 2 healing may be quite different from either of the above two hypotheses.

At a complete loss for a theory about Type 2, the time had come to test the theory of Type 1. Following the theory, the test I set up was to train myself to go into the state of consciousness indicated and see if—as the theory predicted—positive biological changes would occur in the healee's body. If this worked, the next step would be to try to train others to do this. The others would be individuals like myself who had never done this type of healing before, and who were not accustomed to having paranormal experiences of any sort. If the theory pointed out that certain activities had certain results and, that when these activities were carried out the results occurred, it would at least prove the theory to be a fruitful one.

I had therefore to teach myself to go into an altered state of consciousness of a particular type. For at least a moment, I had to *know* that the cosmos was run on field-theory lines, that All is One, and to do this somehow "centered" about the uniting of another person and myself in the Clairvoyant Reality. The next question was *how* to do this.

The writings of the various mystical traditions are a vast resource of training techniques for problems of this sort. I experimented with a wide variety of these techniques, trying with each one to understand its purpose, to relate that purpose to my goal and then to my particular personality organization.

Any way of dividing up these techniques into classes is bound to be faulty. Not only is there a great deal of overlap, but all techniques have as one of their goals a tuning and training of the personality similar to the way an athlete tunes and trains his physical structure. However, bearing this in mind, some general classifications can be made. One of these is a division into meditation techniques, rhythm techniques (as the Dervish dances, the chanting of Mantras, and the Hassidic body movements), and assault-on-the-ego-techniques (such as fasting, the use of hallucinogenic agents such as LSD, and various methods of the *Via Ascetica,* the way of the ascetic). It was clear from what I knew about myself—and found out further in experimenting —that the meditation techniques were closest to my own easiest path.

These meditation techniques are all partially ways of learning to discipline the mind, to make it learn to do what you want it to do. No one who works at one of them for five minutes is left in the slightest doubt that

his mind is as undisciplined as—in St. Teresa's phrase
—"an unbroken horse."

(Plato described the undisciplined state of our minds
by using the analogy of the ship in which the sailors
have made a mutiny, and locked the captain and the
navigator in the cabin below. One sailor after another
—none of whom knows how to navigate—takes the
wheel as the whim strikes him and steers for awhile.
The ship thus follows a completely random course. The
task of a man, said Plato, is to release the captain and
navigator and take control of the ship of our minds so
that we can determine and steer toward our goals.
Plato's teacher—if not Plato himself—was trained in
the Eleusinian mystical tradition, and his life and
philosophy represented well the best in the mystical
tradition.)

One way of classifying meditation techniques is the
threefold division into what has been called in the East
the Inner Way, the Middle Way, and the Outer Way.
In the Inner Way, one concentrates on the spontaneously arising contents of one's own mind, upon the
images and feelings that arise. In the Middle Way one
strives for stillness of the mind; one withdraws from
both internal and external perceptions. It has been
called the Way of Emptiness. In the Outer Way one
concentrates on and meditates on an externally given
perception; one relinquishes spontaneity and disciplines
the mind to stay with this perception until it blends
with oneself. One contemplates one thing, following
the statement of William Blake: "If the gates of perception were cleansed, all things would appear as they
are, infinite."

These divisions are not clear-cut, and various meditation techniques cut across these arbitrary lines. A Zen
Koan, for example, is both a meditation technique of
the Outer Way and an assault-on-the-ego technique, in
that what is being meditated upon cannot be dealt with
by the ego operating in its usual manner. The Thera-
veda techniques in which one concentrates on a spontaneously generated rhythm of one's own (as the rise

and fall of the chest in breathing) are a combination of rhythm and meditation techniques.

Another way of classifying mystical training technique is major avenues of approach: the body (as in Hatha Yoga), the feelings and intuition (perhaps the most widely used avenue; examples include Bhakti Yoga, the way of Meher Baba, and the monastic practicing his prayers, devotions and deepening his ability to love), or the route of the intellect. From what I understood of myself, and of American culture generally, it seemed that the way of the intellect would be best and fastest for my purposes. In the East this is known as the Narodhi Samadhi. In the West it was the approach followed by the Habad school of Hasidism. It starts with an intellectual understanding of the structure of the two ways of being at home in reality, which I have described earlier as the Sensory Reality and the Clairvoyant Reality. From this point, one trains himself to perceive and "be" more and more in the Clairvoyant Reality through various (primarily meditation) techniques. For myself, I had thus chosen the meditation approach, the Outer Way and the intellectual Samadhi.

The Outer Way (the Way of Forms or Way of Absorption) has been more commonly used in the West than the other two paths. In the West it is often called contemplation and we hear of the lives of the contemplatives, as the Christian followers of this path were called. In the East it has been called "one-pointing," or the Buddhist "bare attention." The clearest book on this subject I know of is Evelyn Underhill's *Practical Mysticism*,[20] from which I learned much.

Using contemplation as a central exercise, I gradually devised a series of techniques which it seemed would, if practiced enough, lead me to the state of consciousness that appeared to be associated with the positive biological changes that occurred in successful psychic healing. It took me about a year and a half of experimentation and practice until I felt I could achieve this state.

At the end of this time I felt ready to try. If the theory was right and what was being stimulated was the individual's own self-repair systems, I did not see how I could do any damage. If the theory was invalid, nothing would happen. It seemed ethically legitimate to try it.

Once again—as when I discovered that physicists also believed in the Clairvoyant Reality—I found myself surprised at what occurred and surprised at my surprise. This time I was surprised that positive biological changes *did* occur to healees when I was able to go into the special altered state of consciousness. So deep are the prejudices ingrained in us about the nature of reality being that of the Sensory Reality that I—in spite of all the intellectual understanding and the intensive training program I had put myself through—still somewhere felt that it could *not* work, that it was all fantasy and that "reality *was* reality." I was surprised at positive results and surprised that I was surprised.

The results of the "healing encounters" I now began to have fell into five classes:

1. I went into the altered state of consciousness and nothing happened so far as the healee was concerned.
2. I went into the altered state and positive biological changes occurred in the healee's body.
3. I went into the altered state and positive psychological changes occurred in the patient.
4. I went into the altered state of consciousness and there were telepathic exchanges between the patient and myself.
5. I was unable to go into the altered state of consciousness.

There were all possible combinations also between numbers 2, 3, and 4. Further, again to my surprise, there was no particular relationship between these that I have been able to discover. A patient might consciously observe nothing psychological during the session and still have positive physical changes. He might observe a very strong "calming," "relaxing," or "tranquilizing" effect with or without telepathic exchanges and with or without physical effects. The presence of one of these three factors appears at this time to have nothing much to do with the presence or absence of others.

In order to show the different types of results, I will describe some healing encounters which give a fairly accurate overall picture.

The general procedure followed in the healing encounters was simple. After enough general conversation so that we knew each other a little and felt reasonably relaxed together, I would ask the healee to simply get comfortable physically and to let his mind do as it pleased—not to cooperate in any particular way or to "try" to do anything, but to let happen whatever happened. I would then find myself a comfortable standing position (for no particular reason except that I concentrate more easily standing), close my eyes, and conceptualize this particular healee being in both realities at the same time. I would attempt to reach a point of being in which I would *know* that he not only existed as a separate individual inside his skin and limited by it, but that he also—and in an equally "true" and "real" manner—existed to the furthest reaches of the cosmos in space and time. When I *knew* for a moment that this was true and that I also coexisted with him in this manner—when, in fact, I had attained the Clairvoyant Reality—the healing work was done. Generally, I tried for two or three such moments in each encounter to "make sure," although this is probably more a statement about my own insecurity than it is about anything else.

Often I would use various types of symbols to help myself reach this point of knowing. For example, I might use the symbol of two trees on opposite sides of a hill with the tops visible to each other. From one viewpoint, they looked like two separate trees, but inside the hill, the two root masses met and were one.

The two trees were really one and inseparable. Further, their roots affected the earth and the earth the rocks until I could know that in the whole planet and cosmos there was nothing that was not affected by them and affecting them. This sort of symbolization, different in each case, as the healee and I are different in each healing encounter, would often be useful in helping me reach the Clairvoyant Reality with the healee and myself centered in it. With practice, the situation often arose where no symbols were needed, where I could move immediately to the point of complete *knowledge* of both realities at once. Each healing encounter was different, symbols which would be useful in one would be empty and sterile in the next.

There is certainly something that the healee can do to increase the probability of a positive response to the healing. At present, however, I do not know what this is. In spite of experimentation (still continuing) on having the healee relax, meditate, or do half a dozen other things, I do not know at this time what the best activity (if, indeed, there is one best way for everyone) is for him to do. Curiously, belief in the efficacy of healing of this kind does not seem to be a factor. Our results seem to be as good with skeptics as they are with believers.

Sometimes, if the Type 1 healing described above goes well, I feel the palms of my hands begin to tingle and to realize that I "want" also to do a Type 2 ("laying on of hands") healing with this person. When I have this impulse, I follow it, but never force it or try to do a Type 2 when it does not "feel" right to do so after a strong Type 1 encounter with the healee. The whole procedure rarely takes less than ten minutes or more than fifteen. There comes a certain point when it "feels" complete; there is the sense that whatever could be done has been done. It is then time to stop.

Frequently, I will go through this procedure and have a feeling of having been deeply into it, and as far as the healee is concerned all that has happened is that he relaxed for fifteen minutes in a comfortable chair. So far—in spite of a belief that in science the failures need study exactly as much, if not sometimes more than the successes—I have been able to find no clues as to why this happens with many healees, nor any ideas as to how to predict in advance which healees will respond in this way. The factors are certainly there, but so far I must not been able to analyze them.

With some healees, there is a positive physical response apparently associated with the healing encounter. Although coincidence has a long, long arm and some of these cases are certainly "false positives" (that is, the positive physical response occurred for some other, unknown reason and the relationship in time to the healing encounter was coincidence), the successes have been frequent enough and impressive enough to persuade me that this research is worth continuing.

A woman, well known to me, 75 years old, had had a painful arthritis and swelling of both hands for over a year. Although she could hold and use a pencil, or a knife and fork, it was impossible for her to bring her fingers closer than one inch from her palm. Attempts to do so, or pressure from outside the fingers brought severe pain. Persuaded by members of her family to let me try psychic healing, she agreed and said she was not "against it," but did not believe in it. She asked what she should do during the time I was working. I replied that she should read a newspaper and she did so.

I started with a Type 1 approach and in the course of about ten minutes felt that I had achieved the filling of consciousness with the field-theory viewpoint several times. I then moved into a Type 2 with her left hand only. It seemed to me that this was a strong Type 2, as I had the perception of a good deal of energy between my palms which were on both sides of her left hand.

After about five minutes of the Type 2 I felt that the experience was over and stopped. We chatted a moment and she told me she had felt nothing unusual. I asked the other members of her family to come back in (they had gone into the next room when I started the healing). Her husband asked her if there had been any effect. She replied, "No, it's just the same as it was," and to demonstrate this "flapped" the fingers of both hands. To everyone's surprise—certainly including hers and mine—they swung easily to the palm and out again. She now had full and painless movement in the fingers.

This has not changed in the full year since the healing encounter. She had been taking Predisone (a Cortisone preparation) for three days before the healing, but up to one minute before the healing encounter, it had no apparent effect.

The following healing encounter occurred quite early in the work before I had set up the basic rule of *never* doing a Type 2 without a strong Type 1 first. By and large, Type 2 results (when done alone) tend to be transient; Type 1 results strongly tend to be permanent.

A woman known to me, asged thirty-six years, had intermittent, very large "cold sores" for over twenty years. Two or three times a year she would get one on her lip and it would take approximately thirty days to heal. She and her family knew the phenomena thoroughly and what to expect each time.

I held one hand on each side of her face, not touching the affected area, for about twenty minutes in a strong Type 2 healing. Afterwards she reported that during the twenty minutes she had been conscious of several periods of heat, and one of "tingling" in the lip area. About one half hour later she left my office to drive home (a drive of about an hour); en route she felt suddenly a strong "tingling" in the lip area, she looked at it in the rear-view mirror, and in her words, "I nearly had an accident I was so surprised. I pulled off the road and sat for ten minutes watching the new skin regrow. The dead skin in the center did not seem to change, but new skin slowly grew over the whole raw pink area." When she arrived home, her son and her husband both reacted in surprise to the complete unexpected change and almost complete healing of the cold sore.

The next day it had returned about one-third the size it had been when she arrived in my office the day before, and disappeared over the next week.

A woman, aged thirty-eight years, had an over-stretched cartilage of the knee. Her physician had termed it a "loose joint" and told her that if she was very careful and did not put any weight on it while it was in a bent position, it would recover in a year to eighteen months, or if she immobilized it in a cast, in four to six months. The knee joint was quite swollen, had no strength to bear weight when moving from a full bent (90-degree angle) position to a straight position, although once straightened she could walk on it, and was constantly painful. She came into the end of one of the training seminars I was holding (see p. 156 ff) and all ten people present did a Type 1 healing with her. She said afterwards that she felt very relaxed, calm, and "loved" during the ten-minute session. For me at least, it was a very strong Type 1 with full focus established several times. This was in the early afternoon. By that evening the swelling was reduced and the pain had lessened. On awaking the next morning there was no more sensation of pain in the area, its full strength had returned, and the swelling—according to her physician—was about half of what it had been. This lasted for several months, and the swelling gradually diminished to normal. In the following eighteen months, there has been no recurrence.

This case concerns a fifteen-year-old boy who broke his back on a trampoline. A letter dictated by his father, a surgeon, on November 1, 1971, and written by his mother, reads in part that the "period of detraumatization is over, and we must face the fact that 'medically' Chris is where he will be forever. That means: No feeling below the chest. Some feeling on the backs of the hands and the thumb and first finger. Movement of the lesser flexor muscles in the arm so that he has limited movement and strength in his arms—with supportive braces he may be able to use his arms to a limited degree. Indomitable inner strength and a smile that still knocks you dead."

On November 7, a group made up of sudents who had been at one of the healing seminars and were now working at an advanced workshop did a distance healing with Christopher. We had a letter about him and a picture, and the group—none of whom had ever met Christopher—were deeply involved. Chris, however, did not know of our existence or that anyone was going to do a psychic healing with him. He was in Denver and we were in Greenwich, Connecticut. An earlier healing had been held Friday evening, but it was on Sunday between 11:55 and 12:15 in the day that the group really "turned on" in a very strong long-distance, Type 1 healing. In the early afternoon (2–3 P.M.?) Denver time, Christopher suddenly called out that he could "feel" his legs. It soon became apparent that he could not only feel pressure sensations, but "could even tell which of his toes was being touched at any given time." The father said (to the woman who had written the letter to us, a close family friend) "that there is no explanation for this since the period of detraumatization was well over and no hope was held for any further improvement or restoration in Chris's physical condition."

However, all results must be evaluated cautiously. The most dramatic single result I had occurred when a man I knew asked me to do a distance healing for an extremely painful condition requiring immediate and intensive surgery. I promised to do the healing that night, and the next morning when he awoke a "miraculous cure" had occurred. The medical specialist was astounded, and offered to send me pre- and post-healing X-rays and to sponsor publication in a scientific journal. It would have been the psychic healing case of the century except for one small detail. In the press of overwork, I had forgotten to do the healing! If I had only remembered, it would have been a famous demonstration of what can be accomplished by this method.

Coincidence has a long, long arm and the unexpected *does* often happen. All reports of medical improvement by psychic healing (or by any other therapeutic technique) must be interpreted with this in mind. It is also true, however, that a technique must be evaluated in terms of its results, and not in terms of a previously held theory. If the application of a theory produces results in the predicted direction, its fruitfulness has been demonstrated and previously held theories which imply that these results could not occur must be abandoned or modified.

The third group of cases reported psychological effects only and no positive effects. Almost invariably (and there were no negative or disturbing psychological effects) these were reported in terms like "I felt very calm and relaxed," "It was as if I were tranquilized," "I felt so peaceful," "It was as if a great wave of warm love came over me." Although this comprises a considerable group of healees, and is a definite and consistent phenomenon, in a pure research sense these cases must be regarded as failures, since no physical changes were observed. There is a difference between results of an experiment from which one learns something new (it is hoped one learns something from *all* results) and results that conform to one's predictions.

In the fourth group of cases there were strong

indications of telepathy exchanges between the patient and myself during the healing encounter. To put this more accurately, I should state that there was a movement of images and information *within* the Gestalt that had been formed and that included the two of us.

A woman well known to me, aged twenty-eight, had an area of psoriasis on the abdomen which had shown no signs of clearing up over a five-week period, in spite of various prescribed topical treatments. A Type 1 session was divided into two ten-minute periods with a ten-minute rest period in between. In the first period I visualized her as a part of the "All," and connected to it through white bands (the love she felt and had felt for others during her life) and by black bands (her perceptions of others and events). She is a writer with a very sharp, perceptive eye.) During the rest period she reported first having had the sensation of waves of heat pouring over her and then a pattern of alternating lighter and darker waves of light intensity. I told her nothing of what I had been conceptualizing. During the second period, I was able to conceptualize her very strongly and one-pointedly in the same way and began to merge the bands of black and white into grays—symbolizing her relationships as "love-knowledge" (in Maslow's sense) rather than love *and* knowledge separately.

At the end of the session she was obviously deeply moved, and just wanted to sit quietly and not talk for a few minutes. Then, after drinking some water, she said that it had seemed to her as if she was surrounded by black and white clouds fanning out from her like the spokes of a wheel. They presently began to revolve around her, going faster and faster until the spokes of black and the spokes of white began to merge and blur. She then said to herself "They are outside of me. I'm inside. What would happen if I let them in?" She let them in, and after the session said that they were still inside and outside and she felt that they always would be. On questioning, she would not say that it had been a "good" or "bad" experience (although she now felt very good), but that it had been an "ecstatic" experience and that she now felt "as if I had just made love." She was deeply moved by the experience and we talked in generalities for a half hour.

This is a person I know quite well and have much respect and affection for. The next day she reported that there had been—during the night—a period of intense itching of the psoriasis and a sense that her entire abdomen was "breaking out" with it. In the morning the area was—to her inspection—unchanged. She said that she had since the session "a deep feeling of calm and competence."

And another relevant example: An exceptional healing session with a woman of sixty-five with multiple myeloma. I had met here a few times fifteen years ago. Through a mutual friend she knew of this work. I saw her at her house. A *very* strong Type 1 session. During it, the main symbol system I used was to visualize "A thousand Ilses," each a moment younger than the previous one, each holding the next youngest in her arms and (a word I have not used before) "approving" of her. From the future, older Ilses also formed a line following the same procedure. A gap was in the future part of the line, and I placed myself in it. At this point, the Gestalt solidified very strongly, went from black and white into full and rich color (unusual for me) and really filled the total field of my consciousness. To my surprise, the imagery took on a life of its own and one of the younger girls—in middle adolescence—left it and with a wicker basket over her arm went into a brightly lit field gathering flowers near some trees. This seemed only good, so I let it happen and simply lived with and participated in the picture for some time.

Afterward I asked Ilse what her experience had been. She replied that three things had happened. First, she felt a great deal of pleasant heat throughout her entire body and now felt very good and relaxed. Secondly, she had two strong images. The first concerned an incident at twelve that she felt had changed her entire life. In the town in Northern Germany where she had been raised there were two kinds of pretty girls: those with black hair, blue eyes, and white skin like her sister's, and those with blond hair, fair skin, and blue eyes. "And there I was with mud-colored hair, slate gray skin, and these washed out pale blue eyes." When the nurses dressed up her sisters, they "did not even bother to put a bow in my hair, it was hopeless." One day her mother had gone downtown and she went to her mother's room for something. She caught sight of herself in her mother's full-length miror. "I realized that I was not pretty, but that I *approved* of myself. Since then I have always *approved* of myself and it has made a great difference in my life." (The word "approve" was both times spoken with real emphasis.)

The second image was of herself, as a young girl "gathering flowers in a bright, sunlit field with trees. I was putting them into a wicker basket on my arm."

After the session it was apparent from both our feelings that there was a deep and warm relationship. We sat talking as two people who have had a long, caring relationship for sometime. When I left, she spontaneously kissed me on the cheek, which for a person of her personality and background as I understand it was a highly atypical action.

In the fifth group, I was simply unable to go into the altered state of consciousness with the patient healee. There are experientially two separate phenomena here. In the first, the patient actively does not want the healing. This is a clear experience that one of my students in psychic healing has described as "feeling as if you were running into a rubber wall." Often a person has been "persuaded" by family or friends to try this type of healing and does not want to. The feeling that results when the healer tries is unmistakable; it just cannot be done. Put bluntly, it is impossible to "unite" with someone who does not want to unite with you.

The second class of those with whom I could not go into the altered state of consciousness is not so easy to define. Sometimes it was probably due to a fatigue state or distraction of my own that I could not transcend. At other times, it may have been due to someing in the healee or to the "mix" our two personalities formed. We know so little about the best (and worst) healer-healee pairings that at this stage all we can do is be aware of our ignorance and our wish to overcome it. The experience in these cases was simply that I could not move into the world of the One; the symbols I used remained empty and just images, the world of the many remained the world I was in.

As it became clear that the first stage of testing the hypothesis of "how" psychic healing worked checked out, the time for the second stage drew closer. This was to determine if it could be taught to others. In the past, the ability to "do" psychic healing had always been regarded as "a gift of grace" or due to a special personality organization. Although I had never done any psychic healing before, it was possible that I had the special personality organization (or "gift or grace") and the reason I had never done it was because I had never tried to. From this viewpoint, the theory and self-training might be irrelevant to the results. I might, for all I knew, have been a "natural" healer and had this ability activated by my interest. The only way to test this was to see if the theory could be used to train others. If it worked there, if following the procedures indicated by the theory could lead others to the ability, I could be reasonably sure that the theory was valid and had not worked the first time merely by coincidence.

The first training seminar was held in September, 1970. I let it be known at the annual convention of the Association for Humanistic Psychology that I was interested in holding such a training seminar. With ten participants (mostly psychologists and others who were interested in the human potential movement), I went off to a private Florida estate which had been offered by Margaret Adams, the owner. The three and a half days scheduled was a very short time, but most of the participants learned to do Type 1 healing. Later seminars were scheduled for five days and although the pace was still terribly exhausting, it proved possible to teach the majority of participants how to go into both Type 1 and Type 2 states during this time.

Participants were selected for the seminars on the basis of several qualifications. A strong ego structure was needed, as the exercises used are often quite powerful types of meditation and the time available is too short to allow for members going on "trips" with them. Second, a good ethical approach to life is, from my point of view, important. And third, I selected the kind of people I felt I would like to be associated with in a new field. In the first five seminars I generally also ruled out people who had had a number of psychic experiences or who had ever been involved in psychic healing. The reason for this was that I was less interested in training those already in this area than I was in trying to see if individuals who had never been so involved could be trained. It is important to note, however, that the very act of applying for a seminar in itself was a selection system. Academic or formal qualifications were not considered as standards for acceptance, as I believe that they mean very little. I tend to agree with a patient of mine who once observed that she knew a lot of Ph.D.s and M.D.s who were educated far beyond their intelligence!

The procedure at all the seminars was structurally similar. First came a theoretical discussion of the concept of the Sensory Reality and the Clairvoyant Reality. (All students were asked to read my monograph on the subject [21] *before* we started so we did not start from scratch.) A series of exercises composed the bulk of the seminar. These were designed to accomplish three purposes:

1. To strengthen the structure of the ego—a sort of personality calisthenics.
2. To loosen the individual's usual concepts of dealing with space, time, the location of the self, etc., and to make him emotionally aware that there were alternative valid ways of conceptualizing in these areas.
3. To move in a step-by-step progression until one arrived at the altered state of consciousness theoretically associated with psychic healing.

At the end of this series, the group did Type 1 healing on each other and had a good deal of practice at this. On the last day, a small group of individuals with medically described physical problems would come in, one at a time, and the group would hold healing encounters with them. At one point or another, depending on the fatigue level of the group, a short series of exercises leading to Type 2 healing would be held.

Five days is a very short time for this procedure, but it proved feasible. The pace was exhausting, three sessions a day with each session ending when the group was too tired to go on. The pace was so intense and the pressure so heavy that it was necessary to hold the sessions in a residential setting and in a nonurban atmosphere so that the contact with nature could refresh the participants. At present, I and some of the advanced students who receiving training in teaching the seminar are experimenting with other forms of structure such as several intensive weekends in a row.

Overall, this general format proved successful. As I

learned more and more how to put the exercise series together and how to pace the progress, and as I learned from the contribution of those involved, the seminars improved, and more and more of the participants learned how to go into the altered states. At the seminar in September, 1971, all the students became quite proficient at this, continued to practice it after the seminar and—working together—became an amazingly strong healing circle. It was this group that, at a three-day follow-up advanced seminar, was involved in the case of the boy with the broken back described on p. 124.

It was clear from these results that if one followed the implications of the theory, a training method for psychic healing could be devised. If one then went through the training, it was possible for most people to become fairly effective at psychic healing, and further practice improved this ability. This seemed the most important type of test I could devise of the validity (or fruitfulness) of the theory. Other tests of the more usual "experimental" type have been devised, and one carried out (these are reported elsewhere [22]) but the healing approach seems to me to be the most critical test of the general theory of the paranormal implied in the concept of the Clairvoyant and Sensory Realities.

There is still, of course, a tremendous amount we need to learn about psychic healing. We do not know its limits or in what types of physical problems it is most effective. We do not know its implications for emotional problems, or how it can best be integrated with standard medical and psychotherapeutic procedures. We know little about how to select the best candidates for training, or how to set up the best healer-healee pairings. We need to know much more about training, about the comparative effectiveness of group and individual healing, and about how to form healing groups. We have no adequate theory for Type 2 healing, and we have only impressions about the comparative effectiveness of the two types or if, indeed, they are more than experientially different. We have no idea how to predict which healing encounters will be associated with positive biological changes and which will not. We are very much at the beginning of this work.

8 | a summing up of a beginning

And so—in this report of a research project in progress —we have followed a long road. In attempting to understand further the problem posed by the existence of the paranormal, we have had to probe into the nature of reality as we know it today. It is part of the faith of science that all phenomena that exist must exist under the category of natural law, and that none exist under the categories of "magic" or "miracle." The philosopher Henry Rosenthal once said, "There is no such thing as a paranormal event. However some events are less normal than others."[1]

In following this faith and attempting to understand the paranormal in normal terms, it became necessary to change the question usually asked about this class of phenomena. Instead of asking "How does the sensitive *do* it? How does she attain the 'paranormal' information?"—questions that had not yielded results after long and careful work by serious men—I asked a new question: "What is going on between the sensitive and the rest of reality at the moment the paranormal information is acquired?"

This question was, in effect, put to some of the

leading sensitives of our time, through a study of their written material and in direct discussion where possible. It became clear that at the moment they were "acquiring" the paranormal information they viewed the cosmos as if it were constructed in a special way. I termed this way the Clairvoyant Reality and contrasted it with the way we view the nature of reality in our everyday, "common-sense" life, which I termed the Sensory Reality.

The Clairvoyant Reality is a coherent, organized picture of the-way-the-world-works. It is a complete metaphysical system. It implies that when one is using it, certain events (such as telepathy, clairvoyance, and precognition) are "normal" and explainable. Certain other events (such as being able to will or take action toward a goal) are paranormal in this system.

I then realized that two other groups of individuals had arrived at similar conclusions. The mystics and the Einsteinian physicists both agreed with the clairvoyant that there were two valid ways of perceiving reality and on what these two ways were. Except for tricks of language and a few, comparatively minor, disagreements, all were completely agreed on the existence and nature of the Clairvoyant Reality. It proved impossible to differentiate statements describing it that were written by mystics from those written by physicists.

In order to test this theory, I attempted to use it to learn how to accomplish one of the functions long described as "paranormal" and to teach it to others. If the theory predicted that this paranormal function occurred in a certain psychological situation, and I organized this situation and found that the paranormal function occurred, this would be a pretty good test of the theory. Psychic healing was chosen for this test, and following the theory and its implications made it possible for me to learn to be a psychic healer and to teach it to others.

A second test of the hypothesis was made in a similar vein. In this test, the implications of the theory were used to design a training course in clairvoyance.

This study was done with the Maimonides Dream Laboratory, which selected eighteen subjects, nine experimental and nine control. All were pre- and post-tested for clairvoyant ability through their descriptions of copies of paintings in sealed envelopes. The nine experimental subjects received a five-day training program in mystical exercises derived from the theory of Clairvoyant Reality. Judges' evaluations of the results were as follows:

Number of "Hits" and "Misses"

	Experimental Group		Control Group	
Pre-test	Hits	32	Hits	33
	Misses	40	Misses	39
Post-test	Hits	41	Hits	31
	Misses	31	Misses	41

$(x^2 = 22.26. \ 1 \ df. \ p. \ > \ .001)$

This means that there is less than one chance in one hundred that the training did *not* make a difference in increasing clairvoyant ability. From a scientific standpoint these results can be taken as indicating that the training did produce increased clairvoyant ability. At a first, "pilot" study of the ability of the theory to predict training methods for clairvoyance, it can be taken as successful. As an additional aspect of this study, at the end of the training program, I predicted to the Dream Laboratory that when the results were analyzed all but one of the subjects would do as well or better on the post-testing than they had on the pre-testing, but that this one particular subject would do much worse. This prediction was shown to be completely accurate. The full data is being reported in the *Journal of the American Society for Psychical Research.*

It is interesting in this context to note that a study by Dr. D. F. Buzby showed that subjects who perceived the world in a global or unitary manner (as shown by the Embedded Figures Test) showed more evidence of precognition than those subjects who perceived the world "analytically." D. F. Buzby, "Precognition and a Test of Sensory Perception," *Journal of Parapsychology* 31 (1967), pp. 135–142.

A group of other, more conventional, experimental tests of the theory were devised and discussed in another, more technical publication.[2] Of these one has been carried out. The hypothesis to be tested arose from the fact that when in the Clairvoyant Reality one does not *act*, one *is* and *is related*. Action—with its implications of a future goal and therefore of the future being different in nature from the past—is not possible in the Clairvoyant Reality. One cannot, while in it, change the future any more than he can change the future of a film in which he has been an actor. In this reality all events *are*, they do not *happen*.

From this came the hypothesis that if the theory was valid, a prediction could be made about dreams in which one demonstrates awareness of information that could only have been gained paranormally. In a dream, at any particular moment, one can be in the role of participant in the action or in the role of an observer of the action. The prediction was that at those moments of the first demonstration of having acquired this information, the dreamer will be in the role of the observer, not of the participant. This would not always be true due to the retrospective falsification by means of which we "rewrite" and reorder our dreams even as we wake up, but it should be true more often than can be accounted for by chance. At his Dream Laboratory, where a detailed scientific study is being made of ESP in dreams, Dr. Stanley Krippner tested this hypothesis and found the prediction borne out. The other experimental tests of the theory have not yet been carried out.

There is also a third way to explore the validity of a theory. This is to get the reaction of specialists in the field. I know that if you present in some detail a new explanation of the psychological behavior of hysterics to an experienced psychotherapist, he will know, because of his long experiential background with hysterics, if the explanation "feels" reasonable. Does it give him a sense of "Of course, *that* is what has been going on," "That seems right"? If he does not respond in this way, you had better begin to think about going back and starting over: it does not bode well for your theory. The same thing is true in other fields of expertise.

The reaction of the expert is not the final word. He can be wrong for a variety of reasons. Nevertheless, it is wise to get his opinion. By and large, as John Dewey pointed out many years ago, the person who is wearing the shoe knows where it pinches and where it fits comfortably.

After I had completed the work on the basic theory of the Clairvoyant Reality, I gave this material to two experienced sensitives, Rosalind Heywood and Douglas Johnson. (The reactions of Eileen Garrett should not be included in this section. After all, the hypothesis was largely developed from an analysis of her writing; it would not be too surprising if she agreed with it.) Douglas Johnson commented: "It sounds as if they were written by an experienced sensitive. This is how it is for me." Rosalind Heywood said: "My first thought after reading it was 'It's all so obvious. Why does he want to say that? That's how I've always lived.' Then I realized it wasn't so obvious to other people."

The reactions of these two very experienced and serious sensitives was certainly very encouraging. Other sensitives and mediums I have since shown it to or discussed it with have responded in a similar vein. I have had no negative reactions from them.

One of the strongest responses came when I later presented the basic theory and its application to psychic healing in a meeting of the Life Energies Research Foundation.[3] Sitting in the audience were Ambrose and Olga Worrall and Ronald Beasley (one of the leading psychic healers in England). I spoke with some anxiety, for here indeed was a tough and knowledgeable audience. After my talk the Worralls and Beasley came up to the podium and Ambrose Worrall said, "We would like to congratulate you as a team. You are the first person who has really been able to articulate what we have been doing." It was a moment of vast relief for me!

The theory of the Sensory Reality and the Clairvoyant Reality appears to deal effectively and in scientific terms with the "mental" phenomena of parapsychology, with telepathy, clairvoyance, precognition, and psychic healing. It does not deal with the "physical" phenomena in this field, with psychokinesis, the ability of mental activity to affect physical activity at a distance. The experimental evidence for this phenomenon seems to me to be well established (as in the work of J. Fahler, E. Cox, and others), but I have, at this time, no theoretical concepts to "explain" the phenomenon.

One of the implications of the theory concerns a problem with which psychical research has been deeply concerned. This is the problem of "survival," of what happens to the "personality" after the death of the "body." In appendix E I present an exploration of this implication as it was published in the scientific journal *Main Currents in Modern Thought*.

Certain problems are inherent in a theory of the sort presented here. I am going to describe briefly three possible types of objections which, I believe, must be considered when a theory like this one is evaluated. I do not think that the present formulation of the theory has fallen into any of these dangers, but they should be stated here so that others can come to their own opinion.

The first problem that may relate to the present work was succinctly stated by Max Planck when he wrote: "There is nothing more seductively dangerous in scientific work than the introduction of extraneous analogies into the problem at issue." [4] We must consider whether the structural similarities between the world picture of the sensitive, the mystic, and the modern physicist are really extraneous analogies to the problem of explaining clairvoyance and precognition. Only the fruitfulness of the theory—does it lead to useful new data?—will answer the question.

A second problem in the evaluation of this theory arises from the question how man typically behaves when he is actively facing the outer limits of his knowledge, when his exploration of "what is" reaches beyond the borders of his present understanding. Does the similarity of the conceptualizations of the three groups of researchers—mediums, mystics and physicists—stem from the fact that when human beings face the unknown and try to penetrate it, they conceptualize what is beyond the limits of their understanding in a particular way? Since mystics, in particular, come from such a wide variety of cultural backgrounds, the crucial factor here would probably lie in the inherent nature of the human nervous system. I personally do not believe this to be so, but the possibility should be stated so that it can be evaluated.

A third possible theoretical problem in the approach of this book is pointed up by F. C. S. Northrop when he warns that it is important to ". . . avoid the danger, noted by Margenau and appreciated by Bohr, of giving pseudo solutions to physical and philosophical problems by playing fast and loose with the law of contradiction in the name of the principle of complementarity." [5] Although the concept presented here, with its two ways of interacting with reality, has this danger, I do not believe that it is a violation of the law of contradiction. It states rather that different concepts of reality, different ways of structuring ourselves and whatever is *out there,* lead to different possibilities of interaction with reality. Although Northrop's warning points to a real problem, and this book must be questioned in its light, I believe the present formulation is closer to Margenau's viewpoint: "I am perfectly willing to admit that reality does change as discovery proceeds. I can see nothing basically wrong with a real world which undergoes modification along with the flux of experience." [6]

This, so far, is just a beginning. The real subtitle of this book might well be "A Report of Research in Progress." There is never an ending to the exploration of human potential and man's relationship to the cosmos, nor can any one person carry more than the smallest burden for opening new doors of understanding. On the course of my own adventure, I have used and been inspired by the ideas and insights of many great men and women throughout all of recorded human history. My hope in reporting my work is that in some small way—perhaps moving us a step or two further in our quest for understanding—I might have been able to help a little to illuminate the path for those who are excited by the possibilities and are willing to continue the exploration. Which of us will come up with the next "right question"?

part three | the next adventure

If we do not expect the unexpected,
we will never find it.

—HERACLITUS

9 | a new note on a work in progress

A human being is a part of the whole, called by us
the "Universe," a part limited in time and space.
He experiences himself, his thoughts and feelings as
something separated from the rest—a kind of optical
delusion of his consciousness. This delusion is a
kind of prison for us, restricting us to our personal
desires and to affection for a few persons nearest
to us. Our task must be to free ourselves from this
prison by widening our circle of compassion to em-
brace all living creatures and the whole of nature
in its beauty. Nobody is able to achieve this completely, but the striving for such achievement is in
itself a part of the liberation and a foundation for
inner security.

—ALBERT EINSTEIN [1]

I must admit to an ambivalence that I am ashamed of
about whether or not to add this last chapter. I have
always identified myself as a member in good standing
of the company of those who followed the best in the

traditions and practices of modern science. Up to this point I would assume that most "true and free inquirers" would agree that I have followed the rules of the game in my explorations and adventures into the Clairvoyant Reality. There would be comfort and security in the comradeship of colleagues, if I could leave it at that.

But my work has *not* ended there, and I am now stuck with experiences and observations about which it is necessary for me to report—in spite of my clear understanding that many in the community of science will now say, "He's really gone round the bend now, poor fellow."

And yet, despite this hazard, I am satisfied that I have not given up the great tradition, the strict and beautiful standards of scientific inquiry, when I followed the new paths I recently have found necessary to explore.

There is a third way of being-in-the-world that the mystic often knows and strives for, that medium and healer occasionally reach, and that the physicist does not seem to be much aware of.

I had finished the preceding chapters and shown and discussed the manuscript with a number of knowledgeable friends. They congratulated me, spoke well of it, made a host of constructive criticisms, but were disturbed and unhappy about something I could not understand. Rosalind Heywood hinted something was missing, and said that I should look into myself for it. The psychiatrist Robert Laidlaw asked, "Is this *all* of it?" Maria Janis, a serious healer, gave me a copy of Francis Thompson's "The Hound of Heaven" with a note indicating she thought it applicable. Marvin and Ruth Sampson, both deeply knowledgeable about and immersed in the best of the Christian Science tradition, told me they believed there was much more to be done. Mother Placid, Assistant Superior of Regina Laudis Monastery, said I was avoiding something in myself and that I needed to do something about it. Psychoanalyst Gotthard Booth made it plain that he did not regard the book as finished. Finally, Dr. Edgar Jackson, a Methodist minister of vast experience in healing, told me—in no uncertain terms—that it was time he and I went to Europe to look at some of the great Gothic cathedrals of northern France and to do some serious talking.[2] During the trip he gave me the worst dressing down I have ever had in my life. In his gentle, loving voice he told me that I was avoiding the next step in the research, that I was trying to fit data (such as the kind of healing I have named Type 5, in which major biological changes occur in a few moments) into a framework that was too small (the explanation for Type 1 healing), and generally acting as if I were trying to defend my theory against data that did not fit it, rather than to continue my search for truth.

It was a most unsettling and disturbing lecture. I have long respected Edgar Jackson as one of the wisest men I have ever known, a man who had fused both realities and lived his life accordingly. I could no longer ignore what my friends were saying. It was clearly time to go back to work.[3]

When I looked again at the data and at some of my own experiences, it became plain that the theoretical approach I had been using was useful and fruitful, so far as it went, but it did not go far enough. There were too many experiences and occurrences left out: psychokinesis (P.K.); Type 5 healing, which is rare but real; mystical states of "oneness," including some I had experienced that the theory did not deal with; the occasional real efficacy of prayer ("When I pray, coincidences start to happen," wrote a famous British archbishop); and other data of this kind that I had known about, but apparently had scrupulously avoided worrying about too much.

On careful examination, these factors did not appear to "fit" the Clairvoyant Reality concept. (It goes without saying that they do not fit into the Sensory Reality concept either.) These two concepts, however, appeared too solidly based and too useful to discard. The obvious conclusion was that there is a third way of being-in-the-world in which these factors *can* occur, in which they are "normal." Furthermore, there had been on my part a growing dissatisfaction with the concept of the Clairvoyant Reality. I had done, over the past few years, enough consistent contemplation and meditation so that I could usually move into it strongly in a healing encounter. The deeper I could move into the Clairvoyant Reality, however, the more I felt that something was not right with the concept.

Shortly after the talk with Edgar Jackson, I visited the cathedral at Metz, one of the great ones of the Gothic period. The vaulted roofs appear to tumble endlessly upward, inviting and urging you to an experience if you are ready for it. Probably due to the talks with Jackson, combined with the work in meditation I had been doing, I seem to have been prepared for it.

In the Cathedral I did a Type 1 healing with a healee who was in New York City. It was a particularly "strong" healing in which I moved very deeply into the Clairvoyant Reality.[4] After the experience I sat quietly in a pew simply looking at the walls and arches. I realized that I was beginning to have an experience new for me, and I let it happen.

The altered state of consciousness I then experienced was a profound shock to me. Looking back on it afterwards, it seemed to make sense out of a great many things I had read about, and to pull them together into the beginning of a new insight into the problems of healing. I had had a very deep experience relating to my research and would need much analysis of it before it could be integrated with the concepts and methods I had so far.

After Metz, we visited the cathedrals at Rheims and at Cologne. At these two places I was able to repeat the experience and to deepen it. After this, Jackson strongly urged me to go off by myself for a time and really do some work on the problem. When I did this, and began to try hard to look at it with *all* my experience, it began to be clear to me that in the concept of the Clairvoyant Reality I had included two separate states of consciousness. In Type 1 healing these two were also confused. Once I understood this, it became plain that this had been the source of my increasing feeling of unease during the meditations. It became much easier to go into the Type 1 healing state of consciousness when I had separated out the other state of consciousness I had mixed up with it.

The healer in the basic state of consciousness associated with Type 1 healing is in a state of consciousness in which he and the healee are simply and literally perceived as one entity (each with his uniqueness maintained) within a metaphysical system—the Clairvoyant Reality—that permits this. Literally, in this reality, no entity of which one is conscious can be separate from another. When one is conscious of himself and the healee, these two entities automatically merge into one.

Christmas Humphreys described the Kegon Buddhist philosophy of Jijimuge as "the uninterrupted interdiffusion of all particulars with each other. Herein the doorknob *is* the orange and the orange *is* the doorknob, not relatively, comparatively or indirectly, as species of one genus, but absolutely, directly and precisely as declared." [5] This approach to the unity of healer and healee was the basis of the Type 1 healing. When the healer—for a moment—absolutely knows this to be true, that he and the healee are one, the healee sometimes responds with a mobilization of his self-repair and self-recuperative abilities. This state of consciousness was one of the two I had included in the Type 1 healing.

The second state of consciousness I had included was quite different. In this one, the healer knows that he is a part of the whole cosmos as a wave is part of the ocean. There is no separation between him and the rest of the universe, yet he is a unique part. The All affects him as he affects the All. The healee is also part of the All in the same way. The healee is, so to speak, another wave. In this state of consciousness, the healer knows that he is distinct from the healee although both are a part of the same ocean and thereby connected. In moments of the pure knowledge of this, the healer mentally attempts to bring the immense resources of the harmonic energies of the cosmos to bear on the healee, and thus to increase his inner and outer harmony.

This can be stated as another analogy. If the healer is seen as one toe of the total organism and the healee is seen as another, then it is possible for the healer to see himself as separate enough from the healee to wish the best for him, and as connected enough to attempt to implement these wishes. In a manner of speaking, the healer attempts to send messages to the greater One of which he is a part, and tries to influence the One to move to the aid of another small part. To put it differently, the healer prays to the All for the best for another part of it. The word "prays" is indeed appropriate here, since there may be a deep feeling of awe and reverence connected with the full attainment of this state of consciousness. The experience of this reality is shocking and overwhelming at first impact. After my first experience of it, I had no doubt as to the reason I had blocked perceiving its existence for so long. Following the experience, I understood something of the meaning of the statement in the Zohar "God is not nice. He is not an uncle. He is an earthquake." One can be, as I was, pretty shattered by this.

The "All" is the "One," is "God," and at these moments this becomes clear. Very strong feelings of humility and reverence may come to consciousness with the full realization of what one is a part of and of its awesome and overwhelming nature. To *know* that one is a part of the All is to know a little of its size and nature, and it is doubtful if this can be known without the arousal of deeply religious feelings.[6] I have named this state of consciousness the Transpsychic Reality.

In this state of consciousness one *knows* that everything, including oneself, is a part of the One, of the All. This was expressed by Suzuki Roshi when he wrote, "All is God and there is no God."[7] It is what Kabir meant by his poem about the wave and the ocean, what John Donne meant when he wrote, "God is an angel in an angel, a stone in a stone and a straw in a straw." It was expressed by Francis Thompson when he wrote:

Does the fish soar to find the ocean,
The eagle plunge to find the air—
That we ask of the Stars in motion
If they have rumor of thee there?

Not where the wheeling systems darken,
And our benumbed conceiving soars!—
The drift of pinions, would we hearken,
Beats at our own clay shuttered doors.

The angels keep their ancient places,
Turn but a stone and start a wing!
'Tis ye, 'Tis your estranged faces,
That miss the many splendoured thing.[8]

Marcus Aurelius enjoined his readers to "constantly picture the universe as a single living organism."

The concept of "God" is by no means necessary for this state of consciousness. Conceptualizing in this way is useful for some people, not useful for others. One can attain this state of consciousness and use it just as effectively for healing with other systems of concepts.

A particularly useful concept for many individuals, including myself, can be described in terms of energy. Knowing for the moment that you are a part of the total One of the cosmos, and that there are vast energies which maintain the universe on its course (so to speak, the cosmic "homeostatic" forces), you attempt by total concentration and "will" to bend these energies to increase the harmony of the healee, another part of the cosmos. Knowing yourself a part of an all-encompassing energy system, you will the total system to divert additional energies to the repair and harmonization of a part that needs it.

This is quite different from the usual God-oriented

interpretation of the Transpsychic Reality. From my own viewpoint, it is a useful and fruitful conceptualization and one that has enabled me to move deeply into the Transpsychic Reality on various occasions since the experiences in the Gothic cathedrals.

Many mystics have perceived and related to the All in this way. There seems to me little difference between the Zen *Sunyata* (the Infinite One) and Meister Eckhardt's definition of God as an "is-ness," and his warning that only if God is conceived in this way and "not as he is conceived by anyone to be—nor yet as something to be achieved" that one can become with God, "a unit, that is pure unity." [9] It is interesting to compare Eckhardt's statements with the description of a mystical experience by Bernard Berenson:

> It was a morning in early summer. A silver haze shimmered and trembled over the lime trees. The air was laden with their fragrance. The temperature was like a caress. I remember—I need not recall—that I climbed up a tree stump and felt suddenly immersed in Itness. I did not call it by that name. I had no need for words. It and I were one. [10]

One can, in this state, attempt to "will" the cosmic energies to flow toward a particular person to increase his inner and outer harmony. I am indebted to Dr. Robert Laidlaw for the understanding that there is another approach to healing in the Transpsychic Reality one can use and still remain within the "energy" concept rather than the "God" concept system.

Laidlaw's approach (and it seems to me to be in some ways a superior one to the one I had been following which involved the use of "will") is to use the basic concept "If I can perfectly align myself with the harmonies of the universe, then their energies can flow through me toward the healee whom I hold in my consciousness." The effort here is not of will, but of awareness of and harmonizing oneself and one's consciousness to the total harmonies of the All.

This approach also calls for a moment of total consciousness of the Transpsychic Reality and of one's "wish" for the best for another individual. However, instead of using will and determination to try to bend the cosmic energies to your purpose, you try to become so attuned to these energies that you become a clear channel for them. It means a complete surrender of your own will except for your desire for the best for the healee. Here you identify with the All totally, and reach toward the state where you wear the universe like a glove and it wears you.

Thomas Merton has described these two approaches as they are shown in *The Brothers Karamazov*.[11] The first is exemplified by the ascetic Therapont, who frees himself of the world of multiplicity (the Sensory Reality) by will and effort and then uses these to try to influence the world. The second is exemplified by the staretz Zossima, who identified himself with the All in order to try to bring down God's blessing on individuals.

This then was the differentiation of a third state of consciousness. The first had been the Sensory Reality —the everyday, common-sense way of being-in-the-world. The second was the Clairvoyant Reality delineated earlier in this book. The third state, the Transpsychic Reality, now had to be added to these two. It is worthy of note how often in mystical thought the concept of the three states has been described. The most well known in Western culture is perhaps St. Paul's concept of Body, Spirit, and Soul, which seems to be making the same differentiation as I have done here. I must also say that there is a considerable difference between experiencing these states of consciousness and talking or writing about them. The being in these states is a direct experience, but ". . . we remember it, talk about it and record it through the use of concepts, those second-hand bricks of thought by which we build communication and enshrine discovery."[12] We need both, the experiencing and the conceptualizing. As Cary Baynes wrote in her introduction to *The*

Secret of the Golden Flower, "The solution cannot be found either in deriding . . . spirituality as impotent or by mistrusting science as a destroyer of humanity. We have to see that the spirit must lean on science as its guide to the world of reality and that science must turn to spirit for the meaning of life." [13]

Is it possible to train individuals so that they can attain the Transpsychic Reality, with its potential for Type 5 healing, at will, as it has proven possible to train individuals to reach the Clairvoyant Reality with its potential for Type 1 healing? This is a crucial question. I believe the answer is "yes," and at the present time am engaged in designing and experimenting with such a training program. Whether or not it will be effective I do not know, but theoretically it certainly appears to be feasible.

The exercises, as I see them now, are not easy or gentle ones. They start where the training for the Clairvoyant Reality leaves off, and, I believe, can only be accomplished by individuals with a serious background in contemplation and meditation. It would seem that healers trained in attaining both the Clairvoyant Reality and the Transpsychic Reality would be far more effective than healers trained only in the clairvoyant way of being-in-the-world.

One question must again be raised here and clarified. It is the contention of this work that different types of action are possible in each of these three states of consciousness. In the Clairvoyant Reality state one is sometimes able to help mobilize the healee's self-repair systems, even at a distance. In the Transpsychic Reality state one is sometimes able to attain major biological, therapeutic changes in a few moments. How can this be possible? How can the "laws" of reality be broken by activity inside one's own head? Isn't this impossible on the face of it?

There is no one metaphysical system that "correctly" describes reality. Each valid system (and who knows today how many of these there are?) includes different "basic limiting principles," different definitions of what is "normal" and what is "paranormal" within them. A valid system is only useful to you if what you are trying to do accords well with its basic limiting principles. It is inadvisable to try to cross a busy highway in the Clairvoyant or Transpsychic Realities, if one wishes to continue biological survival from the viewpoint of the Sensory Reality.

As I look at what I have written in this book, it seems to me that it is largely based on the following proposition: the metaphysical system you are using is the metaphysical system that is operating. A metaphysical system is a set of assumptions about how the universe is put together and functions. We always have one whether or not we are aware of it. The assumptions we use about the nature of reality make up the system. The system determines what is possible and impossible, normal and paranormal, within it. Thus, if, in the physicist's phrase, "matter is discontinuous," then separate entities cannot affect each other without an intervening variable. If "matter is continuous," as in the mystic's statement "Thou canst not stir a flower without the troubling of a star," then, in the physicist's words, "any local agitation shakes the entire universe."

Science has given up the search for the "true" metaphysical system, the one system that "correctly" describes the structure of reality. Whether, to use the same example, matter is viewed as continuous or discontinuous depends on what your viewpoint is and what problem you are dealing with at the moment. In this view, man does not only discover reality; within limits he invents it.[14] There is a maxim by Goethe: "Whatever is fact was already in theory."

In an altered state of consciousness we use a different metaphysical system. If we really use a different metaphysical system (and not just think or talk about it), we are in an altered state of consciousness. These two phrases are different ways of describing the same thing. An altered state of consciousness means that we are perceiving and reacting to the universe as if it were run on a different set of laws and principles than those which we "normally" believe to be operating. This is clearly not so simple as it sounds, and there are many limitations and qualifications necessary. Nevertheless, it seems to be true that, within certain definite limits, there is at least a choice as to which metaphysical structure you can choose and operate successfully within.

I do not know what most of the limitations are. Certainly one is the necessity for coherence. The system must be coherent and structurally valid (in its own terms). Another limit is the complete belief in it. One must *know* it is valid to operate within it. There are doubtlessly many other limitations as yet unclear to me. What we do have are three systems within which the human being is apparently capable of functioning. In each of these, different actions are possible and impossible. The first one—the Sensory Reality—is necessary for biological survival and clearly has some sort of priority over the other two for us, although I am not quite sure what I mean by this. The second—the Clairvoyant Reality—is the one in which clairvoyance, telepathy, precognition, and Type 1 healing occur. The third—the Transpsychic Reality—is the one in which true "prayer" is possible, with its (sometimes) remarkable effects.

Having experienced the Transpsychic Reality in the cathedrals of Metz, Rheims, and Cologne and, since then, elsewhere, I cannot doubt its existence. Furthermore, it is described in many of the mystical writings, although it is often confused (as I had confused it myself) with the Clairvoyant Reality.

Very often, as one progresses in research, what has seemed to be one phenomenon is resolved into more than one. Thus, in the first stages of the research into healing, it had seemed to me that Type 1 and Type 2 healing were the same phenomenon. Similarly, I had later confused the Clairvoyant Reality and the Transpsychic Reality as being the same state of consciousness. With this confusion of the two states of consciousness, I had believed that a very strong Type 1 healing could become a Type 5. Since, however, Type

5 calls for a type of change *beyond* the body's ability at self-repair this was not satisfactory, although I apparently "deliberately" did not notice this. It would be hard to place, for example, a well known case of Rebecca Beard's into a Type 1 explanatory system. In this case, a thirty-eight-pound ascites tumor (a liquid tumor) disappeared overnight. During the night the healee did not get out of bed and the bed was not wet. It is hard to imagine the body having the ability to dispose of approximately thirty-eight pints of liquid in this way. The immense resources of the One and the tremendous energies it brings to bear, however, would not seem likely to be strained by it. However, it is in the Transpsychic Reality that we (sometimes, rarely) can bring these energies into play, not in the Clairvoyant Reality.

Very often in mystical writings, the Transpsychic Reality is seen as a "higher" state of being than the Clairvoyant Reality.[15] This may be one of the reasons for the repeated warnings in every serious mystical school that the *siddhis*, the "miracles," ESP, and the like, are dangerous to inner development, that too much personal investment in them prevents growth. In essence, these seem to be statements that the Clairvoyant Reality can be so attractive in the status-giving powers it includes that it can prevent one from progressing into the Transpsychic Reality way of being-in-the-world.

From my own point of view at this time, no way of being-in-the-world is "higher" than another. One may be far more difficult to attain (as indeed the Transpsychic Reality is) but each is valid on its own terms.

In order to discuss the Transpsychic Reality more fully, I have made a table of comparisons of all three altered states of consciousness. As can be seen from Table 2, these are indeed completely different states of consciousness, different metaphysical systems with different possibilities in each of them.

What can one "wish" or "will" in each of these real-

Table 2 | Comparison of Three Types of Consciousness

	Sensory Reality	Clairvoyant Reality	Transpsychic Reality
Perception Mode	Sensory equipment.	Knowledge through uniting with: being one with.	Knowledge through being a part of the whole and so perception of other parts through the whole.
Action Mode	Action involving interaction between separate entities.	Uniting with.	"Prayer"—attempts to mobilize the energies of the One for another part of it.
Possibilities	Action-to-an-end. Cause and effect sequences. Physical action. Self-interest.	ESP phenomena. Type 1 healing.	"Coincidences starting to happen." Type 5 healing.
Impossibilities	ESP phenomena. Action without an intervening variable. Type 1 and Type 5 healing.	Action to an end. Wishing or willing. Separate units or entities. Self-interest.	Any entity *not* being a part of the whole. Self-interest.

Time	"Time's Arrow." Steady movement from future to present to past.	The eternal now without past, present, or future, but sequences remain.	The eternal now. Loss of sequence?
Space	Measured in inches and light years.	An illusion. All is one.	Real but completely unimportant. Parts of the whole are separated by it, but being one with the One, this does not matter at all.
Energy	A useful concept. The way entities affect each other and the way we describe processes within entities. The ability to produce action or effect. That which does work.	Not a useful concept. One cannot "do work" in this reality. However, being in this altered state of consciousness can affect energies in the bodies of healee and healer from the viewpoint of the Sensory Reality.	A useful concept. Through mental action one attempts to bring the immense energies of the total universe to bear on another part of it in order to increase the harmony of that part.
Feelings mobilized by the state	All the variations described by the psychologists and others.	Calm, peace, serenity. Centeredness.	Awe, humility, deep religious feelings. Serenity, calm.

ities? What types of motivation and action are possible?

In the Sensory Reality one can will and act for oneself or for other separate entities, or against oneself or others. There is a constant interplay of energies affecting separate units in the plenum, and one can will and act to affect these energies in any way one chooses. One affects other entities through the use of the energies one controls. These energies range from the sound waves of speech to the thrown rock or bomb. In this reality, and only in this one of the three, one can physically "act."

In the Clairvoyant Reality one can only wish to *unite* with another part of the cosmos; to the degree that one is in this state of consciousness one is only motivated to unite with it, become one with is, merge with it. The reasons for wishing to go into this state of consciousness are varied, but once in it, one unites with another person, entity, or chunk of the universe, and that is all. Any wishing or willing to accomplish anything beyond this implies separate entities and action between them, and this disrupts the Clairvoyant Reality. The "uniting," once one starts it, must be done for its own sake, not for any result it will have. In the words of the Bhagavad Gita, "Let then the motive for action be in the action itself, not in the event." Introducing a "purpose" into the Clairvoyant Reality disrupts it and returns one to the Sensory Reality. The "uniting," however, can have definite effects. When perceived (at some level of perception) by the healee, it can mobilize his self-repair systems and lead to Type 1 healing. In the healer's own body, it can also change the flow and direction of energies, reduce tensions, and produce a calming effect and a sense of serenity. In addition, the uniting leads to ESP-types of perceptions, and since there is no bar to the flow of information *within* the one entity that now exists, these perceptions are often remembered on the return to the Sensory

Reality.[16] Telepathy and clairvoyance are normal in the Clairvoyant Reality. In this reality, however, one cannot "wish" or "will" anything—either good or bad —for the person with whom one is uniting. This willing or wishing something immediately implies two entities, which cannot exist in this metaphysical system and disrupt it, and returns us to the Sensory Reality in which the "paranormal" is impossible.

In the Clairvoyant Reality, the concept of "energy" is not a useful one. Literally, one cannot "do work" in it. Since action, willing, or wishing are "paranormal" in this metaphysical system, one can only observe and be. That there can be energy changes within the healee's body as a result of his perception of the uniting is certainly true, but the person in the Clairvoyant Reality cannot *use* energy in any way.

The Transpsychic Reality—and I confess to knowing least about this one and to feeling remarkably tentative as I write—also has definite limitations in this area. Prayer is one way of conceptualizing the mode of action and communication in this reality, and true prayer must be done purely. One can only really pray for the best for another part of the whole, for its increased harmony. Prayer that is specific beyond this disrupts the Transpsychic Reality. It implies greater knowledge of what is "best" for one part of the All by another part, and thus leads to a division and separation of the parts from the whole that disrupts this way of being-in-the-world and returns one to the Sensory Reality. Certainly the compassion one feels for another's pain or illness can lead one to pray for him, to go into the Transpsychic Reality, and sometimes this seems to lead to quite startling results. "Religion," wrote R. H. Blyth, is "the infinite way we do finite things." [17]

In addition, the prayer must be "pure," that is, without reference to one's own best interests. It must be done in a moment of such "intense" caring for the best in the other part of the All that one can say of that moment, again in the words of the Gita:

One to me is fame or shame
One to me is loss or gain
One to me is pleasure or pain

If one uses a conceptualization other than the religious one and attempts to accomplish healing in the Transpsychic Reality by "mental action" rather than by "prayer," the position stated above is still the same. When in this reality, it is inconceivable to attempt to move the energies of the cosmos to attain greater disharmony for another part of the All. To attempt this increased disharmony immediately removes you from the Transpsychic and back to the Sensory Reality in which you are at liberty to hate and to harm, but cannot accomplish anything of a "paranormal" nature. The negative emotion precipitating an attempt to harm another person has the same effect as attempting to be specific about what help you are trying to accomplish; it introduces a divisiveness and a separation into your conceptualization, and this destroys the coherence of the metaphysical system. The necessity for absolute and selfless caring also exists in the "mental action" and "energy" conceptualization. The healer's concentration and will must be so completely focused that there is simply no room left for self-interest.

As I discussed the concept of the Transpsychic Reality with various colleagues, this problem came up again and again. Repeatedly, they asked whether it was not just as possible to do harm with these energies of the cosmos as it was to heal. It forced me to do a good deal of thinking about this.

I do not believe that the universe is concerned with our standards of good and evil. Electricity is neutral; it can be used to help or to kill. So too, it seems to me, are the rest of the energies of the universe.

There is certainly a widespread belief among many religious people that "God is good." I do not understand this statement. It seems at best a tremendous reduction, a bringing down to our value system of something far beyond it.[18]

Nevertheless, I do not believe it is possible to use these energies to harm. You can only get in touch with them when you are willing to give up your usual sense of identity, when you want to be *more* in harmony with the rest of the universe rather than less in harmony. This means—since at these moments you perceive the universe as one dynamic Gestalt—that you also must want more harmony for any other part of the cosmos that is in your consciousness. To "hurt" or to "harm" is to reduce harmony, not add to it. To "heal" is to increase inner and outer harmony, not lessen it. It is impossible, I believe, to enter the Transpsychic Reality while we are holding a reservation in our minds that part of this reality should be excluded.[19] The metaphysical system breaks down as soon as we make the exception, and returns us to the Sensory Reality. We can try to heal, but not to harm, in the transpsychic way of being-in-the-world.

In the "prayer" or "mental action" of the Transpsychic Reality, we are attempting to mobilize what the Sufi mystics call "Baraka" for another person. Although we may have been brought to this state by compassion for a particular ill or pain of the person, we cannot determine in what way the Baraka—the immense harmonic energies of the One—will manifest itself. If we do succeed in our attempt to bring the harmony of the All to bear more strongly on the part with which we are concerned, it may show in ways we did not even conceive of, or it may show in a direct alleviation of the situation that aroused our feelings in the first place.

The analogy with Type 1 healing is interesting. In a successful Type 1, the individual's self-repair systems may be mobilized on quite a different problem than the one the healer had in mind. In a successful intercessory action of the Transpsychic Reality, the benefit accruing to the person prayed or willed for may not be the specific benefit hoped for by healer and healee. Such results induce a good deal of humility and help prevent power trips quite effectively!

Indeed, every serious mystical school warns against assuming you know what is good for another person. There is the Hasidic story of the rabbi traveling with his disciple. At one village a poor man—he owned only a cow—gave them the best of everything he owned and the fullest hospitality and respect possible. In the morning when the man and his wife had gone to work, the rabbi killed the cow. In the next village a rich man treated them with contempt and had them sleep in the barn. In the morning, the rabbi pointed out to his disciple that a part of the wall around the rich man's house was in disrepair and insisted that they spend the entire morning repairing it for him. Later the disciple asked the meaning of these actions. The rabbi replied, "In the poor man's house I saw the Malach Hamovis —the Angel of Death—in the corner. He had come for the poor man's wife. I was able to give him the cow instead. Under the rich man's wall a secret treasure is buried. If he had repaired it himself, he would have discovered it!" There is a similar tale in the Sufi mystical tradition.

Clearly then, we can wish or will different things and in different ways in the three ways of being-in-the-world. In the Sensory Reality, we can wish anything for ourselves or other separate entities and act as we will within the confines of the basic limiting principles of this reality to achieve these ends, whatever our motivation. In the Clairvoyant Reality, we can only unite with another part of the All. Our motivation must be to do only this, whatever the original motivation that led us to go into this altered state of consciousness may have been. As many mediums have learned to their cost, to *try* to achieve a specific goal while in this state disrupts it and prevents the achievement of any paranormal information.[20]

In the Transpsychic Reality, one can will or pray for the best for another part of the All, so long as it is done wholeheartedly and purely. If one is deeply in the Reality when praying this way, sometimes remarkable benefits (sometimes even those you had in mind!) accrue. This can include Type 5 healing on occasion.

Does it include other types of healing as well, such as Tony Arigo's undoubted painless, shock-free, and infection-free surgery with his carelessly cleaned knife and no anesthetic? (Type 3.) And the Chapman-Lang type of healing that operates with invisible (to anyone else) instruments on the "etheric body" (a term that seems to mean something to many serious people but which I have never understood) several inches above the skin? (Type 4.) Does it, for that matter, include Type 2 healing with its laying on of hands and frequent perception of what appear to be energies flowing through the afflicted part?

I simply do not know the answers to these questions, nor how these types of psychic healing work. The only one of these three I know anything about is Type 2, which I can do and can teach others to do, but have not the faintest idea as to why it sometimes gets results or what is happening. I don't particularly like it because it tends to lead the healer on power trips and its results are transitory more often than with Type 1 healing.[21] Partially because it is so easy to teach and requires no particular mental work or discipline, I am inclined at this time to believe that it is a function of the Sensory Reality, and is indeed the mobilization and focusing of some as yet undefined type of energy. But I just do not know and would not care to have to defend my present beliefs about it.[22]

Are there other realities within which human beings can function and within which other goals can be attained? Are there, for example, realities that include "entities" ("spirits") which interfere in human affairs, and perhaps negative action ("black magic") on other levels of being than the Sensory Reality, or are these things myth, primitive thinking, and illusion? I do not know.[23] These three realities are the only ones I am aware of at this time. There may be many others. William James—as he does so often—has the last word:

. . . our normal waking consciousness, rational consciousness as we call it, is but one special type of
consciousness, whilst all about it, parted from it by
the filmiest of screens, there lie potential forms of
consciousness entirely different. . . . No account of
the universe in its totality can be final which leaves
these other forms of consciousness quite disregarded.
. . . They forbid a premature closing of our accounts
with reality.[24]

And finally, the answer to my own ambivalence in
adding this material to my book is that the essence of
science is that you must at least *act* as if you are not
afraid. You must follow where the data leads you and
abide by the results whatever your previous theories,
biases, or wishes. And if the data leads, as it did, against
all my expectations and preferences into fields hitherto
left to religion, I had to follow the material and report
it as honestly as I could.

The simplest and most basic statement of modern
Western religion is the statement most often ignored—
or at least misunderstood.

The recurring theme "God is Love" appears to mean
exactly what it says; that there is a force, an energy,
that binds the cosmos together and moves always in
the direction of its harmonious action and the fruition
of the separate connected parts. In man, this force
emerges and expresses itself as love, and this is the
"spark of the divine" in each of us.

When this force is acknowledged and reinforced by
the culture, it is possible for human beings to relate
harmoniously to themselves, to others, to the rest of the
cosmos, and to move toward the most unique and
awesome self-fulfillment.

When this force is ignored or discouraged, the energy
becomes blocked and distorted, and in all human history has been expressed in self-hatred, a hunger for
power, materialistic greed and ultimately, as the de-
humanization of our time makes clear, the real pos-

sibility of man's so disrupting the expression of his energy as to end his part in the cosmic design.

It seems to me that the challenge to science, to man, to the human experiment is, finally and irrevocably, whether or not man can accept that he is a part of the energy of the universe and can only function harmoniously within it through his capacity to love—infinitely.

notes

Preface

1. A somewhat more technical definition of these terms would be as follows: It is established that individuals have made statements at time T whose referents match events occurring at Time $T + N$, and that this matching cannot reasonably be accounted for on grounds of probability, extrapolation of data, or of known techniques of gaining information. This is the meaning of the term *precognition* in this book. Similarly, it is established that individuals in localtion A and at time T have made statements whose referents match events occurring in location B and at time T under conditions of being known at the time to no other person, and that this matching cannot reasonably be accounted for on the grounds of probability, extrapolation of data, or known techniques of gaining information. This is the meaning of the term *clairvoyance* in this book. If, however, these events occurring in location B and at time T are known to any living person, the term *telepathy* is used instead of the term clairvoyance.

2. C. D. Broad, *Lectures in Psychical Research* (New York: Humanities Press, 1922).

169

3. Gardner Murphy, *The Challenge of Psychical Research* (New York: Harper & Row, 1961).

4. Certainly Edgar Cayce was a serious and great medium and demonstrated repeatedly that he had unquestionably paranormal abilities. However, in his unconscious there was as much nuttiness as there is in yours or mine and in his trances much of the material came from these portions of his unconscious. (One reason that the unconscious *is* unconscious, of course, is that much of it is as crazy as a three-dollar bill.) Similarly, research scientists such as Ian Stevenson have done very serious work on the problem of reincarnation. However, work of the kind Stevenson does and the serious aspect of Cayce's mediumship bear no other relationship than general title to the immense mass of garbage which is generally offered to the public in these subject areas.

5. Since this test of the theory involved the application of modern physical field theory, I sent the manuscript to Henry Margenau, who is the leading theoretician of Einsteinian theory today. In the accompanying note I said that a fool could be defined as an able man who was two fields away from his own field of competence and that—in this work—I was probably at least five fields away. He replied that he felt I had legitimately used and applied modern field theory and offered to sponsor the paper for publication. Appendix D is that paper as it appeared in *Main Currents of Modern Thought.*

6. Since this book was written, I have become familiar with the research of Robert Crookall as reported in his *The Interpretation of Cosmic and Mystical Experiences* (London: James Clark, 1969). It is impossible to do justice to this excellent and important book in a brief summary, but if I had read it earlier, my own work would have benefited greatly.

7. G. N. M. Tyrrell, "Presidential Address," *Proceedings of the Society for Psychical Research* 47 (1942–1945), p. 317.

8. L. C. Rosenfield, "Portrait of a Philosopher: Morris R. Cohen" in *Life and Letters* (New York: Harcourt, Brace & World, 1962), p. 352.

Part 1
Chapter 1

1. N. Fodor, *Encyclopedia of Psychic Science* (New York: University Books, 1966), p. 296.

2. The scientific standards of these experiments are extremely rigorous. Dr. Schmeidler is, among her other attributes, an extremely able statistician and experimenter. To deny the statistical validity of these studies means that the validity of the statistical methods upon which a great deal of modern science (from quantum mechanics to population studies) is based must also be denied.

3. E. Gurney, W. H. Myers, and R. Podmore, *Phantasms of the Living* (London: Trubner and Co., 1896), Vol. I, p. 194.

4. These are the four major sources of our evidence of the existence of the "paranormal." In order to give a better picture of our present experimental approach to the subject, we might describe briefly one research program now under way.

At Maimonides Hospital in New York, under the leadership of Drs. Stanley Krippner, Charles Honorton, and Montague Ullman, a long-term study of the paranormal is being conducted. The general design of the research is as follows: The subject ("percipient" or "receiver") goes to sleep at night in a special room in which he is monitored by special instruments that can tell when he is dreaming. (This is known as "R.E.M." technique.) After the subject is asleep, one of the experimenters ("agent" or "sender") goes to a room a good distance away. There he chooses from a large file of envelopes by a random procedure. In the envelope are twelve pictures. At random one is chosen from these and all night the experimenter (the only person who knows which envelope or picture he has chosen) concentrates on this picture. Another experimenter watches the instruments which indicate the subject's sleep state. As soon as they show he has finished a dream, he is awakened and tells his dream into a tape recorder. He then goes back to sleep. In the morning, the tapes of his dreams are typed up and together with all twelve pictures in the original envelope go to a panel of judges. Their job is to try to tell from the dreams of the "receiver" which of the twelve pictures the "sender" concentrated on. Generally speaking, the judges do not have too much trouble doing this.

This type of study not only clearly demonstrates scientifically the existence of telepathy, but also is extremely valuable in studying various important aspects of it such as the questions "What relationships between 'sender' and 'receiver' make it most likely to occur?" It is better if they like each other, know each other well, etc?" What types of subject matter are most likely to be transmitted? Calm, peaceful, exciting, depressing, etc?"

5. U Thant, quoted in *New York Post*, May 15, 1969.

Chapter 2

1. Lawrence LeShan, "A Spontaneous Psychometry Experiment with Mrs. Eileen Garrett," *Journal of Society for Psychical Research* 44 (1968), pp. 14–19.

2. Stanley Krippner and Montague Ullman, "Telepathic Perception in the Dream State: Confirmatory Study Using EEG-EOG Monitoring Techniques," *Perceptual and Motor Skills* 29 (1969), pp. 915–918.

Chapter 3

1. Eileen Garrett, *Awareness* (New York: Creative Age Press, 1943), p. 20.

2. Eileen Garrett, *Adventures in the Supernormal* (New York: Creative Age Press, 1949), p. 164.

3. Louisa Rhine, "Parapsychology Then and Now," *Journal of Parapsychology* 31 (1967), p. 242.

4. Gerald William, Earl of Balfour, "A Study in the Psychological Aspects of Mrs. Willett's Mediumship and of the Statements of the Communicators Concerning Process." *Proceedings of the Society for Psychical Research* 43 (1935), p. 218.

5. Ibid., p. 213.

6. Eileen Garrett, *My Life as a Search for the Meaning of Mediumship* (London: Ryder & Co., 1949), p. 179.

7. Garrett, *Adventures in the Supernormal*, p. 177.

8. Emilio Servadio, *Psychology Today*, trans. J. Shapley (New York: Garrett Publications/Helix Press, 1965), p. 286.

Chapter 4

1. Evelyn Underhill, *Mysticism*, 4th ed. (London: Methuen & Co., 1912), p. 3.

2. C. D. Broad, *Religions, Philosophy and Psychical Research* (London: Routledge and Kegan Paul, 1953), p. 3.

3. Bertrand Russell, *Mysticism and Logic and Other Essays* (London: Longmans, Green and Co., 1925), pp. 9ff.

4. Underhill, *Mysticism*, p. 49.

5. Evelyn Underhill, *Practical Mysticism* (London: J. M. Dent and Sons, 1914), p. 5.

6. W. T. Stace, *Mysticism and Philosophy* (New York: J. B. Lippincott Company, 1960), p. 66.

7. Eileen Garrett, "Religion—Dogma," (Manuscript, Parapsychology Foundation, March–April, 1961).

8. Underhill, *Mysticism*, p. 3.

9. Eileen Garrett, *Telepathy: In Search of a Lost Faculty* (New York: Creative Age Press, 1945), p. 169.

10. Quoted in R. Otto, *Mysticism East and West* (New York: Meridian Books, 1957), p. 67.

11. Quoted in Philip Kapleau, ed., *The Three Pillars of Zen* (Boston: Beacon Press, 1967), p. 297.

12. Quoted in Stace, *Mysticism and Philosophy*, p. 104.

13. Quoted in Otto, *Mysticism East and West*, p. 67. In an interesting statement of this, one mystic wrote, "Eternity is neither long nor short, it is simply an environment." A. Wilder, "Mysticism and Its Witnesses," *Metaphysical Magazine* 5 (1897), pp. 1–20.

14. Gary Snyder, *Earth House Hold* (New York: New Directions, 1951), p. 9.

15. Martin Buber, *Tales of the Hassidim* (New York: Shocken Books, 1947), Vol. 1, p. 7.

16. W. R. Inge, *Christian Mysticism* (New York: Meridian Books, 1950), p. xvii.

17. Rohit Mehta, Introduction to A. W. Osborn, *The Expansion of Awareness* (Wheaton, Ill.: Theosophical Publishing House, 1967), p. 7.

18. Rabindranath Tagore, trans., *One Hundred Poems of Kabir* (New York: The Macmillan Company, 1961), p. 14.

19. Gardner Murphy, "The Natural, the Mystical and the Paranormal" (Second John William Graham Lecture on Psychic Science, Swarthmore College, Swarthmore, Pennsylvania, April 27, 1952), p. 13.

20. Jan Ehrenwald, "Personality and the Nature of PSI Phenomena" (Paper presented at the Seventy-fifth Annual Meeting of the American Society for Psychical Research, New York, September 2, 1967).

21. Aldous Huxley, *They Perennial Philosophy* (New York: Meridian Books, 1970), p. 206.

22. Eileen Garrett, *Awareness* (New York: Creative Age Press, 1943), p. 12.

23. Garrett, *Telepathy*, p. 137.

24. Arnold J. Toynbee, *An Historian's Approach to Religion* (New York: Oxford University Press, 1956), p. 27.

25. J. Robert Oppenheimer, *Science and the Common Understanding* (New York: Simon & Schuster, 1964), p. 69.

26. Underhill, *Practical Mysticism*, p. 38.

27. Quoted in Otto, *Mysticism East and West*, p. 67.

28. Kurt Goldstein, "Concerning the Concept of Primitivity," in *Primitive Views of the World*, ed. S. Diamond (New York: Columbia University Press, 1964), p. 8.

29. D. J. West, *Psychical Research Today* (London: Gerald Duckworth & Co., 1954), p. 194.

30. G. N. M. Tyrrell, *Science and Psychical Phenomena* (New York: Harper & Bros., 1938).

31. Laurens Van Der Post, *The Dark Eye of Africa* (New York: William Morrow and Company, 1955), p. 120.

32. Quoted in A. E. White, *The Unknown Philosopher: Louis Claude de St. Martin* (Blauvelt, N.Y.: Rudolf Steiner Publications, 1970), p. 370.

Chapter 5

1. Quoted in J. DeMarquette, *Introduction to Comparative Mysticism* (New York: Philosophical Library, 1949), p. 195.

2. Alfred North Whitehead, *Nature and Life* (London: Cambridge University Press, 1934), pp. 14ff.

3. J. Robert Oppenheimer, *Science and the Common Understanding* (New York: Simon & Schuster, 1954), p. 69.

4. Max Plank, *Where Is Science Going?* (London: G. Allen and Unwin, 1933), p. 24.

5. Quoted in Henry Margenau, "Einstein's Conception of Reality," in *Albert Einstein: Philosopher-Scientist,* ed. P. A. Schilpp (New York: Harper & Bros., 1959), p. 253.

6. Werner Heisenberg, *Physics and Philosophy* (New York: Harper & Bros., 1958), p. 107.

7. Whitehead, *Nature and Life,* p. 36.

8. Quoted in Schilpp, *Albert Einstein,* p. 61.

9. Whitehead, *Nature and Life,* p. 30.

10. Quoted in Schilpp, *Albert Einstein,* p. 292.

11. Evelyn Underhill, *Practical Mysticism* (London: J. M. Dent and Sons, 1941), p. 24.

12. Quoted in Schilpp, *Albert Einstein,* p. 236.

13. Quoted in Philip Kapleau, ed., *The Three Pillars of Zen* (Boston: Beacon Press, 1967), p. 297.

14. Arthur Eddington, *The Nature of the Physical World* (New York: The Macmillan Company, 1931), p. 467.

15. Quoted in P. R. Reeves, "A Topological Approach to Parapsychology," *Journal of the American Society for Psychical Research* 38 (1944), pp. 272–282.

16. Werner Heisenberg, *Philosophic Problems of Nuclear Science* (Greenwich, Conn.: Fawcett, 1966), p. 81. A. W. Osborn, who is both a scientist and a mystic has phrased this viewpoint beautifully: "We fall in love with the projections of our own consciousness and eventually, come to believe that our children are our ancestors: that matter, which is a constituent of our own minds, is the origin of our minds." *The Expansion of Awareness* (Wheaton, Ill.: Theosophical Publishing Co., 1967), p. 15.

17. Herman Weyl, *Philosophy of Mathematics and Natural Science* (Princeton: Princeton University Press, 1949), p. 116.

18. Lincoln Barnett, *The Universe and Dr. Einstein* (New York: William Morrow and Company, 1966), p. 72.

19. Quoted in Schilpp, *Albert Einstein,* p. 114.

20. Sri Vivekananda, *Jnana-Yoga* (New York: Ramakrishna-Vivekananda Center, 1949), pp. 90ff.

21. Henry Margenau, *The Nature of Physical Reality* (New York: McGraw-Hill, 1950), p. 326. One might compare Margenau's statement within the following quotation from Vivekananda: "The Vedantic position is neither pessimism nor optimism. It does not say that this world is all evil or all good. It says that our evil is of no less value than our good and our good of no less value than our evil." Vivekananda, *Jnana-Yoga,* p. 56.

22. Quoted in Schilpp, *Albert Einstein,* p. 248.

23. Ibid., p. 140.

24. W. T. Stace, *The Teachings of the Mystics,* (New York: Mentor, 1969), p. 76.

25. Oppenheimer, *Science and Common Understanding,* p. 40.

26. Eileen Garrett, "Notes on New Insight in Psychic Research," (Manuscript, Parapsychology Foundation, Nov. 9, 1967).

27. Arthur Eddington, *The Philosophy of Physical Science* (Ann Arbor: University of Michigan Press, 1958), p. 155.

28. Quoted in W. T. Stace, *Mysticism and Philosophy* (New York: J. B. Lippincott Co., 1960), p. 196.

29. Ibid., p. 105.

One difference between the view of the mystic and that of the physicist seems to me to be more apparent than real. This is the question whether there is *mind* in the basic structure of the cosmos, if the universe is conscious.

The mystic sees everything as a manifestation of the conscious One and perceives the universe as made up of mind, of which he is a part. In a peak experience or in LSD-type states, the same sense remains. This world—at first glance—appears to be far from the viewpoint of modern physics.

However, the physicist would say (and frequently has said) that the only structure we can perceive in the cosmos is a reflection of our own mental or nervous-system structure, that our comprehension of reality is ultimately dictated by the nature of our own being. "Nature," wrote von Weizacker, "is earlier than man, but man is earlier than natural science." Quoted in Heisenburg, *Physics and Philosophy,* p. 56.

In this way the two points of view seem very similar. The mystic says he can understand reality because he is a part of it; he is shaped basically in its image or there is a "spark of the divine" in him by means of which he can understand the great divine. The physicist says he can understand reality because he has shaped it in his own image. The two concepts do not appear to be as far apart as they looked at first, but to be more differences of stance and attitude than of fundamental thinking.

The similarity of the mystic's view that the universe is a great thought of which he is a part and the physicist's view that he sees reality only in his own mental image can perhaps be seen clearly in a statement by James Jeans: "In brief, idealism has always maintained that, as the beginning of the road by which we explore nature is mental, the chances are that the end also will be mental. To this present-day science adds that, at the farthest point she has so far reached, much, and possibly all, that was not mental has disappeared, and nothing new has come in that is not mental. Yet who shall say what we may find awaiting us around the next corner?" James Jeans, *The New Background of Science* (Ann Arbor: University of Michigan Press, 1959), p. 46.

30. G. G. Scholem, *Major Trends in Jewish Mysticism* (New York: Shocken Books, 1941), p. 254. This problem has sometimes led mystics to attempt to use what has

been called the *via negativa;* since they find it hard to use words to describe what the mystical experience *is,* they try to use words to describe what it *is not.* The most well known of these attempts is the *Tao Te Ching* by Lao-Tze.

31. Lawrence LeShan, "Physicists and Mystics: Similarities in World View," *Journal of Transpersonal Psychology* I (1969), pp. 1–20. This article is reproduced in this book as Appendix D.

32. R. Heywood, *ESP: A Personal Memoir* (New York: E. P. Dutton and Co., 1964), p. 219.

33. Barnett, *Universe and Dr. Einstein,* pp. 111ff.

34. It has been suggested to me by one physicist that the similarity in views of how-the-world-works expressed by physicists, mystics, and sensitives was due to the fact that the physicists were writing—in these quotations—not as physicists, but in terms of other interests. This is an interesting idea, but it is certainly clear that a large number of these scientists, including Planck, Einstein, de Broglie, Margenau, Oppenheimer, Dirac, Weyl, Bohr, Eddington, Heisenberg, Jeans, and many others, certainly *thought* that they were writing as physicists. Werner Heisenberg, writing of the arrival of physics at this new world-picture, speaks of "the completely unexpected realization that a consistent pursuit of classical physics forces a transformation in the very basis of this physics." Heisenberg, *Philosophical Problems,* p. 13.

One fairly well-known astronomer took the "mystic-physicists test" (Appendix D) and agreed with me that it was impossible to differentiate the world-view of mystics from that of Einsteinian physicists. He then said, "You see the implications of this, of course. We are going to have to reexamine the foundations of relativity theory. It is obvious that there is something very wrong with the theory."

Many physicists find it quite reasonable to say that no one can understand what they are really talking about unless one undergoes the long discipline of learning mathematics. As a culture we tend to accept this statement. Most of us, however, do not accept the similar statement made by many mystics and one cannot understand what they are really talking about unless one undergoes the long discipline of learning meditation.

Chapter 6

1. J. Robert Oppenheimer, "Physics in the Contemporary World," in *Great Essays in Science,* ed. M. Gardner (New York: Washington Square Press, 1961), p. 189.

2. Eileen Garrett, *Awareness* (New York: Creative Age Press, 1949), p. 113.

3. Quoted in P. A. Schilpp, ed., *Albert Einstein: Philosopher-Scientist* (New York, Harper & Bros., 1959), p. 557.

4. Lev Landau, and G. B. Rumer, *What is Relativity?,* trans. N. Kemmett (New York: Basic Books, 1960), p. 37.

5. Max Planck, *Where Is Science Going?* (London: G. Allen and Unwin, 1933), p. 15.

6. Quoted in M. Grossman, *A Tribute to Professor Morris Raphael Cohen,* (Private publication, New York, 1928). Illustrating this viewpoint, the physicist Henry Margenau wrote: "The question then, is not whether matter is continuous but how theories succeed when they regard as a continuum the construct which they take to be their system." Margenau, *The Nature of Physical Reality* (New York: McGraw-Hill, 1950), p. 194.

7. Benjamin Lee Whorf, "An American Indian Model of the Universe," in *The Philosophy of Time,* ed. R. M. Gale (New York: Doubleday & Company, 1967), p. 378.

8. James Jeans, *The New Background of Science* (Ann Arbor: University of Michigan Press, 1934), p. 46.

9. Aldous Huxley, *The Perennial Philosophy* (New York: Meridian Books, 1970), p. 57.

10. Ibid., p. 101.

11. Ibid.

12. Abraham Maslow, *Religions, Values and Peak Experiences* (Columbus: Ohio State University Press, 1964).

13. H. Wiener, 9½ Mystics (New York: Collier Books, 1969), p. 35.

14. Another example of this type of expression of the two ways of being may be in the widespread desire for identification with larger and larger social units. Very

often this expresses itself in ways that simply do not
seem to make sense. It is, for example, very hard to have
a meaningful discussion with a hospital administrator or
college president who constantly drives to enlarge an institution that works excellently at its present size and will
take on an entirely different character as it expands. One
finds it impossible to understand the reasons given for the
drive to enlarge the institution. Typically one is finally
answered with the explanation that the reasons are "obvious." One thing is clear. The serious mystic is not concerned with superficial or with concretistic-magical ways
of solving his need to be part of something larger. He is
not concerned with national borders or baseball teams or
with expanding organizations for the sake of expansion.

15. Kenneth Rexroth, "The Works of Rimbaud," *Saturday Review,* January 14, 1967, pp. 34ff.

16. Abraham Maslow, *Toward a Psychology of Being*
(New York: D. Van Nostrand Company, 1962).

17. W. T. Stace, *Mysticism and Philosophy* (New York:
J. B. Lippincott Co., 1960), p. 136.

Part 2

1. Ernst Cassirer, *Language and Myth* (New York:
Dover Publications, 1953), p. 7.

Chapter 7

1. W. R. Inge, *Christian Mysticism* (New York: Meridian Books, 1950), p. 24.

2. Lawrence LeShan, "Toward a General Theory of the
Paranormal," Parapsychology Foundation Monograph no.
9 (New York, 1969).

3. Harry Edwards, Study Course #1, National Federa-
tion of Spirit Healers, Pt. #14.

4. Ambrose Worrall and Olga Worrall, *The Miracle
Healers* (New York: New American Library, 1968), p. 19.

5. Edgar Jackson, *Understanding Prayer* (Cleveland:
World Publishing Co., 1968), p. 70.

6. Harry Edwards, *Psychic Healing* (London: Spiritualist Press, 1946), p. 26.

7. Jackson, *Understanding Prayer*, p. 70.

8. Agnes Sanford, *The Healing Light*, 8th ed. (St. Paul: Malcalester Park Publishing Co., 1949).

9. Worrall and Worrall, *Miracle Healers*, p. 165.

10. Stewart Grayson, "Psychic Healing," (Lecture, June 4, 1971).

11. Sanford, *Healing Light*, p. 24.

12. Mary Baker Eddy, *Science and Health with Key to the Scriptures* (Boston: Authorized Literature of The First Church of Christian Scientists), p. 14.

13. Nikos Kazantzakis, *Report to Greco* (New York: Simon & Schuster, 1965).

14. Worrall and Worrall, *Miracle Healers*, p. 162.

15. Alexis Carrel, *Man the Unknown* (New York: Harper & Row, 1935).

16. Henry Miller, *The Colossus of Marousi* (Middlesex: Penguin Books, 1964), p. 81.

17. Arthur Koestler, *The Ghost in the Machine* (London: Pan Books, 1967), p. 207.

18. Harry Edwards, *The Truth About Spiritual Healing* (London: Spiritualist Press, 1956), p. 25.

19. Frank Loehr, *The Power of Prayer on Plants* (New York: Doubleday & Company, 1959).

20. Evelyn Underhill, *Practical Mysticism* (London: J. M. Dent and Sons, 1914). Technically speaking, contemplation is a basic form of meditation. In contemplation one learns to look at an object without words, without "talking to oneself" about it. It is a basic and very difficult exercise. The discipline of it, if practiced regularly, tends to have a salutary effect upon the entire personality structure, and several students of the seminars on psychic healing who are themselves professional psychotherapists have reported to me that teaching it to their patients has appeared to have shown positive results. In the training seminars, this exercise is used extensively to help the students learn to discipline and train their minds so that they could move themselves along the route of the intellectual Samadhi. Further, in psychic healing the healer must be able to perceive the patient without his usual biases, prejudices, orientations. Contemplation is the basic approach to "cleansing the gates of perception." Not only does this permit us to look at another person without our usual anxieties, but it helps us to see the patient as part of the total universe without separation from the rest. Contemplation is reminiscent of Gurdjieff's "Law of Intentionality" which might be stated as "You never get any more out of perception than you put into it."

21. LeShan, "General Theory of the Paranormal."

22. Ibid.

Chapter 8

1. Henry Rosenthal, "The Structure of the Paranormal" (Lecture given at the Parapsychology Conference on The Problem of Survival, London, June, 1966).

2. Lawrence LeShan, "Toward a General Theory of the Paranormal," Parapsychology Foundation Monograph no. 9 (New York, 1969).

3. Conference on Human Energies, Wainright House, Rye, N.Y., 1970.

4. Max Planck, *Where Is Science Going?* (London: G. Allen and Unwin, 1933), p. 186.

5. Henry Margenau, "Einstein's Conception of Reality," in *Albert Einstein: Philosopher-Scientist*, ed. P. A. Schilpp (New York: Harper & Bros., 1959), p. 49.

6. Henry Margenau, *The Nature of Physical Reality* (New York: McGraw-Hill, 1950), p. 295.

Part 3

Chapter 9

1. *New York Post*, November 28, 1972.

2. These cathedrals were built as an expression of a great mystical tradition. Their designers were mystics as well as architects. If you are ready to understand what they were trying to communicate in stone and glass, the message can still come through.

3. There is an old Jewish saying that if you meet a man in the street and he tells you that you are a horse, you should ignore him because he is drunk. If you meet a second man who tells you the same thing you should ignore him also. He is a drunk too and it is a coincidence. But if you meet a third man who tells you you are a horse, it is time to think of buying a bale of hay! I had met more than three who told me the same thing. What kind of hay I needed was the next problem.

4. Among other experiences during the healing, I had at one point the distinct impression of the healee being asleep, waking up suddenly, being aware of the healing and then going back to sleep. Afterward when I checked the time I realized I had done the healing at 6:00 A.M. New York time. I mentioned the impression to my wife, Eda. Eda returned to New York before I did and spoke to the healee, who spontaneously told her that she had woken up at six o'clock one morning suddenly, said, "There's Larry," having the distinct impression I was there, and gone back to sleep. She wrote down the incident in her diary and checking showed it to be on the same date.

5. Christmas Humphreys, *The Way of Action* (Baltimore: Penguin Books, 1960), p. 29.

6. It seems as if so many religious practices are associated with a dim memory of this state of consciousness. The word "communion," for example, describes this state, and the taking of communion is a symbolic representation of it, but what is usually perceived during the ritual is a far cry indeed from this way of being-in-the-world. Walter Huston Clark has described most religious organizations as similar to vaccination. They give you a small case of the disease to prevent you from getting a serious case! (Personal communication, June, 1972.)

7. Quoted in Humphreys, *Way of Action*, p. 29.

8. Francis Thompson, *Poems*, J. L. Connolly, ed. (New York: Appleton Century, 1941).

9. R. B. Blakney, *Meister Eckhardt: A Modern Translation* (New York: Dover Books, 1941), pp. 204–205. In

Hebrew, one name of God is "Makom" which translates as "place."

10. Bernard Berenson, *Sketch for a Self-Portrait* (New York: Pantheon Books, 1949), p. 18.

11. Thomas Merton, *Contemplative Prayer* (Garden City, N.Y.: Doubleday Image, 1971), p. 28.

12. Humphreys, *Way of Action*, p. 42.

13. C. G. Jung, *The Secret of the Golden Flower*, trans. R. Wilhelm (London: Kegan Paul, 1931), p. VIII.

14. Rudolph Carnap has written of the importance of the mathematician Henri Poincaré's contribution to our understanding of the nature of reality. Poincaré demonstrated that: "No matter what observational facts are found, the physicist is free to ascribe to physical space any one of the mathematically possible geometrical structures, provided he makes suitable adjustments in the laws of mechanics and optics and consequently in the rules for measuring length." Quoted in H. Reichenbach, *The Philosophy of Space and Time* (New York: Dover Books, 1957), p. v.

15. Thus we have the viewpoint of Pierre Teilhard du Chardin that all history and evolution is a gradual ascent toward a total being in the Transpsychic Reality. In his concept, all other ways of being-in-the-world are steps along the way.

16. There does appear to be one bar to the telepathic exchange of information that can occur in the Clairvoyant Reality. In all the experiences I have had in healing encounters—and in all the serious literature of telepathy I combed—there was not one case of telepathic information being "transmitted" that the original holder of this information really wished to keep secret. I have never known of a good case of telepathy which passed information that the "agent" was ashamed of or guilty about and would not have wanted known. I do not understand the reason behind this, but at this time believe it to be a fact.

17. R. H. Blyth, *Zen in English Literature and Oriental Classics* (Hokuseido Press, 1942), p. 148.

18. W. H. Austin has described the problem that runs all through Christian theology which he calls "the paradox

of the religious ultimate." On the one hand the statement "God is good" is taken to be true. On the other hand the statement "It is impossible to assign any properties to God" is also taken to be true. W. H. Austin, "Complementarity and the Theological Paradox," *Zygon: Journal of Religion and Science* (December, 967), pp. 365–381.

Alan Watts has written: "Human purposes are pursued within an immense circling universe which does not seem to me to have purpose, in our sense, at all." "This is It" in *The Highest State of Consciousness,* ed. J. White (New York: Doubleday Anchor, 1972), p. 446. Very possibly the concept that the universe is positively oriented and its energies and actions benign has been strengthened in the West by the Biblical story of creation where it is told that at the end of each day God looked at His work and found it "good."

19. This is the meaning of Eckhardt's statement: "A man should be so poor that he is not and has not a place for God to act in. To reserve a place would be to maintain distinction." Cited in Thomas Merton, *Zen and the Birds of Appetite* (New York: New Directions Press, (1968), p. 9. In the transpsychic state there can be no "distinctions," no exceptions.

20. On this Eileen Garrett wrote, "Many times, when I have been able to give only negative results, or results not expected by the sitter, I have been asked to *try.* I was always hurt and distressed when this happened, since I knew from experience that conscious effort was the one thing which would produce no results that could be described as super-normal." *Telepathy: In Search of a Lost Faculty* (New York: Creative Age Press, 1945), p. 156. Compare this to the statement of the mystic Madame Guyon: "I tried to obtain by effort that which I could only obtain by ceasing all effort." A. W. Osborn, *The Expansion of Awareness* (Wheaton, Ill.: Theosophical Publishing House, 1967), p. 232.

Mrs. Osborne Leonard wrote: "The best clairvoyance has always come to me spontaneously, usually when I am the *least* expecting it." She reports also of her first attempt to go into trance: as long as she kept *trying* to do so, nothing happened. It was only at a time that she had given up the attempt (because of fatigue, discouragement, and the distraction of an outside person in the room), that she became entranced. G. Osborne Leonard, *My Life in Two Worlds* (London: Cassell and Company, 1931), p. 3.

21. The "power trips" in Type 2 (apparently it *can* work with the healer on a power trip, which is interesting) are manifold and can be beautiful to behold. In my eyes, the prettiest is when the healer disclaims any personal ability or power and claims merely to be a vehicle for God's blessing. So often the clear, unstated message behind this is "And if you say that God chose little old me because I am purer or better than anyone else, why you said it, I didn't. I am just a humble vessel the Lord happened to chose, but we both know he does not choose by accident!"

22. Just because there is a perception of energy in Type 2 healing does not mean that it exists except in the perception. The analogy, mentioned earlier, of alcoholics who see funny animals on the wall may be valid. It is hard to conceive of instrumentation that, forcused on the wall, could detect those funny animals. The "aura" is another excellent example of this problem. Many serious and sincere people claim to perceive it. It may well exist (and, if you wish my personal opinion, probably does), but the perception of an aura by a sensitive is not a proof of its existence.

23. It may well be that I am psychologically blocking on perceiving these other realities, in the same way that a very real anxiety blocked me from perceiving the Transpsychic Reality for so long. Or it may be that they do not exist. I do not know. However, at this point in the development of my understanding, I believe that evil forces and evil spirits are a projection of some of the darker aspects of our own being. The psychological mechanism of projecting outward (and often concretizing) that which we do not like within ourselves is a very widely used human technique. What we do not like in ourselves, we frequently see, and feel threatened by, outside of our-

selves. In the Eastern Orthodox mystical tradition, this vewpoint is accepted. St. Macarius the Great wrote, "The most important work in spiritual struggle is to enter the heart and there to wage war with Satan." Satan is not presented as "out there," but inwardly as a part of one's own heart. *The Philokalia,* trans. E. Kadlowbousky and G. E. H. Palmer (London: Faber and Faber, 1954).

The fact that "evil entities" are frequently reported to be encountered in spiritual work is not surprising in this context. As has been shown in many mystical training groups (as well as in psychotherapeutic experience) inner growth and change—particularly if done at a rapid rate—bring to the surface of consciousness some not-so-lovely parts of ourselves. If these are not understood as coming from inside ourselves they are likely to be projected outward on others or as evil forces and entities.

24. William James, *Varieties of Religious Experience* (New York: New American Library, 1958), p. 298.

appendixes

appendix a | on the non-acceptance of the paranormal

In the development of parapsychology since the 1880s a question that has repeatedly been raised concerns the reasons for the rejection of this field by the scientific community as well as by the community-at-large. This rejection has taken a wide variety of forms ranging from total and angry dismissal of any possibility of validity to a bland ignoring of the data. Recently Eisenbud (9) has presented a new approach to the problem and opened it afresh.

The general refusal to deal scientifically with the material gathered in this field seems to be a phenomenon *in itself demanding explanation*. A wide variety of studies and carefully documented experiences present enough unquestionable data so that one would reasonably expect parapsychology to be an accepted and widely studied field of scientific investigation.

From *International Journal of Parapsychology*, Vol. 8, No. 3 (Summer 1966), pp. 367–86. This paper was written under the auspices of a grant from Frederick Ayer II. I would like to express my gratitude to J. Fraser Nicol and Mrs. Eileen Garrett for their comments and suggestions during the development of this paper.

There have been a variety of explanations given for this lack of acceptance. Carington (5, p. 45) felt that there were two main reasons for the rejection by scientists: 1) that its introduction is perceived as weakening the status of causality and law in science; 2) that "the way will be opened for the introduction in thin disguise of all the magic and superstition which they have fought against so hard and long." Tyrrell, (30, p. 341) in a similar vein, quoted William McDougall's S.P.R. Presidential Address on the subject.

> Men of science are afraid lest, if they give an inch in this matter, the publis will take an ell and more. They are afraid that the least display of interest or acquiescence on their part may promote a great outburst of superstition on the part of the public, a relapse into a belief in witchcraft, necromancy and the black arts generally, with all the moral evils which must accompany the prevalence of such beliefs. For they know that it is only through the faithful work of men of science through recent centuries that these distressing beliefs have been in a large measure banished from a small part of the world.

It is sad that it is no longer possible to accept seriously the picture of the scientific world acting from such salutory motives. From the Peenemunde scientists bending every effort to insure that the concentration camp should inherit the earth to the scientists in many countries now trying to increase the presently attained atomic "overkill" ability exponentially, we have too many examples of the schism between scientific research and public morality. Other expanations will have to be found if we are to hope to understand the problem.

Henri Bergson (2, p. 165) pointed out that each approach to science implies that certain types of data (which fall outside the scope of its method) are invalid and unreal. He believed that the modern approach, dealing with measurement as its prime dimension, had made the basic assumption that "mind" and "brain" are two terms referring to the same thing. With this assumption, science would automatically reject parapsychological findings and interpretations. He saw, therefore, little-verbalized assumptions and implications of the modern scientific approach as responsible for the non-acceptance of parapsychology.

Murphy, (19) writing of the resistance of psychologists to the acceptance of parapsychology, stresses the point that, in scientific terms "ESP does not make sense." He quotes Laplace to the effect that " '. . . the amount of evidence that must be marshalled in favor of a hypothesis is directly proportional to its antecedent improbability.' Since, in a sense, the antecedent improbability of the paranormal is for many psychologists virtually infinity, no finite evidence could carry conviction."

Nicol, (23) in his important review of this subject, lists "four factors operating to produce indifference or hostility to psychic research. . . . These are the apparent irrelevance of psychical research to other scientific fields, the failure of psychical researchers to obtain reproducible phenomena, discordant views on the validity of evidence, and inflated claims to discoveries." The present writer agrees with Nicol as to the importance of these factors, but, as I will try to show in the following pages, they do not account for the total picture. And indeed this is an area of agreement with Nicol also, for although he holds that there ". . . is rational justification for scientists avoiding the subject," he also believes that ". . . many of them give the subject a wide berth on grounds that are purely emotional." (24)

Eisenbud (9) in his analysis of this problem has hypothesized that the non-acceptance (as well as the non-repeatability of experiments in this field) is inherent in the general nature of the universe and of psi forces themselves. He sees psi as an aspect of the structure of the cosmos whose function it is to keep things running smoothly and lawfully—a sort of dynamic connective tissue. In his view, to try to bring psi out into the open and to harness it, is to attempt to use it against its own structure and function. Thus psi forces themselves suppress the irregularity and unlawfulness which their overt emergence brings into being. So to speak, a "feedback" mechanism operates which does not permit psi forces to upset the smoothly running universe they are committed to maintain.

Eisenbud's comments on certain aspects of the behavior of parapsychologists which often seem calculated to *prevent* successful work and progress in this field are cogent and penetrating. However, there are certain problems raised by his approach. He gives a metaphysical answer to a psychological question. This is not a legitimate way of approaching the problem unless it has first been carefully evaluated on psychological grounds. A scientific problem is raised on a specific level. It is on *this* level that an exhaustive attack on it must be made before we try to transpose it to a larger frame of reference. If we raise the level of approach to a problem higher than the level on which it is presented, this is in order to be able to return to the observational level with new verifiable concepts leading to a solution. This is not done by Eisenbud. Further, since his "answer" is not given in a form that can be tested or that can be translated into operational terms, it is—at best—simply an "interesting idea" whose validity we can no further probe. The metaphysical answer he gives may be valid, but it seems unlikely that the time is ripe for it. We should first try to deal with the question of non-acceptance *on the psychological levels on which we observe it*, before we pass to the higher levels of speculative philosophy and cosmological system building. (If this be a curious criticism to make of an article written by "a psychoanalyst of the blackest dye," (as Eisenbud jokingly calls himself) perhaps it is only another indicator of the strange field we are investigating!)

Parapsychology seems to have three choices as to how to proceed from there: how it can try to handle the problem of non-acceptance of its data. First, it can accept Eisenbud's speculation that the problem is hopeless; that the nature of the universe makes a solution impossible. Secondly, it can continue—as it has been doing these 80 years—to use Henry Sidgewick's definition of "sufficient evidence" as "evidence that will convince the scientific world." (27, p. 9) In his second address to the S.P.R., Sidgewick amplified this view:

> If they will not yield to half-a-dozen decisive experiments
> by investigators of trained intelligence and hitherto un-
> questioned probity, let us try to give them half-a-dozen
> more recorded by other witnesses; if a dozen will not do,
> let us try to give them a score; if a score will not do,
> let us make up the tale to fifty. (28, p. 67)

However, the tale is now over fifty, Pelion has been piled on Ossa, and there seems to be little more accep- tance now than there was in 1882. This viewpoint, how- ever, continues. In spite of the fact that we have seen nothing to justify it, the optimism (and approach) ex- presed by Myers, Gurney, *et al.*, in 1884 continues to be held by present day parapsychology.

> When we review the 600 cases (exclusive of dreams) we
> have already printed as material for our book "Phantasms
> of the Living" alone—cases of which a large proportion
> were first hand from persons known to us—we can hardly
> doubt that sooner or later the general fact of these distant
> impressions will be accepted by the majority of candid
> minds. (1, p. 173)

The third choice is to try to understand the psychologi- cal reasons for the rejection of parapsychology: to try to analyze the "resistance" (using the term in its widest sense) to looking at, understanding and dealing effec- tively with the data available. If we could understand this resistance, it is possible that we could find a way of over- coming it.

It is not, of course, suggested here that the second and third courses are mutually exclusive alternatives, but that a combination of these two might be more effective than simply continuing with the gathering of new evidence.

It is the purpose of this paper to try to explore some as- pects of the psychological resistance to the acceptance of the data of parapsychology. To do this, we might start with the fact that there is a good deal of evidence that knowledge of the existence or possible existence of psi phenomena seems to produce anxiety in many individuals. Thus, Upton Sinclair in his "Mental Radio" quotes his wife, Mary Craig Sinclair, who was the percipient in their experiments.

I agree with Richet that the fact of telepathy is one of the most terrifying in existence. (29, p. 172)

Freud in his "Dreams and Telepathy" writes of a dream of the death of an aged aunt.

A time of disagreeable anticipation followed; there would of course be nothing surprising in so aged a woman suddenly passing away, yet it would be very unpleasant for the dream to coincide exactly with the occurrence. (12, p. 64)

William James, after seeing what impressed him as an obviously valid case of psychokinesis wrote:

With the conviction that I saw all there was to see, I have to confess that I am surprised that the phenomena affected me emotionally so little. I may add, as a psychological fact, that now, after four days interval, my mind seems strongly inclined not to "count" the observation, as if it were too exceptional to be probable. . . . I find . . . that I took on nature with unaltered eyes today and that my orthodox habits tend to extrude this would-be levee-breaker. It forms too much of an exception. (19, p. 92)

G. N. M. Tyrrell, in his discussion of the 1889 "Census of Hallucinations," reports that:

When the hallucinations were graded according to the time which had elapsed between the occurrence of the vision and the date when the census question was answered, it was found that the number decreased rapidly as the

date of the occurrence became more remote, thus indicating that this kind of experience tends to be forgotten.
(30, p. 12)

A minister who unexpectedly saw an apparently clear
case of clairvoyance said: ". . . it suddenly made all the
neat walls of my three-dimensional life start to shake and
tremble and I was scared."

A physician was asked how she would feel if someone
whose judgment and integrity she respected offered to
show her a crucial and convincing demonstration of telepathy. She replied, "I feel frightened. All my life experiences make no sense if such an important thing exists and
I never knew it. I have the feling of being defenseless in
the face of these things."

W. F. Prince has examined the approach to psychic research of many of its critics (25). He has documented in
some detail the fact that a large number of able, trained
men, when they cross what he calls "The Enchanted
Boundary" into this field, behave in irrational ways. They
attack and criticize parapsychology in ways that they
would never dream of using in their own fields of competence.

Examples could be multiplied with little difficulty. Eisenbud's article (9), for example, uses a good many examples which could also be used here. In another paper,
"Suggestion at a Distance," he gives a detailed example of
how the anxiety produced by the perception of psi phenomena can cause marked "resistance" in the parapsychological investigator himself and prevent progress from
being made. (8)

Accepting, as an hypothesis at least, that evidence of
the existence of psi seems to produce anxiety in many
people, we can ask "why?" Looked at from this viewpoint
—the question of "why" it should induce anxiety—we can
see a variety of likely reasons. We might start to explore
one of these with a few quotations.

In the history of discovery [wrote Gardner Murphy]
there has always been the blur and the horror of that

which refuses to be assimilated; observations which, however carefully repeated and checked, fall into no predetermined place in the jigsaw puzzle which we conceive to be nature. . . . [They are] irrational, meaningless, an affront to reason. (20, p. 1)

. . . few species of literature are more truly dull than reports of phantasma [wrote James (21, p. 39)]. Taken simply by themselves, as separate facts to stare at, they appear so devoid of meaning and coherence that, even if they were certainly true, one would be tempted to leave them out of one's universe for being so idiotic. Every other sort of fact has some context and continuity with the rest of nature. These alone are contextless and discontinuous.

Tyrrell (30, p. 117) pointed this up further when he wrote that psi phenomena show no coherence or analogy with the world with which we are familiar. He continues,

The reason why thinking and scientific people reject psychical phenomena is not because they lack the power of discrimination, but because, as has been repeatedly said, of the innate pull of nature back towards the sensible world. They intuitively feel that the facts of psychical research will no more mix with the beliefs of common sense than will oil with water. . . . the fear that the dissonant facts, if admitted, will disrupt the scheme of the known and the familiar.

Burner and Postman, two psychologists writing on reactions to incongruous perceptions, said:

. . . for as long as possible and by whatever means available, the organism will ward off the perception of the unexpected, those things which do not fit his prevailing set. Our assumption, and it is hardly extravagant, is simply that most people come to depend upon a certain constancy in their environment and, save under certain conditions, attempt to ward off variations from this state of affairs. (4, p. 648)

A pattern begins to emerge here. Psi phenomena seem to threaten the basic concepts of the universe—the *weltanschauung,* the *lebensgefuhl*—of modern individuals. We live in a perceived world of law and order, of sequential cause and effect—a world in which space and time are limiting factors. It is on this view that we have built our own personality structure, our action and reaction patterns, and our sense of security. We may not find it an ideal world and may even resent its limitations, but it *is* the world of the 20th century and our homeland. What then if these basic laws of the universe are threatened? What if we are faced with apparent evidence that they may be illusions—that space and time can sometimes be discounted or ignored; that sequences of events can occur which are irelevant to the logic of cause and effect?

With the constant interaction between the individual's view of the world and his view of himself (from the first taking the prevailing *Zeitgeist* into his own personality through all the learning of how to act, of what patterns of behavior are "right" or "best" in terms of his perceived world), it becomes clear that a disturbance of the orderly structure and laws of the universe that we perceive is bound to threaten to have profound effects on the personality of the perceiver. The preceived intensity of the threat is hard to overestimate. How we act is a vital part of how we see ourselves. But if the perceived rules change, we will not know how to act, what to do or think. We shall be lost in chaos on the outside and no identity within. One might reasonably expect a certain amount of anxiety at this prospect! This would be particularly true in the 20th century with its immense emotional investment in the materialistic metaphysic. Jung wrote of the present ". . . irresistible tendency to account for everything on physical grounds." (17, p. 9)

Parenthetically, we might add that the Classical and Hellenistic Greeks, caught in something like the same position, worked out an ingenious answer which, perhaps unfortunately, does not seem to be applicable for us today. They retained their concept of a stable universe, but as a part of it they included the unstable Gods. The Gods could affect specific situations (and thus an intelligent general would take the auspices before giving battle) but not the long-range patterns and stability. In the last analysis, even the Gods were subject to the Fates. The stability of the cosmos was maintained, but there was room for what we would call today "parapsychological phenomena" also. Primitive cultures (as R. Neale has pointed out [22]) view the "non-normal" or "magical" as terribly dangerous, but necessary. They control the perceived danger by hedging in the magical with a formal structure of detailed, highly repetitious ritual. Their general assumption is that if a practitioner makes an error in the ritual, he will lose—at least—his life.

Some indications of how the human organism responds to a perceived breakdown of his expectations about the structure of the world is shown in a well-designed study by Bruner and Postman. (4) They used tachisticopic exposure of playing cards and thus could measure how long a visual exposure was necessary before a subject could recognize a card. Mixed in their series, unknown to the subjects, were some especially designed "incongruous" cards with the color and suit reversed. Thus there might be a nine of hearts with black pips or a two of spades with red pips. Normal cards were recognized correctly to their standard at an average of 28-millisecond exposure; the incongruous cards took an average of 114 milliseconds. The verbal reactions of the subjects to the reversed cards showed some sense of the stress that they were under. The following quotes from two of their subjects are revealing.

> I can't make the suit out, whatever it is. It didn't even look like a card that time. I don't know what color it is or whether it's a spade or a heart. I'm not even sure now what a spade looks like! My God!

> I don't know what the hell it is now, not even if it's a playing card! (4, p. 659)

The greatest percentage of their subjects showed a pattern they called "Dominance"—a complete rejection of the incongruous elements. Faced with a red six of spades, the subject would call it either a six of spades or a six of hearts and suppress all recognition of the incongruous element. "The perceptual result conforms with past experience . . ." (4, p. 654) This response would be stable. "Perhaps the greatest single barrier to the recognition of incongruous stimuli is the tendency for perceptual hypotheses to fixate after receiving a minimum of confirmation." (4, p. 659) This seems akin to Ducasse's description of the ". . . . disease of the reason where paranormal phenomena are concerned." (6, p. 20)

Perhaps we deal with a smiliar situation to the one we see in the attitude of many people towards psi phenomena. They seem to choose one extreme or the other. Either the universe is run completely on "mystical" lines or else it is run completely on "mechanistic" lines and psi evidence is either error or falsification. There seems to be no middle ground for many.

This approach to the problem has been stimulated by the work on "cognitive dissonance," a concept first advanced by L. Festinger in 1957 in his work on psychological reactions in conflict situation.

The word 'dissonance' in its ordinary meaning, refers to an inharmonious, inconsistent, discrepant relation between two things. The usage in the theory is similar to this. A cognition is something a person knows about himself, about his behavior, or about his surroundings. Dissonance is said to exist when two cognitions, occurring together, are inconsistent with each other according to the expectations of the person. . . . These expectations of what goes with what are built up on the basis of past experience, including notions of logical relations, cultural mores, and learned empirical correlations among events.

The central hypothesis of the theory is that the presence of dissonance gives rise to pressure to reduce that dissonance, and that the strength of the pressure is a direct

function of the magnitude of the existing dissonance. . . .
Dissonance is conceived as a motivating state comparable
to other drive states. Successful reduction of dissonance is,
for example, comparable to successful reduction of a state
of hunger. (10, p. 256)

Here we see an approach in which the conflict between
perceptual and cognitive expectancies on the one hand,
and the perception of psi phenomena on the other is seen
as creating, in itself, a drive state to get rid of itself. Certainly psi phenomena provide a major discord with usual
and accepted ways of being-in-the-world. The techniques
by which an individual removes the dissonance, perhaps
can usefully be conceived of in terms of the psychonana-
lytic concepts of "rationalization," "defensive denial," "la-
cunae of memory," "resistance," etc.

Further work in this area, such as that by Brehm, (3)
demonstrates that once a choice has been made of different possible ways of reducing dissonance, the chosen way
was invested with a high emotional value and the rejected
ways denigrated. There are advantages and disadvantages
to each possible way of reducing cognitive discord (as in
choosing the path of a mechanistic orientation vs. that
of a mystical orientation) and this, in itself, produces
conflict. This conflict is frequently reduced by "derogating
the source of the disagreement." Here, perhaps, is part
of the motivation for some of the attacks made on parapsychology and parapsychologists.

We see in the general concept of cognitive dissonance
an approach to the rejection of parapsychology by our society. It is by no means a new approach—the rejection of
the inherent incongruities involved *because* they were incongruities has been repeatedly recognized by parapsychologists. However, Festinger's concept may provide a
tool to understand—and perhaps deal with—this problem
in more detail.

There are, of course, other ways of approaching the
problem. The validity of one explanation does not invali-
date others. And it seems likely that more than one set of

factors is in play here. Thus it is also apparently true that the recognition of the validity of psi phenomena would be anxiety producting in that it is likely to raise repressed fears and fantasies. Freud in his "The Uncanny" (11, p. 54) points out that the child must learn that thoughts and feelings do not have the same sort of physical reality as do actions so that he can accept his "bad thoughts" without fearing that they will kill or destroy others. The childhood view of "omnipotence of thought" must be overcome. As Eisenbud has pointed out in his "Telepathy and the Problems of Psychoanalysis," (7) if he later begins to make observations that seem to indicate that thoughts "do" have power, the old anxieties (as, being human, he has had and does have "bad thoughts") can begin to threaten him.

Freud also showed that "intellectual uncertainty" was not enough to produce the sensation of the "Uncanny." (12, p. 35) "An uncanny effect occurs when repressed infantile complexes have been revived by some impression, or when the primitive beliefs we have surmounted seem once more to be confirmed." (12, p. 55)

Here we speculate on the mobilizing of old fantasies of omnipotence produced by observations of paranormal phenomena. Freud also describes the uncanny as produced by ". . . the over-accentuation of psychical reality in comparison with physical reality." (12, p. 50) This seems to be another aspect of the anxiety produced by psychic phenomena; so often the sense of the "Uncanny" is associated with these observations.

In a similar way, we see the projection of this perceived danger in the report of an experience by Mrs. Eileen Garret. She tells (15, p. 441) of how, as a child, she had a clairvoyant experience indicating the death of a relative in childbirth and told it to her guardian. This was later confirmed. She was then ordered by her guardian, "Don't ever again speak of things that you *see* like that, for they might *again* come true." In the guardian's fantasy, thoughts had dangerous power and must be suppressed.

Another aspect of the anxiety raised, concerns our sense of the security of our own sanity.

A psychiatrist, with a long interest in, and much knowledge of, the field of parapsychology, said, "If I saw an apparition and it turned out to be valid, I would be afraid of my sanity." If sanity can be defined as acceptance of basically the same cosmology as is held by other members of the culture—the same world view—then accepting the reality of psi phenomena (which certainly seems to imply a different cosmology) would lead to feelings of being threatened with insanity. And to accept the implications of psi factors may seem to the individual to be an acceptance of an unsane point of view.

Another facet of this has been pointed out by Mrs. Eileen Garrett. (14) This is the fact that psi phenomena are seen as aspects of one's mind over which one has no control. The mind acts autonomously. This brings feelings of dissolution and a sense of personal incoherence and disorganization that can be terribly frightening in its implications of insanity.

As was pointed out previously, one cannot really separate the view of the structure of the world from one's view of oneself and of one's own personality structure. Our own personality structure is built according to the nature of the universe and man as we perceived it.

> Wherever a person grows up [writes Kurt Goldstein in his great classic, *Human Nature* (16, p. 196)], his environment is of a specific nature, and this provides the cultural and social contents of his developmental socialization; that is, the determination of the specific character of the potentialities of any individual is oriented by the contents of his milieu.

There is a constant and crucial interaction between the inner self and the perceived outer world and each has major influence on the other. (We need only take one example to demonstrate this. The dissolution of the personality of the "marginal man" is a widely reported anthropological phenomenon. The individual whose culture with its view of the world has been destroyed, but who is too much a part of this view to accept the world view of the culture that destroyed his own, is in a bad position indeed. By the views of both the old and of the new culture, he is at least "unsane" if not "insane", and, under the impact of the stress, his personality structure tends to crumble.) If the view of the outer world is threatened by the acceptance of psi factors—and ours is a culture that has made a tremendous investment in the mechanistic concept of the cosmos; in Descartes' "clockwork universe" —we are terribly threatened in our very being. We feel that our personality structure may not survive the change. This is indeed a catastrophic threat. A threat of this sort, as Goldstein has shown so profoundly (16) produces very great anxiety and a variety of defensive reactions.

> The very existence of the organism is tied up with the possibility of finding an adequate milieu within its environment. Normally, the adaptation of the organism to its environment—that is, congruency between the two— is developed to such a degree that existence is guaranteed.

> The organism ordinarily does not react at all to stimuli which are inadequate to it. Such stimuli can become effective only if they are very strong and force themselves upon the organism; then it is driven into the catastrophic situation, not only because it is unable to react adequately, but also because it is so shocked and disturbed in its functioning that, for a longer or shorter period, it is unable to react at all. (16, p. 89)

The ego structure of the 20th century individual seems related to, and dependent on, the mechanistic logic and scientific materialism of the 20th century view of reality. If this view is threatened, so is his ego structure. With a threat of this magnitude, perhaps it is an intelligent reaction to deny any possibility of the validity of psi phenomena! A more constructive view is one that has been adopted by many parapsychologists. This is to view psi phenomena as belonging to an aspect of physical reality about which we know very little. It sees our ignorance as responsible for the apparent contradictions between psi phenomena and what we believe we know about the working of the rest of the cosmos. The analogy with lightning and our growth in understanding it when we grew to "understand" electricity is often used. Knowledge of electrical forces brought the lightning—previously seen as unpredictable and willful—under natural law.

(Although this viewpoint may be "constructive"—in the sense of reducing anxiety and of providing a philosophical basis for research—it is not necessarily valid. Poincaré has pointed out that modern man uses the concepts of cause-and-effect and of determinism in the same way as ancient man used the Gods: to bring a sense of order to the universe. He goes on to say that this was not because it was the truest system, but because it was the most convenient. "A theory of science," continues Poincaré, "is not necessarily a law of nature.") (Quoted by Mazur [161].)

We have not written here of the social pressure against the acceptance of psi. This pressure can be strong enough in itself to account for some individual's negative reaction.

> To think otherwise than our contemporaries think is somehow illegitimate and disturbing; it is indecent, morbid or blasphemous, and therefore socially dangerous for the individual. He is stupidly swimming against the social current. (17, p. 7)

In a letter to Thomas Davidson, William James wrote in 1885: "We shall be lucky if our scientific names don't grow discredited the instant they subscribe to 'spiritual' manifestations." (21, p. 64) The situation has not really changed since then. Recently a scientist of my acquaintance was offered a University post for which he was ideally equipped. When, however, it came to the notice of his prospective employers that he was taking an active interest in parapsychology, the offer was withdrawn. However, this presure, severe as it is, is not enough to account for our data. (Neither William James nor the scientists mentioned above slackened their interest in parapsychology because of it!) There are far too many individuals with courage and scientific conviction to permit data and concepts of this magnitude to be suppressed by social stigma and discrimination.

One might also suggest that psi can raise another sort of anxiety. This might be the fear of knowing oneself. If one is suddenly aware of new ways of knowing; if there are new, uncharted paths to knowing, what might it reveal to one about oneself that one does not wish to know? The repressed drives and feelings; the self-actualization not attained; the potentialities not fulfilled. These, indeed one feels, are better left in darkness and the idea that a new source of knowing could bring them suddenly to light may indeed be enough to raise anxiety in the stoutest heart.

This article does not pretend to be a definitive exploration of its subject; it is rather a beginning—a pointing in a direction—which, it is hoped, will provide clues for further work in this area. It seems necessary to explore the resistance to the data of parapsychology since the amount and scientific validity of data available does not appear to be relevant to its acceptance.

It is often wise to know the structure of the difficulties that lie in front of one in the solution of a quest. If they are known, ways can perhaps be found to go around, over, or under them. It seems important to understand the nature of the psychological resistances to the acceptance of psi phenomena. With sufficient understanding of a problem, it is a faith of science that it can be solved.

Bibliography

1. Barrett, W. F., Massey, C. C., Moses, W. Stanton, Podmore, F., Gurney, E., and Meyers, F. W. H. A Theory of Apparitions. *Proc. S.P R.,* 2, 1883–1884, pp. 157–186.
2. Bergson, H. S.P.R. Presidential address. *Proc. S.P.R.,* 27, 1914–1915, pp. 157–175.

3. Brehm, J. Post-decision Changes in Desirability of Alternatives. *J. Abnorm. Soc. Psychol.*, 52, 1956, pp. 378–384.

4. Bruner, J. and Postman, L. On the Perception of Incongruity: A Paradigm. In: Beardsley, D. C. and Wertheimer, M. *Readings in Perception*. D. Van Van Nostrand & Co., New York, 1958.

5. Carington, W. *Telepathy*. Methuen & Co., London, 3rd ed., 1946.

6. Ducasse, C. J. Some Questions Concerning Psychical Phenomena. *J.A.S.P.R.*, 18, 1954, pp. 3–20.

7. Eisenbud, J. Telepathy and the Problems of Psychoanalysis. *PSA Quar.*, 15, 1954, pp. 3–20.

8. Eisenbud, J. Suggestion at a Distance. *Parapsychology*, IV, 3, 1962–1963, pp. 99–106.

9. Eisenbud J. Psi and the Nature of Things. *Intl. J. Parapsy.*, 5, Summer 1963, pp. 245–268.

10. Festinger, L. and Bramel, D. The Reactions of Humans to Cognitive Dissonance. In: Bachrach, A. J. (Ed.) *Experimental Foundations of Clinical Psychology*. Basic Books, New York, 1962.

11. Fraenkel, E., Sur la Raison de la Resistance Contre la Parapsychologie. *La Tour Saint-Jacques*. 6–7, 1956, pp. 168–174.

12. Freud, S. *Studies in Parapsychology*. Collier Books, New York, 1963.

13. Garrett, E. J. *Awareness*. Creative Age Press, New York, 1945.

14. Garret, E. J. *Adventures in the Supernormal: A Personal Memoir*. Garrett Publications, New York, 1949.

15. Garrett, E. J. Personal communication, November 1964.

16. Goldstein, K. *Human Nature in the Light of Psychopathology*. Harvard University Press, Cambridge, 1940.

17. Jung, C. The Basic Postulates of Analytical Psychology. In: Smith, A. J. *The Psychic Source Book*. Creative Age Press, New York, 1951.

18. Mazur, M. The Therapeutic Function of the Belief in Will. *Psychiatry*, 43, 1960, pp. 45–52.

19. Murphy, G. Trends in the Study of Extrasensory Per-

ception. *The American Psychologist,* 13, 1958, pp. 69–76.

20. Murhpy, G. *The Challenge of Psychical Research.* Harper, New York, 1961.

21. Murphy, G., and Ballou, R. *William James on Psychical Research.* Viking Press, New York, 1960.

22. Neale, Robert E. Personal communication, October 21, 1964.

23. Nicol, J. F. Some Difficulties in the Way of Scientific Recognition of Extrasensory Perception. *Ciba Foundation Symposium on Extrasensory Perception,* 1956, pp. 24–38.

24. Nicol, J. F. Personal communication, November 1964.

25. Prince, W. F. *The Enchanted Boundary,* Boston Soc. Psychic Res., Boston, 1930.

26. Servadio, E. Parapsychologie Unglaub igkeits Reaction. *Ztschr. f. Parapsychologie und Grenzebiete der Psychologie,* 2, 1958, pp. 1–9.

27. Sidgewick, H. First Presidential Address. *Proc. S.P.R ,* 1, 1882–1883, pp. 7–12.

28. Sidgewick, H. Address to the S.P.R., Second Meeting. *Proc. S.P.R ,* 1, 1882–1883, pp. 65–69.

29. Sinclair, U. *Mental Radio.* Albert and Charles Boni, New York, 1930.

30. Tyrrell, G. N. M. *Science and Psychical Phenomena.* Harper and Brothers, London, 1938.

appendix B | when is uvani?

An Approach to a Concept of Spirit Controls

In all serious cases described as "paranormal," the normal laws of space and time are violated. We have been unable to "explain" this, and that has been the central problem of physical research. We *know* that these laws of space and time cannot be violated, that exceptions cannot occur. We also *know*—and have clearly and scientifically demonstrated in the laboratory and elsewhere—that they are sometimes broken. In spite of all our efforts we have been unable to resolve this problem. We have had to leave them, in Jacob Needleman's words, as "bubbles of mystery floating around in an otherwise 'normal' universe." [1]

Is it fruitful to try to approach the paradox in a new way? Let us try and begin by asking: "Are there classes of things (entities) to which the normal laws and limitations of space and time apply and classes of things to which they do not?"

Looked at in this manner it becomes evident that there *are* two classes of things. The first class we might describe as "structural entities." These are things with length, breadth, and thickness. They are *always* subject to the "normal" laws of space and time. Things of this sort (in this condition) cannot, for example, move faster than the speed of light. They have a definite physical existence during their duration and—as even Bishop Berkeley was forced to agree—go on with this existence whether or not they are at a particular moment in anyone's consciousness. (One can be hit on the back of the head by a falling meteorite of which no one—except perhaps God—was aware.) Of this class of things we can meaningfully ask the question "What is is?" and expect to be able to get a reasonable answer at whatever level the question is put. It is concerning this class of entity that Dean Swift wrote:

Matter, as wise logicians say,
Cannot without a form subsist:
And form, say I as well as they,
Must fail if matter brings no grist.[2]

The second class of things we might call "functional entities." These do not have any length, breadth, or thickness. They cannot be detected by any form of instrumentation although their effects often can be. They are not bound by the "normal" laws of space and time and often can, for example, move faster than light. If I point a telescope at Aldebaran and then swing it to focus on Altair, something very "real," the *point of focus* of the telescope, has moved faster than light. Or, if I take two long rulers laid overlapping with a very narrow angle between them so that at one end they overlap and at the other end there is a small separation, I can locate a definite *point of divergence*. Then, if I snap the separated ends together, this point of divergence will move along the rulers at a speed (at least theoretically) faster than light. Other examples could be given.

There are curious and difficult entities. In a famous incident, Ludwig Wittgenstein was asked what a mathematical point was since it had no length, breadth or thickness. He replied, "A mathematical point is a place to start an argument!" In this profound answer, Wittgenstein pointed up the functional rather than the structural nature of this entity.

The existence of these entities also differs considerably from that of the structural entities. They do not have a continuous existence whether or not they are being mentally conceptualized. Indeed they fit rather well the formulation that Bishop Berkeley attempted to establish—they exist *only* when they are held in a mind; only when being conceptualized, being considered to exist. There is no reality to a mathematical point unless it is being conceptualized as such. You cannot be affected by the focus of a telescope when no one is thinking of it. Put in a better way, a functional entity can have no effect on other entities (and so—for all intents and purposes—ceases to exist) unless it is being conceptualized as existing.

Of this class of entities we cannot ask the question "What is it?" and expect a reasonable answer. We can, however, ask other questions such as "When is it?" and hope to obtain a satisfactory reply. (A mathematical point is when it is conceptualized as the intersection of two lines.)

The question "where" a functional entity is "when" it exists cannot always be answered. With some functional entities, as our mathematical point, we can answer it and locate it in both space and time. With others, a melody for example, we cannot answer the question. We can locate the melody in time, when it is being conceptualized, but not in space.

In essence we might say: A functional entity *is* what it does and when it does it. Further, it only *is* (does anything) when it is being conceptualized by a perceiving and conscious entity.

Let us pause for a moment and ask about "things" with no length, breadth, and thickness. Can they really exist? *Are* there really entities about which one cannot successfully ask "what" or sometimes "where," but can, perhaps, ask "when" and "why" and which do not exist between perceptions of them? Mathematical points are all very fine, but are there others more meaningful for our lives?

Let us take one example and explore it briefly. No one would doubt the *reality* of an emotional experience. We *know* it is real. To the question of "where" was it? how much space did it take up? we can only respond with a helpless shrug. To the question "what," we can only reply with analogies—"I felt 'warm' or 'close' or 'tender' "—with descriptions of physiological correlates, or with a shift into poetry, music, or art. We cannot qualify it although we can compare the intensity of two emotional experiences. We communicate about it best by appeal to another's similar experience, but as the phenomenologists have shown, no one can really know another's experience. Any answer to "what" is, in the last analysis, a hopeful description of analogous terms. However, "when" is possible to answer ("It started yesterday when I met him at 3 o'clock") and "why" is at least theoretically possible ("He reminded me of the time when I . . ."). Does the emotional experience exist between the times it is being experienced? Certainly we would say it does not. (The question of conscious and unconscious levels of perception is not germane to the main thrust of this argument.) Indeed the old statement "in the eye of the beholder" points up clearly the functional entity nature of beauty, for instance, a "thing" which can deeply and strongly affect us. What is one man's "beauty" repels another man. There is, for example, a structure of face and figure that we—with our cultural and invdividual background—regard as "beautiful." The face and form are parts of a structural entity that continues during its duration with or without perception of it. The "beauty," however, is in existence—by our criterion of theoretically conceivable detectability— only when it is being perceived as such, when it is conceptualized as existing.

To the obvious question "Can a functional entity affect a structural entity?" we must answer in the affirmative. A mathematical point has an effect on a surveyor and presently on a steam shovel and a railway line. One can be profoundly affected by the point of aim of a hidden rifleman!

The essential point of this formulation is that it presents us with two classes of entities, one of which is *not* bound by the "normal" laws of space and time (that is, it can behave "paranormally") and can affect the other class of entities, which *is* bound by these laws. We must explore and see if this will help us deal with the problems of psychical research.

Does, for example, a serious spirit control (Uvani, the major spirit control of Mrs. Garrett; Feda, the major spirit control of Mrs. Osborne-Leonard; Chang, the spirit control of Douglas Johnson) fill the conditions we know so far, belonging to the class of functional entities? Certainly we have never been able to detect any physical structure related to, let us choose, Uvani. He (whatever Uvani turns out eventually to be; the pronoun "he" seems more polite than "it"!) has beyond a doubt shown the ability to behave paranormally, to acquire information, the possession of which clearly violated the laws of space and time.[3]

Does Uvani exist between those times at which he is conceptualized as existing? If we take as a rough gauge of what we mean by "existing" the ability to influence other entities then Uvani does not exist between conceptualizations. (Modern science takes "detectability" as the criterion for existence. It was by this criterion that the Michelson-Morley experiment is construed as "proving" that the ether does not exist.) When in existence, Uvani can influence the behavior of structural entities such as the medium, the sitter, etc.

One of the differences between the two types of entities is that one can ask "what" a structural entity is and expect to get a reasonable answer, but one must ask "when" a functional entity is. We have been trying to ask "what" Uvani (or Feda, etc.) is for Lo! these ninety years and have not been able to come to answer or even to derive a satisfactory theoretical method of arriving at one. The usual two explanations (that Uvani is a spirit as he claims to be or that he is a multiple-personality split-off) are unfruitful, unprovable in any way we can think of, and do not even "feel" right. They are, as Alan Gauld has called them, "vacuous hypotheses." It is a faith of science that if serious people unsuccessfully seek long and hard for the answer to a question, they are asking the wrong question. This is clearly the case here. Very well then, if we cannot ask "what" a functional entity is, we can ask "when." So, "when" is Uvani?

Two rather interesting incidents come to mind here. In the first, Rosalind Heywood told me of a time when she was talking to Abdul Latif, a major spirit control of Eileen Garrett. She decided to use her own highly developed paranormal abilities to perceive Abdul Latif. "I put out my antennae and it seemed to me that he only existed for the subject under discussion." [4]

In the other incident, parapsychologist Ira Progoff asked Uvani while Eileen Garrett was in trance on another occasion, "How have you been since last we met?" Uvani, an otherwise invariably calm and self-possessed persona, became completely confused and unable to answer the question. In fact he could not seem to *understand* it although he asked Progoff on various other occasions how Progoff had been since last they met and was obviously capable of understanding both the implications of the questions and the answers. [5]

In these incidents, the spirit controls certainly seem to be indicating that they follow the rule of existence of the functional entity—that they exist only *when* they are conceptualized as existing.

I have elsewhere described the state of consciousness during which paranormal processes occur, calling this the Clairvoyant Reality (CR). This state of consciousness is particularly oriented to the perception of *relationships* rather than to the perception of *structure*. [6] In it, and in the world-picture which it accepts as the valid metaphysical system, relationships are seen as primary and individual structures and the separateness of these structures is seen as secondary or illusory. This same metaphysic is accepted as valid by both the serious mystic and by the Einsteinian physicist. Thus we might quote Arthur Eddington to the effect that "Perhaps the nearest approach to a formulation of the general theory of relativity is that we observe only *relations* between physical entities." [7] A large number of statements of this kind by both physicists and mystics (often indistinguishable as to which of the two persuasions was followed by the author) have been given elsewhere.[8]

Seen in this light, the CR is primarily a way of perceiving functional entities. We begin to see another reason for hypothesizing that paranormal events and functional entities are related.

Very well then, "when" is Uvani? Is this a fruitful question? Does it help us to see further to ask it? Let us try some answers. Uvani is "when" Eileen Garrett moves into a particular state of consciousness in the presence of a perceived need of a sitter. When she conceptualizes the world in a particular way (the CR) and, in this Weltanschauung, conceptualizes Uvani as existing, he exists. Further, he is conceptualized as having certain characteristics. Under these conditions, a functional entity with these characteristics comes into existence and functions according to them.

Clearly it is not as simple as this. For a functional entity with certain characteristics to come into existence (to be able to affect structural entities), a highly coherent Weltbild, a world-picture permitting these characteristics, must be fully believed in by the perceiving structural entity. This is as true for "the square root of minus one" as it is for Uvani. (It is useless to ask "what" $\sqrt{-1}$ is. One can ask "when" it is and how it affects other functional and structural entities. We can get answers to these questions, but not the "what" question.) Not only must the Weltbild be accepted, the functional entity itself must be clearly conceptualized as potentially and actually existing.

However, given these conditions of acceptance of a proper Weltbild for it and the belief in the functional entity, it can come into existence. Now we begin to see "when" Uvani is. Does this help us?

To be helpful, a concept must explain the previously inexplicable and explicable data we have and also predict new data. Let us try to see if our concept here is fruitful.

It does seem to be able to explain the data we have. (This may be because it is so general, but, at this stage of the game, that is acceptable.) Certainly it explains why we have never been able to devise even a theoretical method for satisfactorily determining "what" a spirit control is. And why we have never been able to devise instrumentation that would detect a spirit control directly. (If a telescope is focused on a wall a mile away, the point of focus exists. However, we cannot, even theoretically, detect it by any instrumentation in the wall or monitoring the wall. Yet it exists and, if properly conceived and perceived by a structural entity who has, for example, a cannon handy, can drastically affect the wall.)

In a curiously circular way we explain Uvani's characteristics by saying that those are the characteristics he has. This procedure is invalid—at least since the end of the medieval period—when dealing with structural entities. It is the procedure we claim is valid when dealing with functional entities. (The characteristics of "gravity" are those characteristics we give it when we wish to explain the tables of observations we make on solar phenomena. The functional entity "gravity" is a very useful one and enables us to explain old data and to predict new data, but its characteristics are explained by saying that those *are* its characteristics. To the question "what" is gravity we can only respond with a helpless shrug. The question "when" we can answer. We cannot detect it directly by instrumentation, but can certainly detect its effects.)

Being able to "explain" past observations is all very well. The crucial test is, however, whether it will predict new observations. Again, let us try.

We take the liberty of approaching Uvani in a roundabout method through another aspect of the paranormal. We go to psychic healing. The evidence is clear enough. There is a type of "treatment" of physical problems that falls outside our presently accepted explicatory systems. The "healer" conceptualizes in a certain way. The "healee" responds (sometimes) with positive biological changes.

Sometimes there is no apparent biological change. The healee may or may not know that the healer is "working" with him, may or may not believe in the whole idea, and may or may not be in the physical presence of the healer. Whatever is going on here?

I have elsewhere described the behavior that the serious healers believe is relevant to the healing. (And statements by healers such as the Worralls, Ronald Beasley, and Edgar Jackson indicate that they believe this analysis to be correct. Further, my doing these behaviors has produced positive healing results, and the same has been true of individuals I have taught them to.) This set of behaviors consists of the healer accepting a world-picture in which the most important aspect of "things" is their interrelatedness and connectedness and in which isolation and separation are illusory. Accepting this fully—for at least a moment—it completely fills the field of the healer's consciousness; he conceptualizes a special functional entity that fits organically and naturally into this metaphysic. This is that the healee is no longer a separate structural entity bound and isolated within the limits of his skin, but (with his uniqueness and individuality complete) is a part of a functional entity that includes the entire universe or at least the healer himself and a good-sized chunk of the universe. For one moment, the healer's consciousness is completely filled with this concept. When the healing occurs, this is what the healer has been doing.[9]

The healer has followed our rules for bringing into existence a functional entity: first, conceptualizing the proper metaphysical system and fully accepting its validity; second, conceptualizing a functional entity organically fitting into this world-picture and into the present situation as perceived with the use of this world-picture and fully accepting its validity. This newly brought-into-existence functional entity, perceived by the healer, and probably at some level by the healee, has effects on their structural entities. Have we begun to see some light directed into the paranormal aspects of psychic healing? The basic problem has been bridging the gap between healer and healee. Except when we are forced to it—as in the case of gravity—we are today acutely uncomfortable with anything that smacks of action-at-a-distance. It smells of the paranormal to us. In our normal world of space and time, it *is* paranormal. Functional entities, however, are not limited by such criteria. And a functional entity that includes both healer and healee makes the gap between them disappear. Hey! Presto! Our psychic healing is no longer paranormal. What a convenient concept this one of the existence of two kinds of entity is turning out to be.

However, it is all very well to present a theory about how the gap is bridged and to "explain" the effect of this on the structural entity of the healee. (I have done this last elsewhere by hypothesizing that it places the healee in something closer to an "ideal organismic position" and thereby stimulates his own self-repair mechanisms to operated at a level closer to their potential.) Will this theory, however, predict new data? This is the nitty-gritty of a theory. Without this predictive ability all we have is interesting talk and pleasant games.

So, if healer and healee are included in a functional entity and the healer conceptualizes a functional entity that has positive therapeutic effects on the patient, the patient often responds with positive biological change. In the Weltbild the healer is using, a functional entity of this sort is perfectly reasonable. However, equally reasonable is a similar functional entity that has positive therapeutic effects on *both* the healer and the patient, on all parts of the entity, not just one part. If a functional entity of this sort is conceptualized, the therapeutic effects should be as great on both and we should be able to observe this. Now we begin to approach an experimental situation. Healers are well known for their inability to heal themselves. (There are one or two confusing cases, but basically the evidence is clear.) A change in the conceptualized functional entity should change this with no loss of healing effect on the (previously) healee. Certainly this is a testable prediction.

Other testable predictions can also be made now that we have the basic concept that functional entities can be hand-tailored so long as they fit organically into the Weltbild used. A wide variety of tests are now theoretically possible, of which the above is an example.

(Of course another testable prediction is that no one is going to come up with an instrument to directly detect the "energy" used in a Type 1 healing. This type of prediction, however, is not of much use scientifically unless you can *prove* that no one can come up with such an instrument. Or unless someone does—even theoretically—invent one, in which case you throw out the whole theory!)

What I have described here is an approach to the problem of the paranormal. It *is* true that the normal laws of space and time cannot be violated by structural entities. Functional entities, however, can violate some of these laws with impunity. (Which of the laws can be broken by a particular functional entity depends on its characteristics and the characteristics of the Weltbild within which it organically belongs.)

If we conceptualize the serious spirit controls as functional entities, the data we have becomes more understandable and it seems possible to predict new data.

Modern physics has used the concept I have called the "functional entity" to great advantage. The electron is perhaps a good example. The electron has, in Henry Margenau's words, "no determinate position." [10]   James Jeans has written, "It is probably as meaningless to discuss how much room an electron takes up as it is to discuss how much room a fear, an anxiety or an uncertainty takes up." [11] Eddington has said "that an electron is not in one place, but is smeared over a probability distribution," and J. Robert Oppenheimer writes, "The electron cannot be objectified in a manner independent of the means chosen for observing or studying it." [12] Clearly, we are not describing a structural entity in these terms. If science has found its electron, the square root of minus one, gravity, and a host of other functional entities useful, it may be worthwhile to see if we can find it useful to conceptualize the spirit controls in this way.

222 / The Medium, the Mystic and the Physicist

Notes

1. Personal communication, 1969.
2. Quoted in W. B. Yeats, *A Vision* (New York: Collier, 1970), p. 4.
3. A typical example of this is shown in my paper, "The Vanished Man," *Journal of the American Society for Psychical Research,* 1967, pp. 132–142.
4. Personal communication, 1965.
5. Unpublished manuscript, Parapsychology Foundation, 1967.
6. Lawrence LeShan, "Toward a General Theory of the Paranormal. A Report of Work in Progress" (New York: Parapsychology Foundation, 1969), pp. 41–61.
7. Ibid., p. 83.
8. Lawrence LeShan, "Physicists and Mystics: Similarities in World View," *Journal of Transpersonal Psychology* I (Fall 1969), pp. 1–20.
9. I have been writing here of the type of healing associated with the Worralls, Agnes Sanford, Rebecca Beard, Edgar Jackson, etc.—what I have elsewhere termed "Type 1 healing." The Chapmen-Laing and the Arigo types may well be quite different sorts of phenomena. I simply do not know at this time. Further, the "laying-on-of-hands" type, "Type 2," may or may not be a variation of Type 1. There seem to be theoretical reasons for coming to the conclusion that it *is* a variant and theoretical reasons for coming to the conclusion that it is not! It is hoped that further work will resolve this dilemma.
10. Henry Margenau, *The Nature of Physical Reality* (New York: McGraw-Hill, 1960), p. 326.
11. Quoted in L. Barnett, *The Universe and Dr. Einstein* (New York: William Morrow and Company, 1969), p. 28.
12. Arthur Eddington, *The Philosophy of Physical Science* (Ann Arbor: University of Michigan Press, 1958), p. 50.

appendix c | human survival of biological death

An Approach to the Problem Based upon the Orientation of Field Theory in Modern Physics

We distinguish between living and dead matter: between moving bodies and bodies at rest. This is a primitive point of view. What seems dead, a stone or the proverbial "door-nail," say, is actually forever in motion. We have merely become accustomed to judge by outward appearances; by the deceptive impressions we get through our senses. We shall have to learn to describe things in new and better ways.

—MAX BORN (1)

He goes from death to death who sees the many here.

—THE VEDANTA

The metaphysical wealth reposing largely untapped in modern physical theory is enormous and challenging to the investigator.

—HENRY MARGENAU (2)

From *Main Currents in Modern Thought,* Vol. 26, No. 2 (November–December 1969), pp. 35–57. This paper was written under the auspices of a grant from Dr. Frederick Ayer II. I am indebted to Edgar N. Jackson for very real help with some of these conceptualizations.

223

In man's deep concern with the implications of biological death and whether or not it means his total destruction, he has long searched for an answer to the question "Does the death of the body mean personal annihilation or does some part of the individual continue to exist?" In all the centuries of this search, no generally acceptable answer has been found. Different explorers of the problem have come to different conclusions, and one answer seems as well or poorly proven as another.

It is part of the faith of science that if serious people work diligently on a problem for a long period of time and cannot arrive at a satisfactory answer, they are asking the wrong question and a new one is needed. "If," writes Suzanne Langer, "we want to have new knowledge, we need a whole host of new questions." (3) The hardest part of scientific research, and the part that takes the longest time, is finding the right question to ask. Very often what has appeared to be a complete impasse in one or another area of our quest for comprehension of the world and ourselves has been broken through or bypassed when a new question was formulated.

For this reason, it seems advisable to try to ask new questions about human survival of death. Perhaps if we devise enough questions and explore their implications, we may be able to learn a little more about this dark and crucial problem.[1]

Let us try one restatement of this question and see where it leads us:

What is the nature of the relationship between the human being and the rest of reality, and how does this change with biological death?

By the term "relationship" we do not mean here the narrower concept of energy and matter exchange such as occurs in respiration and nutrition. We shall be concerned rather with such qualities as "individuality," "separateness," "uniqueness of the individual"; with how "separate" he is from outside reality and how much he must be considered as "part-of-a-whole," "one aspect-of-a-total," "part-of-a-Gestalt." We are asking how much we can or must consider the individual person a "unit," and how much we can or must consider him a part of a larger pattern of being from which we cannot meaningfully separate him.

As we look at this question, it becomes apparent that we have historically used two quite different approaches in our attempts at solving the problems of "what-is-the-nature-of-things." We might today call these two the approach of Newtonian mechanics ("classical physics") and the approach of field theory ("modern physics").[2]

In its most basic orientation to the overall nature of things, classical physics is very close to the "common-sense" approach. It operates on the assumption that one should be primarily oriented to individual, unique units ("things" and "events") and only secondarily to how they combine into classes of units, classes of classes of units, and so forth. The basic angle of approach is to the individual unit, the individual object or event. A recognizable perception can be responded to—at least theoretically— with the statement "Oh, that is a so-and-so." This means, in effect, "I recognize that *first* as an individual entity, a unitary 'thing,' and secondarily, I classify it as a unique member of the class of so-and-so's." The focus is on the individual unit of being, separate in the recognition from the rest of reality, and this individuality is considered most "real." The placing of it in classifications is only for the purpose of making it easier to think about and to remember. We know in this viewpoint that classifications are essentially false to reality, as no two entities are exactly alike ("One cannot step into the same river twice . . ."), but use them for the sake of convenience. In this approach, two entities are considered similar (belonging to the same class) when the differences between them make no difference in relation to the problem at hand.

In field theory the matter is quite different. The primary, most "real" aspect of an entity is its part in the larger pattern, and our perception of it cannot be responded to by an "Oh, that is a so-and-so." To perceive it at all, apart from the total field, is to perceive it as a subsystem, an artificially separated aspect of a field of stresses, a pattern. Only secondarily do we classify it as an individual entity for purposes of symbolic manipulation. Thus, from a field-theory viewpoint, we cannot legitimately say, "Here is an electron," but can say at best, "Here is an area where the field is strong," (4) or else we must switch back to the viewpoint of classical physics and say, "Here is a place and time where an instrument registered a reaction."

The field theory approach is first to the total Gestalt, and this is what is perceived as "real." Parts of this total Gestalt may be considered individually as subpatterns, but it is recognized that this is only for the purpose of making it easier to conceptualize and communicate about them. The separation is seen as essentially false to the reality. Thus in consideration of the Tao, the "All" of existence, the "Real," Lao-Tze divided the Tao into the Tao of Heaven (T'ien Tao), the Tao of Man (Jen-Tao), and the Tao of Earth (T'i Tao), but made it completely clear that this was only for the purpose of making it easier to grasp the concept; all three were "really" aspects of a total harmony of being that could not be meaningfully divided. Similarly, Max Planck wrote:

In modern mechanics . . . it is impossible to obtain an adequate version of the laws for which we are looking, unless the physical system is regarded *as a whole*. According to modern mechanics (field theory), each individual particle of the system, in a certain sense, at any one time, exists simultaneously in every part of the space occupied by the system. This simultaneous existence applies not merely to the field of force with which it is surrounded, but also to its mass and its charge.

Thus, we see that nothing less is at stake here than the concept of the particle—the most elementary concept of classical mechanics. We are compelled to give up the earlier essential meaning of this idea; only in a number of special border-line cases can we retain it. (5)

Describing this viewpoint historically, Einstein wrote:

Before Clerk Maxwell, people conceived of physical reality—insofar as it is supposed to represent events in nature
—as material points, whose changes consist exclusively
of motions. . . . After Maxwell they conceived physical
reality as represented by continuous fields, not mechanically explicable. . . . This change in the conception of
reality is the most profound and fruitful one that has
come to physics since Newton. (6)

Each of these two very different conceptualizations of
reality has been widely used by man, and each is applicable to certain types of problems. This is to say that certain problems have been shown as soluble by the use of
the common-sense, classical physics, "individuality-first,
classification-second" approach, and certain other problems
(which did not appear soluble when reality was organized
in this way) were solved when dealt with in the field-
theory, "Gestalt-first, individuality-second" approach.

The differences inherent in these two ways of considering reality should not be underestimated. They lead, for
example, to very different conclusions as to the nature of
various attributes of reality. Basic qualities such as time,
space, and causation, which seem from the common-sense
viewpoint to be absolute, unchangeable, and to be "matter
on which all reasonable men would agree," completely
change their essential structure when the field theory
conceptualization is used. Thus, in the "common-sense"
classical physics world-picture, events "happen" as time
flows inexorably and steadily from the future, through the
present, and into the past. In the field theory world-picture,
events "are," and we—so to speak—stumble across them
as we perceive narrow successive "slices" of the space-
time totality.[3]

With tremendous differences such as this one in our
two conceptualizations, it seems natural to demand,
"Which one is closer to the *true* structure of reality?"
Tempting as this question may seem, we have learned in
the last fifty years that it is not one that we can legiti-

mately ask. In science, the goal of understanding the true nature of reality is, in Max Planck's words, "theoretically unobtainable." (7) What we *can* legitimately ask is, "What logically follows if we can conceive reality to be structured in certain ways and proceed as if it were so structured? What happens, what do we observe, and what can we learn and accomplish?" (As Henry Margenau put it, "The question, then, is not whether matter is continuous but how theories succeed when they regard as a continuum the construct which they take to be their system.") (8) This is all we can ask, and we cannot legitimately escape the question by refusing to condede that we *are* organizing and structuring reality. Willy-nilly we *do* structure it, and our perception of reality is an amalgam consisting of unknown and unknowable proportions of ourselves and whatever "reality" may be. There is, wrote the mystic Evelyn Underhill, "a game of give and take between consciousness and outside reality," (9) and few philosophers or physicists today would disagree with her. Percy Bridgman phrased the same concept differently when he said: "In general we should never think about outside reality without also thinking of the nervous machinery in our heads by means of which we acquire knowledge of the world." (10) From the fact that these two ways of conceptualizing reality have been used by man so widely and usefully, however, one may conclude that—whatever their relation to "ultimate reality" may be —they are at least two ways that are valid for man. For our purpose in this paper, we are examining two ways of organizing and structuring reality. Before proceeding to explore the assets and limitations of each and their implications for the problem of human survival of bodily death, let us look briefly at the ways that they have been described in the past by three of our more serious explorers of "what is": [4]

These two ways of thinking, the way of time and history and, in screening it, dimly reveals it; and therefore each of man's efforts to comprehend the world in which he lives. Neither is comprehended in the other nor reducible to it. They are, as we have learned to say in physics, complementary views, each supplementing the other, neither telling the whole story.

—J. Robert Oppenheimer (11)

[There is a] distinction between two facets of truth which cannot be focused into a unity by the imperfectly united faculties of the Human Mind. In the Human Psyche there are two organs: a conscious volitional surface and a sub-conscious, non-volitional abyss. Each of these two organs has its own way of looking at, and peering through the dark glass that screens reality from man's inward eye, and, in screening it, dimly reveals it; and therefore each mode of the imperfect apprehensions calls its findings "the truth." But the qualities of the two different facets of a latent unitary truth are as different as the nature of the two organs of the human psyche that receive these "broken lights."

—Arnold Toynbee (12)

The soul has something within it, a spark of super-sensual knowledge that is never quenched. But there is also an-other knowledge in our souls, which is directed toward ob-jects; namely knowledge of our senses and the under-standing: this hides that other knowledge from us. The intuitive higher knowledge is timeless and spaceless, with-out any here and now.

—Meister Eckhardt (13)

For heuristic reasons we shall discuss these two ways of structuring the universe as if they were completely sepa-rate, although reality, as we can know it, is rarely so neatly divided into packets. In actuality they seem to be points near opposite ends of the spectrum of conceptuali-zations, each one shading into those adjacent.

Each of the two ways has its assets and liabilities. What can be accomplished easily with one world-picture can often be done only with immense difficulty—if at all—with the other. Anthony Flew quotes an old Spanish proverb that goes: " 'Take what you want,' said God, 'take it and pay for it.'" (14) We find ourselves here in a somewhat similar situation. For certain types of problems, such as those involving molar interactions of certain types of perceived entities, the approach of classical physics is vastly preferable. One could—theoretically at least —solve the problem of how long a lever must be to move X pounds of granite Y feet if Z pounds of force are available by recourse to field-theoretical methods, but who in his right mind would want to? On the other hand, there are problems involving entire ranges of energy interchanges which can only be solved by a field theory approach. (As an example of these, we might refer to the problem of the speed of light remaining constant regardless of the relative motion of its source and observers.)

For theoretical reasons we consider the classical physics conceptualization as a "special case" of the field theory conceptualization—a case applicable within a certain limited range. The fact that this limited range is the one within which most of our perceptual systems operate, and in which our everyday problems appear to us to exist, does not change the situation.[5]

One interesting aspect of the difference between the problems for which we would choose one approach, and those problems for which we would choose another, is that those problems for whose solution we must today go to field theory are mainly those that, from the viewpoint of classical physics, are "extreme conditions." They usually lie in areas that are outside the theoretical limits of human perception. These are areas in which we cannot directly perceive and in which the essential nature of our perceptual apparatus would have to change radically in order for us to be able to perceive events in the same sense that we perceive them in the ordinary range in which they operate. The change to our perceptual apparatus necessary for us to directly perceive subatomic particles staggers the imagination in a way that does not occur if we try to conceive a change that would permit us, for example, to directly perceive further into the infrared end of the visual spectrum. Similarly, at the other end of this scale of things, when we conceive of directly perceiving the vastly large (as distances in interstellar or intergalactic space), no imaginable change in our nervous system would enable us to measure light years and parsecs as we measure feet and yards. Those ranges in which we can directly perceive or can imagine nervous-system modifications which would enable us to perceive are those ranges in which problems can usually be solved by classical physics. Those ranges in which we can neither directly perceive nor imagine nervous-system changes which would enable us to perceive seem to be those ranges in which problems most frequently must be solved by field theory.[6]

With this brief introduction to these two ways of conceptualizing reality, let us return to the question of human survival of biological death. (Much further description and discussion can be found in such books as those by Max Planck, Alfred North Whitehead, [15] and Henry Margenau, and in very different terms by Sri Vivekananda, [16] Meister Eckhardt, and others.)

We can now see that the answer to our question may be related to the conceptual system we use. We shall have to explore the answers we get when using each of the two we have described, and then compare these answers. If they turn out to be different, we shall have to decide what to do about the difference. Let us start with classical physics.

In this viewpoint, we concede that an object exists (is real) under any one of three possible overlapping conditions: (1) if we can directly perceive it; (2) if we can directly perceive its effects; and (3) if we must hypothesize it to account for perceived effects which we cannot account for in any other way. In other words, we do not consider it to be "real" unless it is a perception or necessary to explain a perception.[7]

The only exception to these three criteria for existence is one based on experience. If we leave an object in a place where we can no longer observe it or its effects (for example, placing a shoe in a closet, locking the closet, and leaving the house), we assume—on the basis of past experience—that it will be there when we return (barring special conditions such as burglars or the evaporation of a liquid) and that therefore it exists and is real in the interval between our locking and unlocking the closet.[8] But apart from this exception we must consider things to exist only if we perceive them or if they are necessary to explain what we do perceive.

The converse of these criteria for considering that an entity exists is that it does not fulfill our necessary conditions. If we do not have one of these reasons for believing it to exist, it is considered to be nonexistent. From this viewpoint, everything that is real has effects that are perceptible. Nothing else has existence. It is under this criterion that the Michelson-Morley experiment was interpreted as proving that the ether did not exist.

Further, from this viewpoint, an entity *ceases to exist* when it no longer fulfills one of the three conditions for being real and is not under the umbrella of the special exception of being able (at least theoretically) to return to one of them (as our lonely shoe in the closet). When the electric switch is turned off, the light generated by the bulb ceases to exist. When the wave has broken on the shore, the wave no longer exists. When the orchestra has stopped playing, the music no longer is in existence, although our memories of it may be clear and strong.

We believe the self-awareness and consciousness of other people to be "real" because, on the basis of our experience with ourselves, we consider the existence of their conscious "I" the only way to explain the behavior we observe in them. It is necessary for us to accept that other are conscious, as it is the only way we know to explain our perceptions of them. The self-awareness and consciousness of others is accepted as real under the third condition: as necessary to explain their perceived behavior. It is a "construct," something that we cannot perceive but that we decide exists, in order to explain something we do perceive.

However, the acceptance of the existence of the consciousness of others is only necessary as long as they continue bodily (biological) activity. Once this ceases it is not only no longer necessary to believe it still exists but, by the classical-physics method of structuring the universe, it is necessary to believe that it has ceased to exist. It can no longer be perceived directly. It no longer has effects that can be perceived. We no longer need to postulate its existence to explain any of our perceptions. As the wave broken on the shore has ceased to exist in this viewpoint, the personality and self-awareness of others cease to exist once biological death has occurred. Of both wave and personality we accept that the physical substratum goes on in altered form: the water of the wave as molecules of water in the ocean, the body of the person as chemical atoms in the earth. Of both we may retain memory. But, in this world-picture, wave and personality are no longer in existence. They are no longer real. From the viewpoint of classical physics, the common-sense, Newtonian mechanics method of structuring reality, it is an inexorable conclusion that biological death means the annihilation of the consciousness and self-awareness of the individual.

We must now see what follows if we use the field-theory method of conceptualizing reality, and again raise the question of the personality surviving the dissolution of the body.

In field theory, a subpattern is considered to be "real" under three conditions, *all* of which must be fulfilled if the criteria for existence are to be met:

1. It must be necessary to complete our constructs about reality. Its absence must leave an inharmonious gap in the relationships of things. To state this in another way, our observations in the classical-physics viewpoint lead us to certain constructs which form the structure of the field-theory model of reality. The specific construct whose reality is under question must form hitherto-unincluded observations into a harmonious relation with the rest of the model. Not to include them would leave them irrelevant to the model, which—since the model is of the "all" —is unacceptable.

2. It must be the simplest construct we can make which will fit our observations into the larger model. It is considered to be real to the degree it does not have avoidable or "inelegant" complexities. In Einstein's words, "Our ex-

perience justifies us in believing that nature is the realization of the simplest mathematical ideals." (17)

3. The primary requirement—and the one which includes the previous two—is that of harmony and coherence. It must mesh smoothly and functionally into the
larger Gestalt (the general model) and function according
to the same laws which we attribute to the whole. To the
degree that it meshes harmoniously and follows the same
laws as the rest of the conceptualization, it is considered
to be "real"; to the degree it does not, it is considered to
be an invalid ("unreal") construct.

It is thus primarily its functional characteristics which
determine the "reality" of a construct, not its structural
characteristics. The bunghole in the barrel, as Eddington
points out, (18) is considered in field theory to be real and
an integral part of the barrel.[9]

From a field-theory viewpoint, the existence of the conscious, self-aware "I" would be considered to be "real,"
and must be conceptualized in certain ways. It fulfills the
three criteria as follows:

1. It is a definite, clear, and compelling observation we
each make. Not only do we each *know* of its existence,
but Descartes's "I think, therefore I am" has given us an
emotionally satisfying proof of the matter. To leave out
such a strong "protocol observation" as this one would
violate the first requirement; the model would be incom-
plete. (Further, it appears to be needed in the theory. It
is, for example, the conscious "I" that cannot distinguish
acceleration from gravity in Einstein's classic example.)

2. So far as the second requirement goes, it is the simplest construct we can make to account for our observations. This goes further than the existence of our own "I";
it is also the simplest construct we can make to account
for the observed behavior of others.

3. It is with the third requirement that we come to the
crux of the matter. This is the requirement of harmony
and coherence.

We can only fit our construct of the "I" into the field-
theory viewpoint by conceptualizing it in a way that is

harmonious with the rest of the model. It must follow the general conceptual rules of field theory and function in accord with the general dynamic laws which we have attributed to the model—those that operate in this world-picture. To do this, we must conceptualize the "I" as boundaryless in the continuum; as not being "separate from" or "isolated from" the rest of "what is"; as not being limited by specific events such as the perceived ceasing of biological activity.

"If the theory of relativity is correct, even in its special form, the meaning of independent particles is an absurdity because their states cannot be specified in principle." (19)

This is the heart of the matter. Each of us *knows* that he has a self-aware "I." We can legitimately paraphrase the above quotation by saying, "If the theory of relativity is correct, even in its special form, the meaning of an independent 'I' bounded by specific events such as birth or death is an absurdity." In a field-theory approach we must be consistent, and our conceptualization (including that of the "I") must be legitimate within the approach. "Independence," "individuality," and "bounded by" are concepts that are not consistent with the approach. (This of course, is what the serious mystics, with their field-theory viewpoint, have been telling us for centuries.)

Since this is a difficult and complex matter, let us go back and approach the problem of "survival" in the field-theory conceptualization from a different angle. Let us start with a statement of the physicist Louis de Broglie in which he describes the field-theory viewpoint concerning the way the universe "works":

> In space-time, everything which for each of us constitutes the past, the present and the future is given in block, and the entire collection of events successive of each of us which forms the material particle is represented by a line, the world line of the particle. . . . Each observer, as his time passes, discovers, so to speak, new slices of space-time which appear to him as successive aspects of the material world, though in reality the ensemble of events

which constitutes space-time exists prior to his knowledge of them. (20)

P. W. Bridgman has pointed out that "in domains in which our ordinary space and time concepts fail, the ordinary notions of creation must also fail and be replaced by others." (21) The implications of this are clear: in field theory we are in such a domain, and it is not only our "ordinary notions of creation" that must be replaced, but also our ordinary notions of annihilation.

In this approach, reality is seen as a harmonious, unified field of dynamically balanced stresses existing in— and being—the space-time continuum. No part of it can be legitimately separated from the rest except for purposes of symbolic manipulation. In the most profound sense, the field is without limits or boundaries, within or without, in space or time. Terms such as "isolated from" or "separated from" have only subjective meaning at best and no objective reality, and this is also true for the terms "past," "present," and "future." Indeed this is so literally true that the physicists L. Landau and B. Rumer could write that the words that two events occurred "at one and the same time" are "as meaningless" as the words that they occurred "at one and the same place." (22) Instead of saying "this too shall pass away," one says, "this is, was, and will be." It is from this viewpoint that Jesus is quoted as saying "Before Abraham was, I am"; it is only from this viewpoint that such a statement (and many other statements made by mystics) makes any sense.

Let us restate this differently. The viewpoint of classical physics and of common sense *geometrizes* the world in terms of boundary points, lines, and surfaces, and is concerned with the relationships of these. With such a viewpoint, boundaries and limits are seen inherent in the structure of reality and are basic to all conceptual derivation. A lake is perceived as limited by the land around it, a life by the terminal points of birth and death.

Field theory does not accept this. In Margenau's words, "The central recognition of the theory of relativity is that geometry is a construct of the human intellect."

(23) It recognizes this type of geometrizing as one set of ways of conceptualizing reality, and goes beyond this set to a boundaryless conceptualization of reality. In this boundaryless world-picture there are no limiting points, lines, or surfaces, nor such termination events as birth and death. Geometry, which includes boundaries and surfaces, is considered to be useful in the "limited case" and as a tool for special purposes, but is not seen as inherent in reality.

With this type of perception of "what is," what are we going to conclude about the biological death of a mystic who, let us say, "once in his life" has conceptualized the cosmos in this way? If we accept as true what all serious mystics tell us—that in their moments of mystical "enlightment" they *do* organize and perceive the world in this way—we have a curious problem. Once this individual has "stepped out of time," once he has perceived and interacted with "what is" as if the field-theory viewpoint were valid, he has been outside our common-sense time scheme. Once he "has done" this (or "will do" it, since the two are the same), it "never can be" ("never has been") revoked. He remains "forever" a part of the unified cosmos. He *is*. What then is the significance of his bodily death?

"I cannot decide," wrote Hugo Bergmann in 1929, "by physical means who is living now, Plato or myself. For the difference is a psychological one. Now is the temporal mode of the experiencing ego." (24) J. Choron, in his classic *Death in Western Thought*, points out clearly that the problem of survival rests directly on the problem of the nature of time. (25)

From the field-theory viewpoint, it is not only the mystic who *is*, who exists as an organic part of the total space-time continuum, but *all* "entities," "unities," "objects," and "events." They exist "always" in the total field which constitutes the cosmos, although they may be outside the range of perception. In this conceptualization the term "now" has no real meaning. With the universe so structured, the wave that has broken on the shore has not ceased to exist; it was, is, and will be. These terms, with their implications of pastness, presentness, and futurity, are false to reality. There are many different states of the same system in the continuum, but to say that one state "is" and another "was" is a distortion. All we can say is that we only perceive a narrow, changing slice of the total manifold, but our limited perceptual range does not affect the reality of existence of *all* states of the system in the continuum.

In this sense, field theory leads as inexorably to a concept of "survival" of biological death as classical physics does to a concept of total annihilation at bodily death. In the sense that all things that "were," "are," or "will be" exist forever in the continuum, the individual continues to be.

This, however, seems to be a pale kind of survival, "disembodied" and not even very interesting. Is there anything more we can say about it from the viewpoint of field theory? To do so we must make a detour and consider the question of consciousness: what it means and how it feels in a world structured by the common-sense method, and in a world structured by field theory.

What *can* we say about consciousness and self-awareness in a cosmos structured from a field-theory viewpoint? How does my existence feel to me when I am using this conceptualization? Perhaps there is a way in which we can get some clues.

We know how consciousness "feels" under the common-sense conceptualization of reality with which we normally operate. We know that the viewpoint of common sense and that of field theory are not completely separate, but are, rather, two points close to opposite ends of a spectrum of conceptualizations. There is a progression of mental states in which we move along this spectrum, in which our concepts of reality progress from the everyday view of common sense and classical physics to the field-theory viewpoint. Let us examine this progression of mental states and see how consciousness changes—which of its attributes change, and how—as we move along this spectrum.

The progression might be loosely defined as follows: (1)

ordinary consciousness; 2) the state of inspiration where there is deep concentration and mental focus on the relationship of entities, with a sudden new insight into these relationships; (3) the "peak experience" as defined by A. H. Maslow; (26) (4) the extrovertive, or "spontaneous" mystical experience; (5) the introvertive or "acquired" mystical experience; and (6) the complete mystical state (*parinirvana*).

These states of consciousness have been described by thousands of individuals who have participated in each state. Two things must be emphasized about these descriptions, particularly those of the mystical states. First, they are individual and self-generating. Persons reporting them come from every culture and every period of which we have records. Frequently without knowledge of other reports, they clearly describe the same phenomena, although the explanatory language may vary widely.[10] Second, these reports are not made by crackpot, fringe groups. The evidence comes from some of the most serious, respected, and important figures of history, and their reports cannot be dismissed lightly on grounds of naïveté or psychosis.

Structurally, these reports indicate a progression in the way the universe is perceived and structured—a progression from the common-sense to the field-theory viewpoint. The attributes of consciousness, "how it feels," also change as we move along this progression. We might describe four overlapping areas in which there is almost complete agreement by the experiments. Each of these aspects (or facets of what may be a unitary change) increases in intensity and in the total of permeating consciousness as we progress along the spectrum:

1. A definite knowledge and sense of individuality and self-awareness exists, but this is secondary to a basic sense of being part of, and totally in harmony with, the rest of the cosmos. Being primarily a part of the whole—a subsystem—does not destroy one's sense of individuality, but one perceives himself more and more as an indivisible part of the indivisible "all." Relatedness is primary, individuality secondary, but very real.

2. There is a sense of peace, of "rightness," of being completely at home in the universe. The inner and outer harmony are so great that action to change what is becomes increasingly unthinkable. In Rosalind Heywood's words, "If you hear music being played perfectly, you don't say, 'Play it out of tune.'" (27)

3. The sense of peace and harmony make for nonaction, but this is not a "passive" state. One feels at his highest peak in terms of energy, zest, "joy," in terms of exultancy and exaltation. The mind is clear and very alert. Awareness of oneself and the rest of reality increases as he mounts the spectrum.

4. There is a *knowledge* that time and space are illusions of the senses and that one is boundaryless in the continuum. One *knows* he is not confined within the limits of his skin and not dependent on the body for existence, and that the usual belief that this is so is illusion which one's vision now penetrates.

These four aspects of how consciousness "feels" all increase in intensity as the individual comes closer and closer to structuring reality in a field-theory way, until they totally permeate consciousness in the advanced mystical state. What are the implications of all this?

Before we go further, we should reemphasize one aspect of a field-theory approach. It is not only the outside world that is structured and organized as an indivisible field of relationships; the individual himself is a part of that field and cannot be separated therefrom:

> The development of atomic physics . . . forces us to an attitude recalling ancient wisdom, that when searching for harmony in life one must never forget that in the drama of existence we are ourselves both actors and spectators.
>
> —Niels Bohr (28)

The old philosophy of physics ceased to work at the end of the nineteenth century and the twentieth century physicist is hammering out a new philosophy for himself. Its essence is that he no longer sees nature as something entirely distinct from himself. Sometimes it is what he creates or selects or abstracts: sometimes it is what he destroys.

—James Jeans (29)

The student asked what was his enemy barring his path to enlightenment. The Zen-master Yasutani-Roshi replied: "Your enemy is your discursive thinking which leads you to differentiate yourself on one side of an imaginary line from what is not you on the other side of this non-existing line.

—Philip Kapleau (30)

In this view, we must include ourselves in the field—a field in which the term "separate from" has no meaning. When we do this, we subject ourselves to the world-picture of field theory, to a set of laws that places us outside the common-sense conception of time.[11] We have gone from the "particular" to the "general," and we cannot undo this action. Our present being—we as we are—is now removed from "inexorable, passing time." For a "moment," we were out of the usual conception of time, and "once" out of it is clearly "always" out of it. And we know what our consciousness was like when we were out of time: we were conscious and self-aware. There is not the slightest doubt of this in the thousands of serious reports of inspirational states, peak experiences, and mystical experiences. Therefore, from the viewpoint of field theory, our "forever" remaining outside of time means "forever" remaining out of it in a state of consciousness and self-awareness. Now the "survival" implied by field theory begins to look less pale and disembodied; it begins to take on more reality.

There seems, however, to be some difficulty here. From a field-theory viewpoint, change is seen as emergence of different states of the same system and all states "survive," i.e., eternally *are* in the cosmos. One might legitimately ask, "Which consciousness of mine survives? The one I had as a child? As an adolescent? The one I will have in my later years?" Clearly, from this viewpoint *all* states survive. The question being asked, however, is not answered by this statement; the central issue is more complex and must be dealt with directly. We shall have to return temporarily to the experience of the mystic for clues.

In her important book *Practical Mysticism,* Evelyn Underhill has demonstrated that the acquired mystical perception (or what we have called the field-theory organization) is accomplished as a result of training, strengthening, and integrating the total organismic being. It is a viewpoint that "emerges" as a result of bringing organization of the personality to its finest possible tuning, and is a function of the highest state of personality integration.[12]

In each state of consciousness all the previous exist, not only as the substratum of the present state, but also in their own form although not usually accessible as such to conscious recall. No one who has been through the voyage of inner exploration known as depth psychology—in which long-past states of consciousness are fully recalled and reexperienced—would deny this.

Similarly, in the mystical experience all other states of consciousness are present, but the individual who has the experience is quite clear about his present state of consciousness. And he is aware that he is more alert and "awake" during the experience, more aware of "being" and of being part of the "All," than he is when he is in other states of consciousness. From the viewpoint of the experiment, from the viewpoint of personality training and integration, from the viewpoint of the spectrum running from the common-sense view of reality to the field-theory view, it is the "highest" experience of consciousness. The more complete the field-theory structuring of reality, the more the experience includes and integrates all "previous" states of consciousness and influences those to come "later." The more fully the individual experiences this view, the more fully he is out of ordinary time and out of the acceptance of individuality and separateness which characterize the common-sense view. The central state of being—the state of consciousness and awareness of the individual—"after" biological death would appear to be no lower than the highest state of consciousness experienced "during" the biological phase of being. "Which consciousness survives?" From this viewpoint, the highest and most aware one that we had in biological life.

This is a complex point, so let us try to restate it in other words. The real question being asked is "If all my moments of being (states of the system I define as 'I') exist permanently in the continuum, which of them would I be most aware of after biological death?" The answer appears to be conditioned by the fact that—from the field-theory viewpoint—the rules of the game do not change with individual events (i.e., bodily death), since to perceive them as unique events or boundary points is illusory. So to the question "Of which moment of personality would I be most aware after bodily death?" the answer would be "the moment of personality in which you were most aware before bodily death." The moment of most awareness is that moment when we organized reality in a fashion closest to the field-theory end of the spectrum— the moment when we were freest of the limited case of common-sense organizing of reality, and closest to the general case of field-theory organizing. To the question of which "I" would I be most aware of, post mortem, field theory seems to respond, "The 'I' of which you were most aware pre-mortem. Why should the rules change?"

This is a crucial point. In a field-theory approach the rules do not change any more with biological death than they do with other specific events. They are invariant under the transformations of time. As Henry Margenau states, "Objectivity becomes equivalent to *invariance* of physical laws, not physical phenomena or observations. . . . Einstein's concept of objectivity takes every pretense to uniformity out of the sphere of perception and puts it in the basic form of theoretical statements." (31)

Our ordinary perception of the creation and annihilation of the individual at birth and death is not made from a "privileged position" from which we see objectively. It is the view from one limited position, and objectivity can only be reached with a theoretical description in which the laws governing reality remain invariant no matter what the position of the observer is.

In conceptualizing the problem of "survival" from a field-theory viewpoint, it is important not to confuse structure and functon. We are tempted, because of our common-sense orientation, to ask, "What survives?" implying that the answer be given in terms of structure rather than in the functional (relational) terms. The easy confusion between these two is illustrated by the famous story about Ludwig Wittgenstein, who was asked, "What is a mathematical point?" He replied, "A mathematical point is a place to start an argument!" His answer is more profound than it might appear at first glance. A mathematical point has no length, breadth, or thickness. The question implies an answer in terms of structure which cannot be given. Wittgenstein's answer wrenched the problem back to its proper frame of reference—to the functional qualities of the point and away from the invalid implications of structure. In a similar vein is the incident, in which the mystic Jacob Boehme was asked, "Where does the soul go when the body dies?" He replied, "There is no necessity for it to go anywhere."

As we have remarked before, each of the two ways of organizing reality that we are considering here has assets and liabilities. In the presence of an immediate stress which threatens the continuation of the biological aspects of our being—our body—the common-sense viewpoint is far superior to the field-theory viewpoint. If one wishes to avoid the approaching truck, dodge the thrown spear, or get food for one's empty stomach, it is far wiser to conceptualize the world in the manner of common sense and classical physics than to conceptualize it after the manner of the mystic and the modern physicist.[13] So long as the body is functioning as a biological unit and one is concerned that it continues so to function, it is essential to retain the common-sense "individuality-first, classification-second" world-picture, at least the largest part of the time. Once it ceases its biological activity, this necessity no longer exists; for example, it does not exist for the next phase of the system. This source gives one no more reason to continue to use this conceptualization.[14]

It may well be that, according to our original definition, we shall have to consider death an "extreme condition" and, as such, a problem that must be solved by a field-theory conceptualization of reality rather than by a common-sense, classical-physics conceptualization. (We defined "extreme conditions" as those areas outside the theoretical limits of our perceptual apparatus—such as the realm of subatomic particles or the realm of interstellar distances—in which we could neither perceive directly nor imagine modifications of our perceptual apparatus that would enable us to perceive directly.) The perception of the "I" of another person after his biological death seems to fulfill these conditions. The validity of the idea of classifying bodily death as an "extreme condition" according to our definition, however, needs further exploration.

Let us try to sum up. We rephrased the usual question concerning man's survival of biological death in order to see if the new way of phrasing would help us understand a little more about the subject than the old phrasing did. We found that this effort led us to try to apply the methodological lessons learned from the Einsteinian revolution in physics. These lessons concern new ways to solve problems in which the organization used by classical physics (common sense) does not seem to be able to lead us to further understanding by using a field-theory organization of the universe.

Analyzing the rules of the game as they apply to what "exists," we found that, so far as "survival" goes, these two problems lead to opposite conclusions. Organizing the world in the manner of classical physics leads inexorably to the conclusion that biological death means total annihilation (nonexistence) of the individual. Organizing the world in the manner of field theory leads as inexorably to a conclusion of survival of biological death.

In attempting to analyze the meaning of this survival, we have drawn upon the immense amount of available data provided by descriptions of consciousness in moments of inspiration, in "peak experiences," and in mystical experience. Mystics, from our viewpoint, are individuals who have succeeded in emotionally and intellectually attaining a field-theoretical view of reality, either through having special personality configurations or through special training. We take this viewpoint from the fact that their descriptions of how-the-universe-works, as comprehended in their moments of mystical perception, match so completely the description of that part of modern theoretical physics that uses a field-theory conceptualization. (31)

In the description of consciousness in moments of inspiration, "peak experiences" and mystical "enlightenment," we find certain psychological attributes increasing in intensity and permeation of consciousness, as one moves along the spectrum from the ordinary, common-sense state of consciousness to the field-theory state of consciousness. We are led to the conclusion that these attributes permeate the consciousness and self-awareness that are "outside" of our usual conceptualization of reality (with its common-sense concepts of space, time, and causality), and that survive biological death.

The relationships between the common-sense approach to reality and the field-theory approach that have been worked out in modern physics indicate that when the two lead to different solutions to a problem, the field-theory answer is of greater validity and includes the other as a "special" or "limited" case; and that the *apparent* validity of the common-sense approach is due to limitations of our perceptual apparatus. The implications of this conclusion for the problem of "survival" seem to be clear.

Notes

1. It is very difficulty for the modern scientist to think about the possibility of the personality surviving biological death because of his assumption that brain and mind are the same. This is accepted as the "truth," and it is rarely realized that this is an assumption and that other conceptualizations are possible. For example, there is the viewpoint taken by Bergson, James, Eccles, Burt, and others which is perhaps best summed up in the words of Sir Charles Sherrington: "Mental

phenomena on examination do not seem amenable to understanding under physics and chemistry. I have therefore to think of the brain as an organ of liaison between energy and mind, but not as a converter of energy into mind or vice versa." (32)

2. These terms are used somewhat loosely here and will be more clearly defined as we proceed. The two approaches which I am trying to differentiate are allied to the *spirit* behind particle theories and field theory.

3. If one is a layman in physics and wishes a personal experience of the differences implied in these two approaches, I might suggests the following small experiment: Ask a modern theoretical physicist the question, "If light travels in waves through a vacuum, *what* is waving?" He is likely to reply with a statement something like this: "Why do you think that, because there are waves, something must be waving?" Several minutes later as you reel back from the merry-go-round of noncommunication and confusion the two of you have stepped into, you are likely to have a sense of how greatly these two ways of organizing reality differ from each other.

4. As I have demonstrated elsewhere (33), at least three groups of individuals use the field-theory approach in their work: serious mystics, serious theoretical physicists, serious clairvoyants. (A "serious clairvoyant" is an individual who has been shown over a period of years of intensive study to be able, under strictest laboratory conditions, to acquire information from other than known channels and about whom there has never been the slightest evidence of chicanery. Typical among these are Mrs. Piper, Mrs. Willett, and Eileen Garrett.

Each of these three groups (mystics, physicists and clairvoyants) state clearly that, when they are functioning in their special capacities, they conceptualize the world in this way. Their attitudes, their techniques, and their goal, of course, differ very widely. As Rosalind Heywood (one of the serious clairvoyants) said in this context, "James Bond and I may both use the telephone, but we say different things on it." (34)

5. One reason we call the common-sense viewpoint a "limited case" of the field-theory viewpoint is the following: all problems that can be solved by a classical physics conceptualization (plus many that cannot) can also be solved by a field-theory conceptualization. The reverse, however, is not true. Further, when we push classical physics to its limits we find that these limits can only be expanded by our switching to a field-theoretical approach. In Werner Heisenberg's words, "we come to . . . the completely unexpected realization that a consistent pursuit of classical physics forces a transformation in the very basis of this physics." (35)

6. Instruments such as telescopes, microscopes, spectroscopes, radio receivers, etc., are similar to our imaginable modifications of the nervous system. What we can do by this type of instrumentation we can conceive of being able to do without it.

7. We may perceive an illusion, but we then concede that the illusion exists. The rule holds. In Kurt Lewin's words, "as far as conceptual derivation is concerned, one may use effectiveness as the criterion for existence. What is real is what has effects." (36) Or in the doggerel of an anonymous verse: "In modern thought, if not in fact, nothing is that doesn't act. So that is counted wisdom which explains the scratch, but not the itch."

8. This seems so borne out by experience and common sense that the contrary point of view of Bishop Berkeley never became widely accepted, and even the good Bishop came to the conclusion that the shoe is always watched by God!

9. The positron might be defined as a hole from which an electron has been removed. The positron is considered to be "real" in this approach.

10. The British philosopher C. D. Broad has put it this way: "To me, the occurrence of mystical experience at all times and places, and the similarities between

the statements of so many mystics all the world over, seems to be a really significant fact. *Prima facie,* it suggests that there is an aspect of reality with which these persons come in contact in their mystical experiences, and which they afterwards strive and largely fail to describe in the language of daily life. I should say this *prima facie* appearance of objectivity ought to be accepted at its face value unless and until some reasonable satisfactory explanation of the agreement can be given." (37)

11. This is as true if someone else had structured the universe in this way as it is if we had done it ourselves. For purposes of clarity only we are exploring the matter as if we ourselves had fully structured the world in this way, e.g., had had a full mystical experience ourself.

12. This viewpoint is agreed on by all the major approaches to mystical training: Yoga training, Zen, the Gurdjieff "work," etc. Spontaneous mystical experience can come to the individual in various ways relating to special personality configurations, special body-chemistry conditions, etc. The most profound mystical experiences, however, are the "acquired" or "trained" experiences.

13. Indeed Ramakrishna states that one cannot survive biologically for more than 21 days if one is conceptualizing continually in the mystic way. (38)

14. It is possible that some individuals, who have been deeply involved with "things" and are so emotionally bound to them, or to unfinished business relating to this world-picture, can only bridge the gap between the two viewpoints partially. They would remain somehow "stuck" with the world-organization of "common sense" and be unable to leave it completely. This could possibly account for some of the more serious data concerning "hauntings" and "apparitions" where —as in the case of the "Ash Manor Ghost"—*something* of the deceased person seems to remain in the area. The data concerning serious "apparition" cases has so much in it that is consistent from case to case

that, after studying it, one hesitates to dismiss it out of hand. The unfinished-business concept seems to make sense out of this data. It is as if some part of the personality remained related to a task to which the person was so emotionally bound, he could not leave it. This part of him carries on in a ritualistic manner. Tyrrell, in a classic study, has pointed out that "apparitions look like human beings, but behave in a markedly somnambulistic fashion." (39) The concept of the deceased remaining tied to a specific need or set of needs would also account for a remarkable observation made by the clairvoyant Rosalind Heywood. She was working with Eileen Garrett (also one of the serious clairvoyants), who was in trance and her "control," Abdul Latif, was ostensibly speaking through her. Mrs. Heywood decided to try to function herself as a clairvoyant at this moment and see if she could perceive Abdul Latif in this way. She says of this experience, "I put out my antennae and it seemed to me that he only existed for the subject we were talking about." This is an extremely provocative comment made by a very serious and highly qualified person.

Although it seems reasonable, in terms of the evidence, to speculate on the concept of a deceased person sometimes remaining partially in a Newtonian mechanics world-picture and thereby sometimes affecting our perceptual apparatus, I see no way, at present, to explore its validity further.

References

1. Max Born, *The Restless Universe* (New York: Dover Publications, 1951), p. 1.
2. Henry Margenau, "Einstein's Conception of Reality," in P. A. Schilpp, *Albert Einstein: Philosopher-Scientist* (New York: Harper & Row, 1959), p. 246.
3. Suzanne Langer, *Philosophy in a New Key* (Cambridge: Harvard University Press, 1957).

4. James Jeans, *The New Background of Science* (Ann Arbor: University of Michigan Press, 1959), p. 113.

5. Max Planck, *Where Is Science Going?* (London: George Allen & Unwin, 1933), p. 24.

6. Margenau, "Einstein's Conception," p. 257.

7. Planck, *Where Is Science Going?*, p. 15.

8. Henry Margenau, *The Night of Physical Reality* (New York: Mc-Graw-Hill, 1956), p. 194.

9. Evelyn Underhill, *Practical Mysticism* (London: J. M. Dent & Sons, 1964), p. 27.

10. P. W. Bridgman, *The Way Things Are* (Cambridge: Harvard University Press, 1966), p. 154.

11. J. R. Oppenheimer, *Science and the Common Understanding* (New York: Simon & Shuster, 1966), p. 69.

12. Arnold Toynbee, *An Historian's Approach to Religion* (New York: Oxford University Press, 1956), p. 27.

13. R. B. Blakney, *Meister Eckhardt, a Modern Translation* (New York: Harper & Row, 1941), p. 35.

14. Anthony Flew, Remarks Made at the Parapsychology Foundation Conference on Survival, London, 1967.

15. Alfred North Whitehead, *Science and the Modern World* (1925).

16. Swami Vivekananda, *Jnana-Yoga* (New York: Ramakrishna-Vivekananda Center, 1949), pp. 90ff.

17. Margenau, "Einstein's Conception."

18. Arthur Eddington, *The Philosophy of Physical Science* (Ann Arbor: University of Michigan Press, 1958), p. 120.

19. Margenau, "Einstein's Conception of Reality," p. 248.

20. Louis de Broglie, "The Scientific Work of Albert Einstein," in Schilpp, *Einstein*, p. 114.

21. Bridgman, *The Way Things Are*, p. 198.

22. L. Landau and B. Rumer, *What Is Relativity?* (New York: Basic Books, 1959), p. 37.

23. Margenau, "Einstein's Conception," p. 246.

24. Hugo Bergmann, *Der Kampf Um Das Kauselgesetz in der Junsten Physic* (Braunschweig: F. Weweg & Sons, 1929).

25. J. Choron, *Death in Western Thought* (New York: Collier, 1966), p. 25.
26. A. H. Maslow, *Towards a Psychology of Being* (New York: Van Nostrand, 1962).
27. Rosalind Heywood, Personal communication, June 16, 1967.
28. Niels Bohr, "Discussion with Einstein on Epistemological Problems in Atomic Physics," in Schilpp, *Einstein*, p. 236.
29. Jeans, *New Background*, p. 1.
30. Philip Kapleau, ed., *The Three Pillars of Zen* (New York: Harper & Row, 1966), p. 154.
31. Margenau, "Einstein's Conception," p. 253.
32. A. Hardy, "Physical Research and Civilization," *Proc. Soc. Psy. Research* (1966), 55, pp. 1–21.
33. Lawrence LeShan, *Toward a General Theory of the Paranormal* (New York: Parapsychology Foundation, 1969).
34. Heywood, Communication, June 16, 1967.
35. Werner Heisenberg, *Philosophic Problems of Nuclear Science* (Greenwich, Conn.: Fawcett, 1966), p. 13.
36. Kurt Lewin, *Principles of Topological Psychology* (New York: McGraw Hill, 1936), p. 19.
37. C. D. Broad, *Religion, Philosophy and Psychical Research* (London: Rutledge and Kegan Paul, 1953), p. 242.
38. Sri Ramakrishna, *The Gospel of Sri Ramakrishna* (New York: Ramakrishna-Vivekananda Center, 1952).
39. G. N. M. Tyrrell, *Apparitions* (New York: Collier Books, 1963), p. 42.

appendix d | physicists and mystics: similarities in world view[1]

It is the purpose of this paper to attempt to show the similarities in the picture of how-the-world-works, the *Weltbild,* which was derived from the research data accumulated in two different disciplines. At first glance, these two disciplines seem to have nothing at all in common. They start with different goals in view, have completely different methodologies, and appear to be *Totaliter Aliter,* separate from each other in every way. Nevertheless, it is interesting to note that in their general description of the universe they appear to be describing the same conclusions. This, in itself, that with all their differences of starting point, method, and goal, the conclusions are isomorphic, would seem to indicate a much greater probability that these conclusions are valid.

The two groups whose conclusions we wish to compare are modern theoretical physicists and serious mystics. To speak of mystics as having a "discipline" and "research data" may appear to many to be seriously distorting the meaning of these words. The usual Western stereotype of the mystic is of a dreamy, unworldly individual with his

From *Journal of Transpersonal Psychology,* Vol. 1, No. 2 (1969).

eyes firmly fixed on a God-inhabited, subjective, faith-oriented view of reality.

However, as one surveys those serious mystics of whom we have extenisve records, some interesting material comes to light. The similarity of their reports, including reports of those who clearly had no contact with each other, is overwhelming. They are clearly describing the same phenomena in ancient India, classical Rome, Medieval Europe and Twentieth Century England. The British philosopher C. D. Broad (1953), in discussing this, states:

To me, the occurrence of mystical experience at all times and places, and the similarities between the statements of so many mystics all the world over, seems to be a really significant fact. *Prima facie* it suggests that there is an aspect of reality with which these persons came in contact in their mystical experience, and which they afterwards strive and largely fail to describe in the language of daily life. I should say that this *prima facie* appearance of objectivity ought to be accepted at its face value unless and until some reasonably satisfactory explanation of the agreement can be given (p. 242).

Evelyn Underhill (1912), one of the most profound and serious mystics of the century, and probably the most learned student of the subject in our times, describes mystics as follows:

The most highly developed branches of the human family have in common one peculiar characteristic. They tend to produce—sporadically it is true, and usually in the teeth of adverse external circumstances—a curious and definite type of personality: a type which refsues to be satisfied with that which other men call experience, and is inclined, in the words of its enemies, to "deny the world in order that it may find reality." We meet these persons in the east and west; in the ancient, medieval and modern worlds. . . . Whatever the place or period in which they have arisen, their aims, doctrines and methods have been substantially the same. Their experience, therefore, forms a body of evidence, curiously self-consistent and often mutually explanatory which must be taken into account before we can add up the sum of the energies and potentialities of the human spirit, or reasonably speculate on its relations to the unknown world which lies outside the boundaries of sense (p. 3).

The overwhelming consistency of the mystics' reports have been admirably described by Bertrand Russell (1925), William James (1958), W. T. Stace (1961), and others.

Basically, the starting point of serious mysticism is that the data given by the senses about reality is not valid as it is so strongly influenced by the nature of man and his perceptual equipment and by his techniques of perception. The mystic believes that by means of special training he can so discipline, tune and train his total organism (much in the way a champion athlete disciplines, tunes and trains his body) that it will be able to transcend these limitations and perceive reality more accurately.

All serious schools of mystical training (Yoga, Zen, Christian Mysticism, the Gurdjieff "work," etc.) agree on the necessity for long and extremely arduous training. Although the training procedures and techniques vary superficially, their basic structure and orientation is very similar. A good decsription of one of these training methods (Zen) can be obtained from Philip Kapleau's book (1967). For those interested in a comparision of training methods, Evelyn Underhill's approach to Christian mysticism (1964) can provide a useful guide.

The goals of the physicist and the mystic are as different as are the training and research techniques of these two groups. The goal of the physicist is to understand and control physical reality. The goal of the mystics is to be more at home in the universe, to comprehend and be a part of reality, and to attain serenity, peace and joy. The interesting thing about these two goals is that the techniques used by the two groups are clearly adapted to them. Both sets of techniques "work"; the physicist has gained increasing understanding and control of reality; the serious mystic certainly reports the deep belief that he has attained a sense of serenity, peace and joy and is more at home in the cosmos. Outside observers of mystics report that they certainly behave and act as if this were true.[2]

With two different theoretical starting points, two different sets of research techniques and different goals (except that both agree that sensory data give at best a very limited picture of reality and their goal is to understand it more fully), let us try to compare the two groups in one area. Since both are trying to understand the nature of reality more completely, and both describe their conclusions on its nature, let us compare their conclusions. This is to say, both arrive at a world-picture and describe it in some detail. There is enough general agreement within each group to make a coherent composite description of its world-picture with which all the trained members of the group would find themselves in general agreement. Let us compare their two *Weltbilds,* these two pictures of how-the-universe-works.

One way to see how similar or how different these two views are might be to take statements or paragraphs that summarize one aspect of the world view and see if we can easily tell whether they were written by physicists or mystics. If the views are very different, we should have no trouble doing this. If the views are very similar, we should not be able to do it very easily; not be able to quickly differentiate whether the writer was a mystic or a physicist; if he was the Buddha or if he was Max Planck!

In the following section of this paper, we propose such an experiment. A list of statements will be presented. Each statement comes from one of the two sets of sources we list (Table 1): one set of sources is comprised of the writings of mystics, the second set of the writings of modern, theoretical physicists. The task of the experiment is to determine from which set each quotation comes.[3] Every attempt has been made not to tear the quotations out of context. The short ones simply seem to reflect well and briefly what the author was saying at greater length. The quotations are taken from material in which the physicists were writing as physicists and the mystics as

Table 1 | *Sources of Quotations*

Mystics	Physicists
Evelyn Underhill	A. Eddington
Dōgen (13th Century Zen	A. N. Whitehead
Master)	H. Dingle
Plotinus	P. Schrodinger
The Dhammapada	P. W. Bridgman
The Suringama Sutra	J. R. Oppenheimer
Suzuki	H. Weyl
Eugen Herrigel	W. Heisenberg
Sri Vivekananda	A. Einstein
The Svetasuatara	L. de Broglie
The Upanishads	Max Planck
Meister Eckhardt	James Jeans
Dionysious the Areopagite	Henry Margenau
Sufi Doctrinal Articles	H. Reichenbach
The Majjhima-Nikaya Sutra	N. Bohr
A. K. Coomaraswamy	B. Russell
Sri Aurobindo	
Zen Classification of Personal	
Growth during Zen	
Training	
St. Augustine	

mystics. The only change or omission not indicated in the texts is that I have occasionally omitted the capitalization of such words as *Absolute, Space, One,* which appear in the originals.[4]

In the first group of quotations, we will be concerned with the problem of the relationship of man to his perceptions; with how objective and complete a picture of reality is given by sense data.

1. "So far as broader characteristics are concerned we see in nature what we look for or are equipped to look for. Of course, I do not mean that we can arrange the details of the scene; but by the light and

shade of our values we can bring out things that shall have the broad characteristics we esteem. In this sense the value placed on permanence creates the world of apparent substance; in this sense, perhaps, the God within creates the God in nature."

2. "Nature gets credit which should in truth be reserved to ourselves; the rose for its scent, the nightingale for his song and the sun for its radiance. The poets are entirely mistaken. They should address their lyrics to themselves and should turn them into odes of self-congratulations on the excellency of the human mind. Nature is a dull affair, soundless, scentless, colorless, merely the hurrying of material, endlessly, meaninglessly."

3. "It is immediately apparent, however, that this sense-world, this seemingly real external universe, though it may be useful and valid in other respects, cannot be the external world, but only the self's projected picture of it. It is a work of art, not a scientific fact; and whilst it may possess the profound significance proper to great works of art, it is dangerous if treated as a subject for analysis. Very slight investigation shows that it is a picture whose relation to reality is at best symbolic and approximate, and which would have no meaning for selves whose senses, or channels of communication, happen to be arranged upon a different plan. The evidence of the senses then, cannot be accepted as evidence of the nature of ultimate reality. Useful servants, they are dangerous guides."

4. "Man disposes himself and construes this disposition as the world."

5. "No doubt we should not speak of seeing, but, instead of seen and seer, speak boldly of a simple unity. For in this seeing we neither distinguish nor are there two."

6. "It is the mind which gives to things their quality, their foundation, and their being."

7. "When we thought we were studying the external

world, our data were still our observations; the world was an inference from them."

8. ". . . the reason why our sentient, percipient, and thinking ego is met nowhere in our world picture can easily be indicated in seven words: because it is ITSELF that world picture. It is identical with the whole and therefore cannot be contained in it as part of it."

9. ". . . all phenomena and their development are simply manifestations of mind, all causes and effects, from great universes to the fine dust only seen in the sunlight, come into apparent existence only by means of the discriminating mind. Even open space is not nothingness."

10. ". . . the stuff of the world is mind stuff."

11. ". . . the game of give and take which goes on between the human consciousness and the external world."

12. "In general, we should never think of the world around us without also thinking of the nervous machinery in our heads by means of which we acquire knowledge of the world."

13. ". . . when searching for harmony in life one must never forget that in the drama of existence we are ourselves both actors and spectators."

In the next group of quotations, we will be concerned with the comparison of the two ways of looking at reality: the "common sense," everyday way of the senses and the other, deeper view of reality.

14. "Over and over again—as being and becoming, as eternity and time, as transcendence and immanence, reality and appearance, the one and the many—these two dominant ideas, demand, imperious insincts of men's will reappear, the warp and woof of his complete universe."

15. "These two groups of thinking, the way of time and history, the way of eternity and timelessness, are both parts of man's efforts to comprehend the world

in which he lives. Neither is comprehended in the other nor reducible to it . . . each supplementing the other, neither telling the whole story."

In the following quote, and in various others, one word in the original was a "give-away," would make it clear from which group the statement came. I have, therefore, offered an alternative to the word; an alternative from the language of the other group. One can read it both ways, with either the first or second statement of each pair in parentheses.

16. "(Satori) (Relativity) theory may be defined as an intuitive looking into the nature of things in contradiction to the analytical or logical understanding of it. Practically, it means the unfolding of a new world hitherto unperceived in the confusion of a dualistically-trained mind. Or we may say that with (Satori) (Relatively) theory our entire surroundings are viewed from quite an unexpected angle of perception . . . logically stated, all its (the world's) opposites and contradictions are united and harmonized into a consistent, organic whole."

17. "The first characteristic, it seems to me, of the new way of seeing is that all things are of equal importance in its sight, the most trivial as well as the most significant by ordinary human standards. They all seem to have acquired an absolute value, as if they had become transparent, revealing a relationship which does not obtain in the ordinary field of vision. This relationship is not horizontal, linking one thing to another and so remaining within the world of objects, but vertical; it plumbs each thing to its very depths, to the point of origination. Things are thus seen . . . from the origin, out of the "being" which manifests itself in them. To that very extent they are all of equal rank, all possessing the illustrious patents of their origin. They are not objects isloated in themselves, to the common ground of their being, and yet this ground can be perceived only through

them, through what exists, although it is the origin of all existence."

The next group of quotations concerns the relationship of cognition and logic to an understanding of reality.

18. "(In science) (In meditation) we realize more and more that our understanding of nature cannot begin with some definite cognition, that it cannot be built on such a rock-like foundation, but that all cognition is, so to speak, suspended over an infinite abyss."

19. "Pure logical thinking cannot yield us any knowledge of the empirical world; all knowledge of reality starts from experience and ends in it. Propositions arrived at by purely logical means are completely empty of reality."

20. "Since, however, sense perception only gives information of this external world indirectly, we can only grasp the latter by speculative means."

21. "As far as the laws of mathematics refer to reality, they are not certain; and as far as they are certain, they do not refer to reality."

This next group of quotations refers to the two aspects of reality: the "absolute" (the four-dimensional continuum, the "one," etc.) and the world of apparent reality.

22. "The absolute (is) . . . everything that exists . . . this absolute has become the universe . . . (as we perceive it) by coming through time, space and causation. This is the central idea of (Minkowski) (Advaita). . . . Time, space and causation are like the glass through which the absolute is seen and when it is seen . . . it appears as the universe. Now we at once gather from this that in the universe there is neither time, space nor causation . . . what we may call causation begins, after, if we may be permitted to say so, the degeneration of the absolute into the phenomenal and not before."

23. "In (the One) (Space-time) everything which for

each of us constitutes the past, the present and the future is given in block, and the entire collection of events, successive for each one of us, which form the existence of a material (object) (particle) is represented by a line, the world line of the (object) (particle) . . . each observer, as his time passes, discovers, so to speak, new slices of (the One) (Space-time) which appear to him as successive aspects of the material world, though in reality the ensemble of events constituting (the One) (Space-time) exist prior to his knowledge of them."

24. "This world has no existence? What is meant by that? It means that it has no absolute existence. It exists only in relation to my mind, to your mind, and to the mind of everyone else. We see this world with the five senses, but if we had another sense, we would see in it something more. If we had another sense, it would appear to us something still different. It has, therefore, no real existence; it has no unchangeable, immovable, infinite existence. Nor can it be called non-existence, seeing that it exists, and we have to work in through it."

25. "If from space and time we should take away the concept of the absolute, this does not mean that the absolute is thereby banished out of existence, but rather that it is referred back to something more specific . . . this most fundamental thing is the (one without a second) (four-dimensional manifold)."

26. "If we watch the shore while sailing in a boat, we feel that the shore is moving. But if we look nearer to the boat itself, we know then it is the boat which moves."

"When firewood becomes ashes, it never returns to being firewood. But we should not take the view that what is latterly ashes was formerly firewood. What we should understand is that . . . firewood stays at the position of firewood. There are former and later stages. We do not consider . . . that Winter becomes Spring or that Spring becomes Summer."

27. "What is the cause of this universe? . . . time, space,

law, chance, matter, primal energy, intelligence—none of these, nor a combination of these can be the final cause of the universe, for they are effects . . . this universe which is made up of the perishable and the imperishable, the manifest and the unmanifest . . . realize that mind, matter, and . . . the power which unites mind and matter are but three aspects of . . . the one reality."

28. "This (divine ground) (block universe) (four-dimensional manifold) is a unified stillness immoveable in itself. Yet from this immobility all things are moved and receive life."

29. "For in the absolute, there is neither space, time nor causation. . . . It is all one."

In the next group, we will be concerned with reality, existence and non-existence.

30. "Thus the material world . . . constitutes the whole world of appearance, but not the whole world of reality; we may think of it as forming only a cross section of the world of reality."

31. "Nor does it (the Supreme) (the continuum) belong to the category of non-existence nor to that of existance."

32. "I am afraid of this word 'reality,' not constituting an ordinarily definable characteristic of the things it is applied to, but used as though it were some kind of celestial halo. I very much doubt if anyone of us has the faintest idea of what is meant by the reality of existence of anything but our own egos."

In the next two quotations (as will be the case in No. 59a and b) we are, for the sake of variety, changing the puzzle a little. Two quotes will be presented. One may be a paraphrase of the other (in the language style of the other group of sources) or both may be valid This is to say, one or both of the quotations are real ones. Decide which (or both) is the legitimate quotation.

33a. "Ultimate reality is unified, impersonal and can be understood if we search, in an impersonal manner beyond the data provided by our senses."

and/or

33b. "1. The ultimate reality is one.

2. The ultimate reality is impersonal.

3. The ultimate reality can be known by reaching supersensory, impersonal knowledge."

34a. "Vaccha asked the Buddha: Do you hold that the soul of the saint exists after death?

I do not hold that the soul of the saint exists after death.

Do you hold that the soul of the saint does not exist after death?

I do not hold that the soul of the saint does not exist after death.

Where is the saint reborn?

To say he is reborn would not fit the case.

Then he is not reborn.

To say he is not reborn would not fit the case."

and/or

34b. "If we ask, for instance, whether the position of the electron remains the same, we must say 'no'; if we ask whether the electron's position changes with time, we must say 'no'; if we ask whether the electron is at rest, we must say 'no'; if we ask whether it is in motion, we must say 'no'."

The following quotations concern the dynamic-static aspect of reality.

35. "(The new view is) (The wise say it is) entirely different. The fundamental concepts are activity and process. . . . Nature is a theatre for the interrelations of activities. All things change, the activities and their interrelation. . . . In the place of the Aristotelian notion of the procession of forms (we have) . . . substituted the forms of process."

36. "(Buddhism) (Modern Science) classifies the world . . . not into different groups of objects but into dif-

ferent groups of connections . . . the world thus appears to be a complicated tissue of events, in which connections of different kinds alternate or overlap or combine and thereby determine the texture of the whole."

37. "(Modern Science) (Deeper understanding) has demonstrated that in the real world surrounding us, it is not the geometric forms, but the dynamic laws concerning movement (coming into being and passing away) which are permanent."

38. "We are deceived if we allow ourselves to believe that there is ever a pause in the flow of becoming, a resting place where positive existence is attained for even the briefest duration of time. It is only by shutting our eyes to the succession of events that we come to speak of things rather than processes."

39. "Substance is one of the most dominant concepts of our familiar outlook on the world of sensory experience, and it is one with which (science) (wisdom) finds itself continually at war."

40. "The belief that what is ultimately real must be immutable is a very common one: it gave rise to the metaphysical notion of substance, and finds, even now, a wholly illegitimate satisfaction in such scientific doctrines as the conservation of energy and mass."

41. "It is a primitive form of thought that things either exist or do not exist; and the concept of a category of things possessing existence results from forcing our knowledge into a corresponding frame of thought. Everyone does this instinctively. . . ."

42. "There is something ineffable about the real, something occasionally described as mysterious and awe inspiring; the property attended to is no doubt its ultimacy, its spontaneity, its failure to present itself as the perfect and articulate consequence of rational thought."

43. "The (body) (hard sphere) has always a definite position in space; (the soul) (electron) apparently has not. A (body) (hard sphere) takes up a definite amount of room; A (soul) (electron) . . . well it is probably

as meaningless to discuss how much room a fear, an anxiety or an uncertainty takes up."

This group is concerned with time, space, matter and causation.

44. "The objective world simply is, it does not happen. Only to the gaze of my consciousness, crawling upward along the life line of my body, does a section of this world come to life as a fleeting image in space which continuously changes in time."

45. "Time, then, is continued in differentiation of life, the ceaseless forward movement of life brings with it unending time; and life as it achieves its stages constitutes past time . . . eternity, as we have said, is life in repose, unchanging self-identical, always endlessly complete . . . the origin of time, clearly, is to be traced to the first stirrings of the (soul's) (mind's) tendency towards the production of the sensible universe with the consecutive act ongoing . . . the (soul) (mind) begot at once the universe and time."

46. "The importance of time is rather practical than theoretical, rather in relation to our desires than in relation to truth. A truer image of the world . . . is obtained by picturing things as entering into the stream of time from an eternal world outside, rather than from a view which regards time as the devouring tyrant of all that is."

47. "This is why (space-time) (sunyata) is said to be a reservoir of infinite possibilities and not just a state of mere emptiness. Differentiating itself and yet remaining in itself undifferentiated, and this to go on eternally in the world of creation . . . we can say that it is a creation of nothing."

48. "However deep the chasm may be that separates the intuitive nature of space from that of time in our experience, nothing of this qualitative difference enters into the objective world which (Hatha Yoga) (Physics) endeavors to crystalize out of direct experience. It is a (One without a second) (four-dimensional continuum)

which is neither time nor space—only the consciousness that passes on in one portion of the world experiences the detached piece which is going to meet it and passes behind it, as history, that is a process going forward in time and taking place in space."

49. "Every attempt to solve the laws of causation, time and space would be futile because the very attempt would have to be made by taking for granted the existence of these three."

50. "Nothing hinders . . . knowledge of (reality) (God) as much as time and space, for time and space are fragments, where as (reality) (God) is one . . . to know (reality) (God) [is to know] above time and outside space for (reality) (God) is neither this nor that as are all those manifested things."

51. "Thus from the outset we can be quite clear about one very important fact, namely that the validity of the law of causation for the world of reality is a question that cannot be decided on grounds of abstract reasoning."

52. "A stone falls and we ask why. This question is possible only on the supposition that nothing happens without a cause. I request you to make this very clear in your minds, for, whenever we ask why anything happens, we are taking for granted that everything that happened must have a why, that is to say, it must have been preceded by something else which acted as the cause. This precedence in succession is what we call the law of causation. It means that everything in the universe is by turn cause and effect."

53. "We must await the further development of (human growth) (science) before we can design a true and detailed picture of the interwoven texture of Matter, Life and Soul. But the old classical determinism of (the everyday view of life) (Hobbes and Laplace) need not oppress us any longer."

54. "Matter expressed itself eventually as a formulation of some unknown Force. Life, too, that yet unfathomed mystery, begins to reveal itself as an obscure energy of sensitivity imprisoned in its material formulation;

and when the dividing ignorance is cured, that gives us the sense of a gulf between life and matter, it is difficult to suppose that mind, life and matter will be found to be anything else than one energy, triply formulated."

In this final group of quotations we are concerned with more general matters; the philosophy of leaders in the field, training methods and goals for students, etc.

55. "When I, on a certain occasion, asked (Professor Einstein) (The Lord Buddha) how he found (his theory of relativity) (Enlightenment) he answered that he found it because he was so strongly convinced of the harmony of the universe."

56. "Behind the tireless efforts of the (searcher) (investigator) there lurks a stronger, more mysterious drive; it is existence and reality that one wishes to comprehend. But one shrinks from the use of such words, for one soon gets into difficulties when one has to explain what is really meant by reality and by comprehended in such a general statement."

57. "It is necessary, therefore, that advancing knowledge should base herself on a clear, pure and disciplined intellect. It is necessary, too, that she should correct her errors, sometimes by a return to the restraint of sensible fact, the concrete realities of the physical world. The touch of Earth is always reinvigorating to the sons of Earth . . . the superphysical can only be really mastered in its fullness . . . when we keep our feet firmly on the physical."

58. "The purpose of training and educating students is to enable them to understand (contemplate) spatial infinity in its homogeneity, the infinity of consciousness, the transcending of space and consciousness, and even the distinction between space and consciousness. Without this training (education), their work is not at the highest level it can be."

59a. "When you try to comprehend the four-dimensional continuum, make every effort to avoid conceptualizing in sensory or corporeal terms. It cannot be represented in this way and images of this sort are wrong and misleading."

and/or

59b. "When thou thinkest of God, if a sensory or corporeal representation (of God) comes to thy mind, chase it, repulse it, negate it, despise it, drive it away, flee from it."

60. ". . . man is the meeting point of various stages of reality."

61. "They are the most thorough-going empiricists in the history of philosophy."

62. "Religion and natural science are fighting a joint battle in a second, never-ending crusade against skepticism and dogmatism, and against superstition. The rallying cry for this crusade has always been and always will be "On to God!"

Discussion

Perhaps the most significant fact about this procedure of dealing with quotations is not that they were impossible to place in one group or the other (language, thought style, minor variations in tone, etc., make it possible for most individuals trained in one of the areas to decide with pretty fair accuracy), but rather the fact that it is a "difficult" task. This difficulty and necessity to think seriously about the correct classification for many of the quotations is, in itself, a good indication of the general similarity of conclusions reached by the two groups we are dealing with.

What are the implications of this similarity of conclusion? [5] Perhaps we can only say here that it gives added weight to our beliefs that there is somewhere validity in our conclusions. If from those searching within themselves and from those searching without come the same conclusions, and (in the obvious absence of very much communication between the two groups) the same results are obtained, we can be a little more certain of their results. There is an old Buddhist idea that seems relevant here.

It is the belief that as one searches more and more deeply into oneself, tearing aside veil after veil of illusion, one comes finally to ATMAN, the true essence of the self. And that as one searches more and more deeply into outside reality, tearing aside veil after veil of illusion, one comes finally to BRAHMAN, the true essence of reality. And that Atman and Brahman are the same.

Table 2 | *Index of Quotations*

Number of Quotation	Category	Author	Reference
1	(P)	Eddington (1931, p. 330)
2	(P)	Whitehead (quoted in J. de Marquette, 1949, p. 15)
3	(M)	Underhill (1912, p. 6)
4	(M)	Dogen (quoted in P. Kapleau, 1967, p. 297)
5	(M)	Plotinus (quoted in W. T. Stace, 1961, p. 104)
6	(M)	Dhammapada (quoted in A. Huxley, 1962, p. 179)
7	(P)	Dingle (1952, p. 266)
8	(P)	Schrodinger (quoted in Fisher, 1967, p. 16)
9	(M)	Suringama Sutra (quoted in S. Cummins & R. Linscott, 1947, p. 145)
10	(P)	Eddington (1931, p. 414)
11	(M)	Underhill (1964, p. 27)
12	(P)	Bridgman (1966, p. 154)
13	(P)	Bohr (quoted in Schilpp, 1959, p. 236)
14	(M)	Underhill (1912, p. 41)
15	(P)	Oppenheimer (1966, p. 69)
16	(M)	Suzuki (quoted in W. T. Stace, 1969, p. 90)
17	(M)	Herrigel (quoted in W. T. Stace, 1969, p. 100)
18	(P)	Heisenberg (1966, p. 132)
19	(P)	Einstein (quoted in P. A. Schilpp, 1958, p. 391)

Number of Quotation	Category	Author / Reference
20	(P)	Einstein (quoted in P. A. Schilpp, 1958, p. 248)
21	(P)	Einstein (quoted in P. A. Schilpp, 1958, p. 250)
22	(M)	Vivekananda (1949, p. 90 ff)
23	(P)	de Broglie (quoted in P. A. Schilpp, 1959, p. 114)
24	(M)	Vivekananda (1949, p. 42)
25	(P)	Planck (1933, p. 197)
26	(M)	Dogen (quoted in A. Watts, 1957, p. 123)
27	(M)	Svetasuatara Upanishad (quoted in W. T. Stace, 1969, p. 30 ff)
28	(M)	Eckhardt (quoted in W. T. Stace, 1961, p. 175)
29	(M)	Vivekananda (1949, p. 93)
30	(P)	Jeans (quoted in Cummins & Linscott, 1947, p. 381)
31	(M)	Dionysius the Areopagite (quoted in W. T. Stace, 1961, p. 196)
32	(P)	Eddington (1931, p. 419)
33a		Paraphrase of Next Quotation
33b	(M)	Sufi Doctrinal Article (quoted in de Marquette, 1949, p. 175)
34a	(M)	Majjhima-Nikaya Sutra (quoted in W. T. Stace, 1969, p. 70)
34b	(P)	J. R. Oppenheimer (1966, p. 40)
35	(P)	Whitehead (1934, p. 36)
36	(P)	Heisenberg (1958, p. 107)
37	(P)	Heisenberg (1966, p. 64)
38	(M)	Coomaraswamy (1964, p. 95)
39	(P)	Eddington (1958, p. 132)
40	(P)	Russell (1925, p. 21)
41	(P)	Eddington (1958, p. 155)
42	(P)	Margenau (1959, p. 250)
43	(P)	Jeans (1966, p. 28)

Number of Quotation	Category	Author | Reference
44	(P)	Weyl (1963, p. 116)
45	(M)	Plotinus (quoted in R. M. Gale, 1967, p. 33 ff)
46	(P)	Russell (1925, p. 21)
47	(M)	Suzuki (quoted in W. T. Stace, 1961, p. 176)
48	(P)	Weyl (quoted in O. C. de Beauregard in R. Fisher, 1967, p. 412)
49	(M)	Vivekananda (1949, p. 92)
50	(M)	Eckhardt (quoted in W. T. Stace, 1961, p. 196)
51	(P)	Planck (quoted in M. Gardner, 1961, p. 243)
52	(M)	Vivekananda (1949, p. 92)
53	(P)	Weyl (quoted in M. Gardner, 1961, p. 244)
54	(M)	Aurobindo (quoted in W. T. Stace, 1969, p. 58)
55	(P)	Reichenbach (quoted in P. A. Schilpp, 1959, p. 292)
56	(P)	Einstein (quoted in P. A. Schilpp, 1958, p. 249)
57	(M)	Aurobindo (quoted by W. T. Stace, 1969, p. 57)
58	(M)	Zen Training Classification (quoted in J. de Marquette, 1965, p. 101)
59a		Paraphrase of Next Quotation
59b	(M)	St. Augustine (quoted in J. de Marquette, 1969, p. 195
60	(M)	Eucken (quoted in Underhill, 1912, p. 34)
61	(M)	Description of Mystics (quoted in J. de Marquette, 1969, p. 195)
62	(P)	Planck (1949, p. 113)

Notes

1. This paper was written under the auspices of a grant from Dr. Frederick Ayer II.
2. It is, perhaps, worthy of note here that the stereotype of the mystic as dreamy and unworldly does not seem to stand up to the data. Every serious historian of mysticism reports the large number of cases in which mystics were active and influential, in which they demonstrated ability as superb administrators (as Teresa of Avila or St. John of the Cross) and that "their business capacity is specially noted in a curiously large number of cases. (Inge, 1950, p. xvii)." It is true, of course, that just as there are dreamy and unworldly physicists, there are dreamy and unworldly mystics; however, in both groups, they do not seem to be the rule.
3. It might be easiest and perhaps most interesting to mark each quotation with a "P" (for Physicist) or an "M" (for Mystic) and later to check your accuracy against the index designated Table 2 at the end of this article.
4. One word of caution: Many of these texts are in translation (i.e., from Latin or Sanskrit) so that phrasings may appear to be more modern in style than they actually were in the original. All translations used, of course, were serious ones that maintained the meaning and content of the original.
5. I have explored some of these implications elsewhere (Towards a general theory of the paranormal: A report of work in progress with an introduction by Henry Margenau: Parapsychology Foundation, Inc.; New York, 1969).

References

Aurobindo, S. *The Life Divine.* Cited by W. T. Stace, *The Teachings of the Mystics.* New York: Mentor, 1969.

Barnett, L. *The Universe and Dr. Einstein.* New York: Morrow, 1966.

Bohr, N. Discussion with Einstein on epistemological problems in atomic physics. In P. A. Schilpp (Ed), *Albert Einstein: Philosopher-scientist.* New York: Harper, 1959.

Bridgman, P. W. *The Ways Things Are.* Cambridge: Harvard University Press, 1966.

Broad, C. D. *Religion, Philosophy and Psychical Research.* London: Routledge and Kegan Paul, Ltd., 1953.

Coomaraswamy, A. K. *Buddha and the Gospel of Buddhism.* New York: Harper Torchbooks, 1964 (1916).

Cummins, S., and Linscott, R. (Eds.), *Man and Spirit: The Speculative Philosophers.* New York: Random, 1947.

De Beauregard, O. C. Two principles of time science. In R. Fischer (Ed.), *Interdisciplinary Perspectives on Time.* New York: New York Academy of Science, 1967.

De Broglie, L. The scientific work of Albert Einstein. In P. A. Schilpp (Ed), *Albert Einstein: Philosopher-scientist.* New York: Harper, 1959.

De Marquette, J. *Introduction to Comparative Mysticism.* New York: Philosophical Library, 1949.

Dingle, H. *The Scientific Adventure.* New York: Pitman, 1952.

Eddington, A. *The Nature of the Physical World.* New York: Macmillan, 1931.

Eddington, A. *The Philosophy of Physical Science.* Ann Arbor, Mich.: University of Michigan Press, 1958.

Eucken, R. *Der Sinn und Wert des Lebens.* Leipzig, 1908.

Fischer, R. (Ed.), *Interdisciplinary Perspectives on Time.* New York: New York Academy of Science, 1967.

Gale, R. M. *The Philosophy of Time.* New York: Doubleday, 1967.

Gardner, M. (Ed.), *Great Essays in Science.* New York: Washington Square Press, 1961.

Heisenberg, W. *Physics and Philosophy.* New York: Harper, 1958.

Heisenberg, W. *Philosophic Problems of Nuclear Science.* Greenwich, Conn.: Fawcett, 1966.

Herrigel, E. *The Method of Zen.* Cited in W. T. Stace, *The Teachings of the Mystics.* New York: Mentor, 1969.

Huxley, A. *The Perennial Philosophy*. New York: Meridian Books, 1962.

Inge, W. R. *Christian Mysticism*. New York: Meridian Books, 1950.

James, W. *The Varieties of Religious Experience*. New York: New American Library, 1958.

Jeans, J. Some problems of philosophy. In S. Cummins & R. Linscott (Eds.), *Man and the Universe: The Philosophers of Science*. New York: Random, 1947.

Kapleau, P. (Ed.), *Three Pillars of Zen*. Boston: Beacon, 1967.

Margenau, H. Einstein's conception of reality. In P. A. Schilpp (Ed.), *Albert Einstein: Philosopher-scientist*. New York: Harper, 1959.

Northrop, F. S. C. Einstein's conception of science. In P. A. Schilpp (Ed.), *Elbert Einstein: Philosopher-scientist*. New York: Harper, 1959.

Oppenheimer, J. R. *Science and the Human Understanding*. New York: Simon & Schuster, 1966.

Planck, M. *Where Is Science Going?* London: George Allen and Unwin, Ltd., 1933.

Plank, M. *Scientific Autobiography* (F. Gaynon, Trans.) New York: Philosophical Library, 1949.

Reichenbach, H. The philosophical significance of the theory of relativity. In P. A. Schilpp (Ed.), *Albert Einstein: Philosopher-scientist*. New York: Harper, 1959.

Russell, B. *Mysticism and Logic and Other Essays*. London: Longmans Green, 1925.

Schilpp, P. A. (Ed.), *Albert Einstein: Philosopher-scientist*. New York: Harper, 1959.

Schrodinger, P. *Mind and Matter*. London: Cambridge University Press, 1959.

Stace, W. T. *Mysticism and Philosophy*. New York: Lippincott, 1961.

Stace, W. T. *The Teachings of the Mystics*. New York: Mentor, 1969.

St. Augustine, *The Confessions*. (E. F. Pusey, Trans.) London: George Allen and Unwin, 1907.

Suzuki, *Essays in Zen Buddhism*. Cited in W. T. Stace, *The Teachings of the Mystics*. New York: Mentor, 1969.

Underhill, E. *Mysticism.* (4th ed.) London: Methuen and Co., Ltd., 1912.

Underhill, E. *Practical Mysticism* London: J. M. Dent and Sons, Ltd., 1964.

Vivekananda, S. *Jnana Yoga.* New York: Ramakrishna-Vivekananda Center, 1949.

Watts, A. *The Way of Zen.* New York: New American Library, 1957.

Weyl, H. *Philosophy of Mathematics and National Science.* New York: Atheneum, 1963.

Whitehead, A. N. *Nature and Life.* London: Cambridge University Press, 1934.

Whitehead, A. N. *Science and the Modern World.* Cited by J. de Marquette, *Introduction to Comparative Mysticism.* New York: Philosophical Library, 1949.

appendix ε | telepathic perception in the dream state

Confirmatory Study Using EEG–EOG Monitoring Techniques

Stanley Krippner and Montague Ullman
Maimonides Medical Center

Summary.—*S*, selected on the basis of his successful performance in a previous telepathy-dream study, spent 8 nights in a laboratory; his sleep was monitored by EEG-EOG techniques. As *E* observed the onset of an REM period, he signalled (by buzzer) an acoustically isolated psychologist to awaken and concentrate on a randomly selected target (art print), the content of which was unknown to *S* or *E*. At the termination of each REM period, *E* awakened *S*, eliciting a dream report. These reports, and *S*'s associations to them, were tape-recorded and subsequently transcribed. The hypothesis stated that there would be a discernible correspondence between the target used on any night and *S*'s dreams on that night. Upon completion of the eight nights, three judges (working independently and blind) rated each of the 8 targets against each of the 8 dream transcripts, using a 100-point scale to indicate degree of correspondence between each target-

From *Perceptual and Motor Skills*, 29, (1969), 915–918. C Perceptual and Motor Skills 1969. These studies are supported by grants from the Society for Comparative Philosophy and the Ittleson Family Foundation.

transcript pair. A Latin-square analysis of variance procedure compared the mean ratings of the 8 critical pairs with the mean ratings of the 56 non-critical pairs. An F of 6.43 (7/28 df) was obtained (p <0.001), confirming the telepathy hypothesis and replicating a previous telepathy-dream study.

The first recorded attempt to induce telepathic dreams experimentally was recorded by Ermacora (1895) who attempted telepathically to influence the dreams of a young girl. Her morning dream recall demonstrated several close correspondences with the images which Ermacora had attempted to transmit, at a distance, during the night. The discovery by Aserinsky and Kleitman (1953) of physiological techniques for the monitoring of dreams made it posisble to move from a conjectural and clinical level of discussion and observation to a scientific level which freed the investigator from the uncertainty of relying on spontaneous dream recall.

The first telepathy-dream experiment with a single S which utilized EEG-EOG monitoring yielded significant results (Ullman, Krippner, and Feldstein, 1966). S was a male psychologist who was paired with an agent (or "transmitter") serving as a staff psychologist at Maimonides Medical Center. On seven non-consecutive nights, S's sleep was monitored by an E in the Maimonides Dream Laboratory. As E observed the onset of an REM period, he signalled (by buzzer) the agent who was located in a distant, acoustically isolated room. The agent then concentrated on a randomly selected target picture (an art print). At the termination of each REM period, E awakened S, eliciting a dream report. These reports, and S's associations to them, were tape-recorded and subsequently transcribed. Upon completion of the study, three judges (working independently and blind) rated each of the seven targets against each of the seven dream transcripts. Data were subjected to analysis of variance (Scheffe, 1959), yielding an F of 10.86 (p<0.01).

Two years later, the two psychologists were again available for an experimental study and it was decided to attempt a replication of the earlier results. A decision was made to complete an eight-night study and to use a Latin-square analysis of variance technique so that target effects, night effects, and sitting (by the judges) effects could also be inspected. The same three judges were obtained to evaluate target-transcript correspondences.

Procedure

It was again hypothesized that there would be a discernible correspondence between the target used on any given night and S's dreams on that night. The selection of art prints was made by four laboratory staff members who were never present on any of the experimental nights. As a result, the range of possible art prints used was unknown to S, to Es, or to the agent.

In the previous study with S, the nightly log of the agent indicated that he had spontaneously dramatized or acted out some of the scenes depicted in the target pictures. In order to facilitate this process, as well as to involve more deeply the agent in the mood and theme of the art print, a staff member prepared a series of objects relating to each of the target pictures. These objects were designed to create a multisensory involvement of A with the target picture. For example, an art print depicting two boxers was accompanied by a boxing glove so that the agent could spend part of the night shadow boxing.

The staff member who selected the multisensory materials sealed each art print in an opaque enveloped. This envelope was enclosed in a larger envelope which was also sealed. Each envelope had a small letter in its upper right-hand corner, matching a letter on an appropriate box of multisensory materials. This staff member who sealed the envelopes affixed his signature on the flap of each envelope. This signature was covered with transparent tape so that any attempt to open the envelope prematurely would be detected. This staff member also affixed his signature to the side of each box of multisensory material.

Again, the signature was covered with transparent tape to detect any attempt to tamper with the materials.

S slept in the dream laboratory on eight non-consecutive nights. As soon as S was in bed, the agent entered an office and selected a single digit from a table of random numbers. At this point, he was given a key by one of the Es; taking this key, he unlocked an attache case which contained the 10 envelopes in which the target pictures had been sealed. The agent counted down through the stack of target envelopes until he reached the number of the randomly selected digit. If the digit were larger than the number of targets remaining in the pool, the agent went through the pool a second time until an envelope was located, the order of which matched the randomly chosen number.

Once the target envelope had been selected, the appropriate box of multisensory materials was located. These boxes were kept in a cabient near the file in which the attache case was located. The agent and E examined both the target envelope and the box to see if the transparent tape had been broken or if the signature showed evidence of tampering. Still under the observation of E, the agent placed the remaining target envelopes back in the attache case and locked it, taking the key and the target materials to his room.

The agent's room contained a table, a bed, a loudspeaker, and a buzzer. S's dream reports could be heard by the agent on the loudspeaker; this procedure served to maintain the agent's interest in the experiment and his continued orientation to the sleeping S. There was no microphone in the agent's room, making it impossible for any vocal cues to be transmitted from the agent to S or from the agent to Es. The agent's room was separated from S's sleep room by three doors and a corridor which was 96 ft. in length.

Upon arriving in his room, the agent opened the target containers, inspected the target material, and began his attempts to influence S's dreams telepathically. The agent was allowed to nap, but an E buzzed the agent whenever the electroencephalographic record indicated that an REM period was about to begin.

During the night, *Es* monitored *S's* sleep on an eight-channel Model D Medcraft EEG to detect emergent Stage I REM (rapid eye movement) periods. At the end of each REM period, an *E* awakened *S* by means of a two-way intercom and elicited a verbal report. These reports were recorded on tape and subsequently transcribed.

Following *S's* final awakening in the morning, an *E* conducted a post-sleep interview with *S* in order to obtain additional associational material. Finally, *S* was asked to make a guess as to what he thought the target picture for the night might have been. At this point, *S's* electrodes were detached, he was taken to breafast, and dismissed.

Once the post-sleep interview had been terminated, a secretarial assistant malied the tape to a transcriber who typed a transcript of the night's verbal report and interview. In the meantime, the agent re-sealed the envelope and the box containing the multisensory materials, affixing his signature to each seal and covering it with transparent tape. These materials were filed in a separate cabinet by the agent until the entire experimental series was concluded.

After transcripts for all eight nights had been collected and transcribed, three outside judges who had not been present during any of the experimental sessions rated each of the eight target materials against each of the eight transcripts. The judges worked blind and independently, using slides of the art prints and of the multisensory materials.

The 64 possible target-transcript combinations were submitted to each judge in a different random order. Eight combinations were judged at a time. Following the completion of each set of eight, the judge mailed his ratings to the dream laboratory and was sent another set. All contacts between the judges and the dream laboratory was accomplished through the mails so as to eliminate contamination in the form of *E* bias effects.

The judging form contained a 100-point scale. The judges were asked to inspect the art print and the multisensory material and to examine the dream transcript for correspondences. The judges' instructions read, in part:

> . . . You are to consider that the target represents an event that has occurred while S was in the sleeping state. You must further assume that the event has in fact influenced the dream either in a direct way or through some process of transformation. The task then becomes one of working from the dream back to the event that affected the dream . . . Using a red pencil, color the space that represents, in your judgment, the correspondence between target material and transcript content.

Results and Discussion

The Latin-square analysis of variance technique which was utilized compared the ratings of the eight critical pairs (e.g., the actual target-transcript combinations for each experimental night) with the 56 non-critical pairs. Means of the three judges' ratings were entered in the matrix. An F of 6.43 (7/28 df) was obtained ($p < 0.001$). The target effects, night effects, and sitting effects were analyzed and did not yield significant results.

The judges' ratings indicated that there was a high degree of correspondence between the art print and the dream transcript on each of the eight experimental nights. For example, the agent randomly selected Hiroshige's "Downpour at Shono" on the second night of the study. S's dream reports for that night read, in part:

> It's as though I was doing some drawing. . . . I had the feeling as though it were in a down position, like a low table. Down on the floor. Seems that's what I meant by "down. . . ." Something about an Oriental man who was ill. . . . A fountain. Two images and a water spray that would shoot up. . . . Walking with someone on the street. Raining. . . . It seemed it was raining a little bit and . . . we had to walk out into the street. . . . It was raining, and it was night and it had a sort of heavy feeling. . . .

The data obtained from this study provided a successful replication of telepathic perception in the dream state. Fortunately, the basic EEG-EOG technique described in this report can easily be utilized by other dream laboratories interested in these phenomena. An independent confirmation of this effect has already been reported (Hall, 1967) and two other investigations are in process.

It may be premature to attempt an explanation of the telepathic effect in dreams as further investigation is necessary. However, current writers are divided as to whether the effect follows a sender-receiver model in which actual transfer of information takes place (Hernandez-Peon, 1968) or whether a telepathic "field" is created in which no new information is perceived but in which memory traces of S are stimulated which correspond to the target picture or object (Roll, 1966). In any event, the phenomenon is a provocative one which deserves further inspection and careful scrutiny.

References

Aserinsky, E., and Kleitman, N. Regularly occurring periods of eye motility, and concomitant phenomena, during sleep. *Science,* 1953, 118, 273–274.

Ermacora, G. G. Telepathic dreams experimentally induced. *Proceedings, Society for Psychical Research,* 1895, 11, 235–308.

Hall, C. Experimente zur telepathischen Beeinflussung von Traeumen. *Zeitschrift fuer Parapsychologie und Grenzgebiete der Psychologie,* 1967, 10, 18–47.

Hernandez-Peon, R. A unitary neurophysiological model of hypnosis, dreams, hallucinations, and ESP. In R. Cavanna and M. Ullman (Eds.), *Psi and altered states of consciousness.* New York: Garrett, 1969, pp. 178–193.

Roll, W. G. ESP and memory. *International Journal of Neuropsychiatry,* 1966, 2, 505–521.

Scheffe, H. *The analysis of variance.* New York: Wiley, 1959.

Ullman, M., Krippner, S., and Feldstein, S. Experimentally induced telepathic dreams: two studies using EEG-REM monitoring technique. *International Journal of Neuropsychiatry*, 1966, 2, 420–437.